KB132726

나의 토익 Listening 목표 달성기

나의 목표 점수	나의 학습 플랜

_____ 점

☐ [400점 이상] 2주 완성 학습 플랜

☐ [300~395점] 3주 완성 학습 플랜

☐ [295점 이하] 4주 완성 학습 플랜

* 일 단위의 상세 학습 플랜은 p.18에 있습니다.

각 Test를 마친 후, 해당 Test의 점수를 ● 으로 표시하여 자신의 점수 변화를 확인하세요.

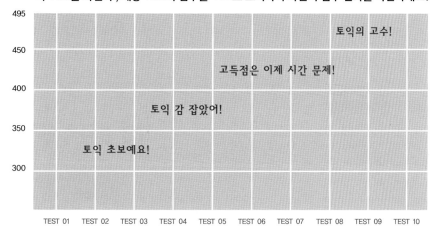

	TEST 01	TEST 02	TEST 03	TEST 04	TEST 05	TEST 06	TEST 07	TEST 08	TEST 09	TEST 10
학습일	/	/	/	/	/	/	/	/	/	/
맞은 개수	개	개	개	개	개	개	개	개	개	개
환산점수	점	점	점	점	점	점	점	점	점	점

* 리스닝 점수 환산표는 p.165에 있습니다.

해커스
토익 LC

실전 **1000**제 **3**
LISTENING

문제집

해커스 어학연구소

무료 토익·토스·오픽·지텔프 자료 제공
Hackers.co.kr

최신 토익 경향을 완벽하게 반영한
해커스 토익 실전 1000제 3 LISTENING 문제집을 내면서

해커스 토익이 항상 독보적인 베스트셀러의 자리를 지킬 수 있는 것은 늘 **처음과 같은 마음으로** 더 좋은 책을 만들기 위해 고민하고, **최신 경향을 반영하기 위해 끊임없이 노력**하기 때문입니다.

그리고 이러한 노력 끝에 **최신 토익 경향을 반영한** 《해커스 토익 실전 1000제 3 Listening 문제집》(**최신개정판**) 을 출간하게 되었습니다.

최신 출제 경향 완벽 반영!

최신 출제 경향을 철저히 분석하여 실전과 가장 유사한 지문과 문제 10회분을 수록했습니다. 수록한 모든 문제는 실전과 동일한 환경에서 풀 수 있도록 실제 토익 문제지와 동일하게 구성하였으며, Answer Sheet를 수록하여 시간 관리 연습과 더불어 실전 감각을 보다 높일 수 있도록 하였습니다.

점수를 올려주는 학습 구성과 학습 자료로 토익 고득점 달성!

모든 문제의 정답과 함께 스크립트를 수록하였으며, 해커스토익(Hackers.co.kr)에서 '문제 해석'을 무료로 제공 합니다. 문제의 정확한 이해를 통해 토익 리스닝 점수를 향상할 수 있으며, 토익 고득점 달성이 가능합니다.

《해커스 토익 실전 1000제 3 Listening 문제집》은 별매되는 해설집과 함께 학습할 때 보다 효과적으로 학습할 수 있습니다. 또한, 해커스인강(HackersIngang.com)에서 '온라인 실전모의고사 1회분'과 '단어암기 PDF&MP3'를 무료로 제공하며, 토익 스타 강사의 파트별 해설강의를 수강할 수 있습니다.

《해커스 토익 실전 1000제 3 Listening 문제집》이 여러분의 토익 목표 점수 달성에 확실한 해결책이 되고 영어 실력 향상, 나아가 여러분의 꿈을 향한 길에 믿음직한 동반자가 되기를 소망합니다.

해커스 어학연구소

CONTENTS

무료 해석 바로 보기

토익, 이렇게 공부하면
확실하게 고득점 잡는다!

01 토익에 완벽하게 대비한다!

최신 토익 출제 경향을 반영한 실전 10회분 수록

시험 경향에 맞지 않는 문제들만 풀면, 실전에서는 연습했던 문제와 달라 당황할 수 있습니다. 《해커스 토익 실전 1000제 3 Listening 문제집》에 수록된 모든 문제는 **최신 출제 경향과 난이도를 반영**하여 실전에 철저하게 대비할 수 있도록 하였습니다.

실전과 동일한 구성!

《해커스 토익 실전 1000제 3 Listening 문제집》에 수록된 모든 문제는 실전 문제지와 동일하게 구성되었으며, 미국·캐나다·영국·호주식의 국가별 발음 또한 실전과 동일한 비율로 구성되었습니다. 또한 **영국·호주식 실전 버전 MP3**로 까다로운 영국·호주식 발음에 확실히 대비할 수 있으며, **고사장/매미 버전 MP3**로 실전 감각을 극대화할 수 있습니다. 이와 더불어 **교재 뒤에 수록된 Answer Sheet**으로 실제 시험처럼 답안 마킹을 연습하면서 시간 관리 방법을 익힐 수 있습니다.

02 한 문제를 풀어도, 정확하게 이해하고 푼다!

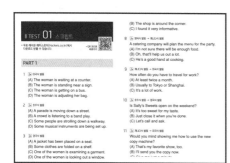

스크립트

수록된 모든 문제에 대한 스크립트를 교재 뒤에 수록하였습니다. 테스트를 마친 후 문제를 풀 때 음성을 정확히 이해하면서 풀었는지, 틀린 문제의 경우 어떤 부분을 놓쳤는지 등을 **스크립트를 통해 꼼꼼히 확인하고 다시 듣는 연습**을 통해 리스닝 실력을 향상할 수 있도록 하였습니다.

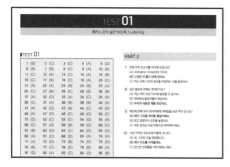

무료 해석 PDF

수록된 모든 지문 및 모든 문제에 대한 정확한 해석을 해커스토익(Hackers.co.kr) 사이트에서 **무료로 제공**합니다. 이를 통해 테스트를 마친 후, 스크립트를 봐도 잘 이해가 되지 않거나 해석이 어려운 문제를 확인하여 **지문과 문제를 보다 정확하게 이해**할 수 있도록 하였습니다.

Self 체크 리스트

각 테스트 마지막 페이지에는 Self 체크 리스트를 수록하여 **테스트를 마친 후 자신의 문제 풀이 방식과 태도를 스스로 점검**할 수 있도록 하였습니다. 이를 통해 효과적인 복습과 더불어 목표 점수를 달성하기 위해 개선해야 할 습관 및 부족한 점을 찾아 보완해나갈 수 있습니다.

03 내 실력을 확실하게 파악한다!

점수 환산표

점수 환산표

정답 수	리스닝 점수	정답 수	리스닝 점수	정답 수	리스닝 점수
100	495	66	305	32	135
99	495	65	300	31	130
98	495	64	295	30	125
97	495	63	290	29	120
96	490	62	285	28	115
95	485	61	280	27	110
94	480	60	275	26	105
93	475	59	270	25	100
92	470	58	265	24	95
91	465	57	260	23	90
90	460	56	255	22	85
89	455	55	250	21	80
88	450	54	245	20	75
87	445	53	240	19	70

점수 환산표

교재 부록으로 점수 환산표를 수록하여, 학습자들이 테스트를 마치고 채점을 한 후 바로 점수를 확인하여 **자신의 실력을 정확하게 파악**할 수 있도록 하였습니다. 환산 점수를 교재 첫 장의 목표 달성 그래프에 표시하여 실력의 변화를 확인하고, 학습 계획을 세울 수 있습니다.

무료 온라인 실전모의고사

교재에 수록된 테스트 외에 해커스인강(HackersIngang.com) 사이트에서 온라인 실전모의고사 1회분을 추가로 무료 제공합니다. 이를 통해 토익 시험 전, 학습자들이 자신의 실력을 마지막으로 점검해볼 수 있도록 하였습니다.

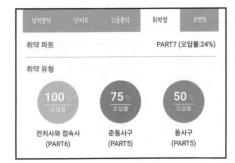

인공지능 1:1 토익어플 '빅플'

교재의 문제를 풀고 답안을 입력하기만 하면, 인공지능 어플 '해커스토익 빅플'이 **자동 채점**은 물론 성적분석표와 취약 유형 심층 분석까지 제공합니다. 이를 통해, 자신이 가장 많이 틀리는 취약 유형이 무엇인지 확인하고, 관련 문제들을 추가로 학습하며 취약 유형을 집중 공략하여 약점을 보완할 수 있습니다.

04 다양한 학습 자료를 활용한다!

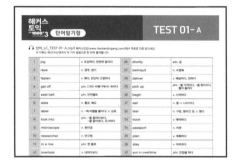

단어암기 PDF&MP3 / 정답녹음 MP3

해커스인강(HackersIngang.com) 사이트에서 단어암기 PDF와 MP3를 무료로 제공하여, 교재에 수록된 테스트의 중요 단어를 복습하고 암기할 수 있도록 하였습니다. 또한 **정답녹음 MP3** 파일을 제공하여 학습자들이 보다 편리하게 채점할 수 있도록 하였습니다.

방대한 무료 학습 자료(Hackers.co.kr) / 동영상강의(HackersIngang.com)

해커스토익(Hackers.co.kr) 사이트에서는 토익 적중 예상특강을 비롯한 방대하고 유용한 토익 학습 자료를 무료로 이용할 수 있습니다. 또한 온라인 교육 포털 사이트인 해커스인강(HackersIngang.com) 사이트에서 교재 동영상강의를 수강하면, 보다 깊이 있는 학습이 가능합니다.

해설집 미리보기

<해설집 별매>

01 정답과 오답의 이유를 확인하여 Part 1&2 문제 완벽 정복!

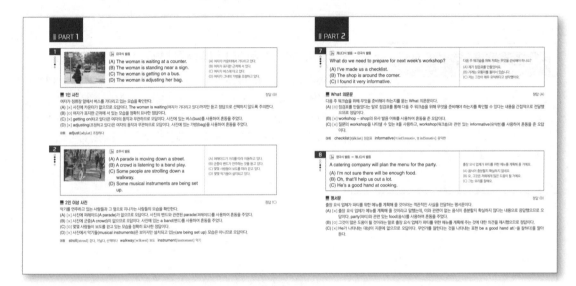

1 문제 및 문제 해석

최신 토익 출제 경향이 반영된 문제를 해설집에도 그대로 수록해, 해설을 보기 전 문제를 다시 한번 풀어보며 자신이 어떤 과정으로 정답을 선택했는지 되짚어 볼 수 있습니다. 함께 수록된 정확한 해석을 보며 문장 구조를 꼼꼼하게 파악하여 문제를 완벽하게 이해할 수 있습니다.

2 문제 유형 및 난이도

모든 문제마다 문제 유형을 제시하여 자주 틀리는 문제 유형을 쉽게 파악할 수 있고, 사전 테스트를 거쳐 검증된 문제별 난이도를 확인하여 자신의 실력과 학습 목표에 따라 학습할 수 있습니다. 문제 유형은 모두 《해커스 토익 Listening》의 목차 목록과 동일하여, 보완 학습이 필요할 경우 쉽게 참고할 수 있습니다.

3 상세한 해설 및 어휘

문제 유형별로 가장 효과적인 해결 방법을 제시하며, 오답 보기가 오답이 되는 이유까지 상세하게 설명하여 틀린 문제의 원인을 파악하고 보완할 수 있습니다. 또한, 영국·호주식 발음으로 들려준 지문문제에서 어휘의 국가별 발음이 다를 경우, 미국·영국식 발음 기호를 모두 수록하여 국가별 발음 차이까지 익힐 수 있도록 하였습니다.

02 효율적인 Part 3&4 문제풀이 전략으로 고득점 달성!

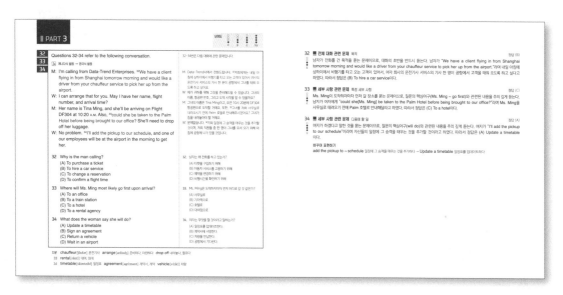

1 지문, 문제, 해석, 정답의 단서

최신 토익 출제 경향이 반영된 지문 및 문제와 함께 수록된 정확한 해석을 보며 지문 및 문제의 내용을 완벽하게 이해할 수 있습니다. 또한, 각 문제별로 표시된 정답의 단서를 확인하여, 모든 문제에 대한 정답의 근거를 정확하게 파악하는 연습을 할 수 있습니다.

2 문제 유형별 상세한 해설 및 문제 풀이 방법

질문 유형별로 가장 효율적인 해결 방법이 적용된 문제 풀이 방법을 제시하였습니다. 대화/지문에서 주의 깊게 들어야 할 부분이나 파악해야 할 사항을 확인하는 단계부터 대화/지문을 들으며 정답을 선택하는 문제 풀이 과정을 읽는 것만으로도 자연스럽게 Part 3 · 4의 문제 풀이 전략을 익힐 수 있습니다.

3 바꾸어 표현하기

대화/지문의 내용이 질문이나 정답 보기에서 바꾸어 표현된 경우, [대화/지문의 표현 → 정답 보기의 표현] 혹은 [질문의 표현 → 대화/지문의 표현]으로 정리하여 한눈에 확인할 수 있도록 하였습니다. 이를 통해 Part 3 · 4 풀이 전략을 익히고 나아가 고득점 달성이 가능하도록 하였습니다.

토익 소개 및 시험장 Tips

토익이란 무엇인가?

TOEIC은 **Test Of English for International Communication**의 약자로 영어가 모국어가 아닌 사람들을 대상으로 언어 본래의 기능인 '커뮤니케이션' 능력에 중점을 두고 일상생활 또는 국제 업무 등에 필요한 실용영어 능력을 평가하는 시험입니다. 토익은 일상생활 및 비즈니스 현장에서 필요로 하는 내용을 평가하기 위해 개발되었고 다음과 같은 실용적인 주제들을 주로 다룹니다.

- 협력 개발: 연구, 제품 개발
- 재무 회계: 대출, 투자, 세금, 회계, 은행 업무
- 일반 업무: 계약, 협상, 마케팅, 판매
- 기술 영역: 전기, 공업 기술, 컴퓨터, 실험실
- 사무 영역: 회의, 서류 업무
- 물품 구입: 쇼핑, 물건 주문, 대금 지불
- 식사: 레스토랑, 회식, 만찬
- 문화: 극장, 스포츠, 피크닉
- 건강: 의료 보험, 병원 진료, 치과
- 제조: 생산 조립 라인, 공장 경영
- 직원: 채용, 은퇴, 급여, 진급, 고용 기회
- 주택: 부동산, 이사, 기업 부지

토익의 파트별 구성

구성		내용	문항 수	시간	배점
Listening Test	Part 1	사진 묘사	6문항 (1번~6번)	45분	495점
	Part 2	질의 응답	25문항 (7번~31번)		
	Part 3	짧은 대화	39문항, 13지문 (32번~70번)		
	Part 4	짧은 담화	30문항, 10지문 (71번~100번)		
Reading Test	Part 5	단문 빈칸 채우기 (문법/어휘)	30문항 (101번~130번)	75분	495점
	Part 6	장문 빈칸 채우기 (문법/어휘/문장 고르기)	16문항, 4지문 (131번~146번)		
	Part 7	지문 읽고 문제 풀기(독해) - 단일 지문 (Single Passage) - 이중 지문 (Double Passages) - 삼중 지문 (Triple Passages)	54문항, 15지문 (147번~200번) - 29문항, 10지문 (147번~175번) - 10문항, 2지문 (176번~185번) - 15문항, 3지문 (186번~200번)		
Total		7 Parts	200문항	120분	990점

토익 접수 방법 및 성적 확인

1. 접수 방법

- 접수 기간을 TOEIC위원회 인터넷 사이트(www.toeic.co.kr) 혹은 공식 애플리케이션에서 확인하고 접수합니다.
- 접수 시 jpg형식의 사진 파일이 필요하므로 미리 준비합니다.

2. 성적 확인

- 시험일로부터 약 10일 이후 TOEIC위원회 인터넷 사이트(www.toeic.co.kr) 혹은 공식 애플리케이션에서 확인합니다. (성적 발표 기간은 회차마다 상이함)
- 시험 접수 시, 우편 수령과 온라인 출력 중 성적 수령 방법을 선택할 수 있습니다.
  - *온라인 출력은 성적 발표 즉시 발급 가능하나, 우편 수령은 약 7일가량의 발송 기간이 소요될 수 있습니다.

시험 당일 준비물

| 신분증 | 연필&지우개 | 시계 | 수험번호를 적어둔 메모 | 오답노트&단어암기장 |

* 시험 당일 신분증이 없으면 시험에 응시할 수 없으므로, 반드시 ETS에서 요구하는 신분증(주민등록증, 운전면허증, 공무원증 등)을 지참해야 합니다.
  ETS에서 인정하는 신분증 종류는 TOEIC위원회 인터넷 사이트(www.toeic.co.kr)에서 확인 가능합니다.

시험 진행 순서

정기시험/추가시험(오전)	추가시험(오후)	진행내용	유의사항
AM 9:30 - 9:45	PM 2:30 - 2:45	답안지 작성 오리엔테이션	10분 전에 고사장에 도착하여, 이름과 수험번호로 고사실을 확인합니다.
AM 9:45 - 9:50	PM 2:45 - 2:50	쉬는 시간	준비해간 오답노트나 단어암기장으로 최종 정리를 합니다. 시험 중간에는 쉬는 시간이 없으므로 화장실에 꼭 다녀오도록 합니다.
AM 9:50 - 10:10	PM 2:50 - 3:10		신분 확인 및 문제지 배부
AM 10:10 - 10:55	PM 3:10 - 3:55	Listening Test	Part 1과 Part 2는 문제를 풀면서 정답을 바로 답안지에 마킹합니다. Part 3와 Part 4는 문제의 정답보기 옆에 살짝 표시해두고, Listening Test가 끝난 후 한꺼번에 마킹합니다.
AM 10:55 - 12:10	PM 3:55 - 5:10	Reading Test	각 문제를 풀 때 바로 정답을 마킹합니다.

* 추가시험은 토요일 오전 또는 오후에 시행되므로 이 사항도 꼼꼼히 확인합니다.
* 당일 진행 순서에 대한 더 자세한 내용은 해커스토익(Hackers.co.kr) 사이트에서 확인할 수 있습니다.

파트별 형태 및 전략

Part 1 사진 묘사 (6문제)

사진을 가장 잘 묘사한 문장을 4개의 보기 중에서 고르는 유형

문제 형태

문제지	음성
1. 	Number 1. Look at the picture marked number 1 in your test book. (A) He is writing on a sheet of paper. (B) He is reaching for a glass. (C) He is seated near a window. (D) He is opening up a laptop computer.

해설   남자가 창문 근처에 앉아 있는 모습을 seated near a window(창문 근처에 앉아 있다)로 묘사한 (C)가 정답이다.

문제 풀이 전략

1. 보기를 듣기 전에 사진을 묘사할 수 있는 표현을 미리 연상합니다.

보기를 듣기 전에 사진을 보면서 사용 가능한 주어와 등장 인물의 동작이나 사물을 나타내는 동사 및 명사를 미리 연상합니다. 표현을 미리 연상하는 과정에서 사진의 내용을 정확하게 확인하게 되며, 연상했던 표현이 보기에서 사용될 경우 훨씬 명확하게 들을 수 있어 정답 선택이 수월해집니다.

2. 사진을 완벽하게 묘사한 것이 아니라 가장 적절하게 묘사한 보기를 선택합니다.

Part 1은 사진을 완벽하게 묘사한 보기가 아니라 가장 적절하게 묘사한 보기를 선택해야 합니다. 이를 위해 Part 1의 문제를 풀 때 O, ×를 표시하면서 보기를 들으면 오답 보기를 확실히 제거할 수 있어 정확히 정답을 선택할 수 있습니다. 특별히 Part 1에서 자주 출제되는 오답 유형을 알아두면 ×를 표시하면서 훨씬 수월하게 정답을 선택할 수 있습니다.

Part 1 빈출 오답 유형

· 사진 속 사람의 동작을 잘못 묘사한 오답

· 사진에 없는 사람이나 사물을 언급한 오답

· 사진 속 사물의 상태나 위치를 잘못 묘사한 오답

· 사물의 상태를 사람의 동작으로 잘못 묘사한 오답

· 사진에서는 알 수 없는 사실을 진술한 오답

· 혼동하기 쉬운 어휘를 이용한 오답

* 실제 시험을 볼 때, Part 1 디렉션이 나오는 동안 Part 5 문제를 최대한 많이 풀면 전체 시험 시간 조절에 도움이 됩니다. 하지만 "Now, Part 1 will begin"이라는 음성이 들리면 바로 Part 1으로 돌아가서 문제를 풀도록 합니다.

Part 2 질의 응답 (25문제)

영어로 된 질문을 듣고 가장 적절한 응답을 3개의 보기 중에서 고르는 유형

문제 형태

문제지	음성
7. Mark your answer on your answer sheet.	Number 7. When is the presentation going to be held? (A) I'm going to discuss sales levels. (B) Sometime on Tuesday. (C) He handled the preparations.

해설 의문사 When을 이용하여 발표가 진행될 시기를 묻고 있는 문제이므로 Sometime on Tuesday라는 시점을 언급한 (B)가 정답이다.

문제 풀이 전략

1. 질문의 첫 단어는 절대 놓치지 않도록 합니다.

Part 2의 문제 유형은 질문의 첫 단어로 결정되므로 절대 첫 단어를 놓치지 않아야 합니다. Part 2에서 평균 11문제 정도 출제되는 의문사 의문문은 첫 단어인 의문사만 들으면 대부분 정답을 선택할 수 있습니다. 그리고 다른 유형의 문제도 첫 단어를 통하여 유형, 시제, 주어 등 문제 풀이와 관련된 기본적인 정보를 파악할 수 있습니다.

2. 오답 유형을 숙지하여 오답 제거 방법을 100% 활용하도록 합니다.

Part 2에서는 오답의 유형이 어느 정도 일정한 패턴으로 사용되고 있습니다. 따라서 오답 유형을 숙지해두어 문제를 풀 때마다 오답 제거 방법을 최대한 활용하도록 합니다. 이를 위해 Part 2의 문제를 풀 때 O, ×를 표시하면서 보기를 들으면 오답 보기를 확실히 제거할 수 있어 정확히 정답을 선택할 수 있습니다.

Part 2 빈출 오답 유형

- 질문에 등장한 단어를 반복하거나, 발음이 유사한 어휘를 사용한 오답
- 동의어, 관련 어휘, 다의어를 사용한 오답
- 주체나 시제를 혼동한 오답
- 정보를 묻는 의문사 의문문에 Yes/No로 응답한 오답

* 실제 시험을 볼 때, Part 2 디렉션이 나오는 동안 Part 5 문제를 최대한 많이 풀면 전체 시험 시간 조절에 도움이 됩니다. 하지만 "Now, let us begin with question number 7"이라는 음성이 들리면 바로 Part 2로 돌아가서 문제를 풀도록 합니다.

Part 3 짧은 대화 (39문제)

· 2~3명이 주고받는 짧은 대화를 듣고 관련 질문에 대한 정답을 고르는 유형
· 구성: 총 13개의 대화에 39문제 출제 (한 대화 당 3문제, 일부 대화는 3문제와 함께 시각 자료가 출제)

문제 형태

문제지	음성
32. What are the speakers mainly discussing? (A) Finding a venue (B) Scheduling a renovation (C) Choosing a menu (D) Organizing a conference 33. What does the woman offer to do? (A) Visit a nearby event hall (B) Revise a travel itinerary (C) Proceed with a booking (D) Contact a facility manager 34. What does the woman mean when she says, "we're all set"? (A) Some furniture will be arranged. (B) Some memos will be circulated. (C) An update will be installed. (D) An area will be large enough.	Questions 32 through 34 refer to the following conversation. W: Joseph, I'm worried it'll be too chilly for the outdoor luncheon we've planned for Wednesday. M: I agree. We'd better book an event hall instead. W: How about Wolford Hall? I'm looking at its Web site now, and it appears to be available. M: Oh, that'd be ideal. That place is near our office, so staff won't have to travel far. W: I can book the hall now, if you want. We need it from 11 A.M. to 2 P.M., right? M: Yeah. Just make sure it can accommodate 50 people. W: It says it'll hold up to 70, so we're all set. M: Perfect. I'll send staff an e-mail with the updated details. Number 32. What are the speakers mainly discussing? Number 33. What does the woman offer to do? Number 34. What does the woman mean when she says, "we're all set"?

해설 32. 대화의 주제를 묻는 문제이다. 여자가 it'll be too chilly for the outdoor luncheon이라며 야외 오찬을 하기에는 날씨가 너무 쌀쌀할 것 같다고 하자, 남자가 We'd better book an event hall instead라며 대신 행사장을 예약하는 것이 낫겠다고 한 뒤, 행사를 위한 장소를 찾는 것에 관한 내용으로 대화가 이어지고 있다. 따라서 정답은 (A)이다.

33. 여자가 해주겠다고 제안하는 것을 묻는 문제이다. 여자가 I can book the hall now라며 지금 자신이 그 행사장을 예약할 수 있다고 하였다. 따라서 정답은 (C)이다.

34. 여자가 하는 말의 의도를 묻는 문제이다. 남자가 Just make sure it[hall] can accommodate 50 people이라며 행사장이 50명의 사람들을 수용할 수 있는지 확인하라고 하자, 여자가 it'll hold up to 70, so we're all set이라며 그것은 70명까지 수용할 것이니 우리는 준비가 다 되었다고 한 말을 통해 행사장의 공간이 충분히 클 것임을 알 수 있다. 따라서 정답은 (D)이다.

문제 풀이 전략

1. 대화를 듣기 전에 반드시 질문과 보기를 먼저 읽어야 합니다.

① Part 3의 디렉션을 들려줄 때 32번부터 34번까지의 질문과 보기를 읽으면, 이후 계속해서 대화를 듣기 전에 질문과 보기를 미리 읽을 수 있습니다.

② 질문을 읽을 때에는 질문 유형을 파악한 후, 해당 유형에 따라 어느 부분을 들을지와 어떤 내용을 들을지 듣기 전략을 세웁니다. 시각 자료가 출제된 대화의 경우, 시각 자료를 함께 확인하면서 시각 자료의 종류와 그 내용을 파악합니다.

③ 보기를 읽을 때에는 각 보기를 다르게 구별해주는 어휘를 선택적으로 읽어야 합니다. 특별히 보기가 문장일 경우, 주어가 모두 다르면 주어를, 주어가 모두 같으면 동사 또는 목적어 등의 중요 어휘를 키워드로 결정합니다.

2. 대화를 들으면서 동시에 정답을 선택합니다.

① 질문과 보기를 읽으며 세운 듣기 전략을 토대로, 대화를 들으면서 동시에 각 문제의 정답을 선택합니다.

② 3인 대화의 경우, 대화가 시작하기 전에 "Questions ~ refer to the following conversation with three speakers."라는 음성이 재생되므로 각 대화별 디렉션에도 집중해야 합니다.

③ 대화가 끝난 후 관련된 3개의 질문을 읽어줄 때 다음 대화와 관련된 3개의 질문과 보기를 재빨리 읽으면서 듣기 전략을 다시 세워야 합니다.

④ 만약 대화가 다 끝났는데도 정답을 선택하지 못했다면 가장 정답인 것 같은 보기를 선택하고, 곧바로 다음 대화에 해당하는 질문과 보기를 읽기 시작하는 것이 오답률을 줄이는 현명한 방법입니다.

3. 대화의 초반은 반드시 들어야 합니다.

① 대화에서 초반에 언급된 내용 중 80% 이상이 문제로 출제되므로 대화의 초반은 반드시 들어야 합니다.

② 특별히 대화의 주제를 묻는 문제, 대화자의 직업, 대화의 장소를 묻는 문제에 대한 정답의 단서는 대부분 대화의 초반에 언급됩니다.

③ 초반을 듣지 못하고 놓칠 경우 대화 후반에서 언급된 특정 표현을 사용한 보기를 정답으로 선택하는 오류를 범할 수 있으므로 각별히 주의해야 합니다.

▌Part 4 짧은 담화 (30문제)

· 짧은 담화를 듣고 관련 질문에 대한 정답을 고르는 유형
· 구성: 총 10개의 지문에 30문제 출제 (한 지문 당 3문제, 일부 지문은 3문제와 함께 시각 자료가 출제)

문제 형태

문제지	음성
<table><tr><th>Department</th><th>Manager</th></tr><tr><td>Accounting</td><td>Janet Lee</td></tr><tr><td>Sales</td><td>Sarah Bedford</td></tr><tr><td>Human Resources</td><td>David Weber</td></tr><tr><td>Marketing</td><td>Michael Brenner</td></tr></table> 92. What is the purpose of the announcement? (A) To explain a new project (B) To describe a job opening (C) To discuss a recent hire (D) To verify a policy change 93. Look at the graphic. Which department will Shannon Clark manage? (A) Accounting (B) Sales (C) Human Resources (D) Marketing 94. What will probably happen on September 1? (A) A job interview (B) A product launch (C) A staff gathering (D) An employee evaluation	Questions 92 through 94 refer to the following announcement and list. May I have your attention, please? I just received an e-mail from David Weber in human resources regarding a new manager. Shannon Clark will begin working here next month. Ms. Clark has over a decade of experience working for multinational corporations, so she brings a wealth of knowledge to our company. She will be replacing Michael Brenner, who is retiring this month. One of the other department managers . . . um, Janet Lee . . . has arranged a get-together on September 1 to introduce Ms. Clark. Food and beverages will be provided. Please give her a warm welcome. Number 92. What is the purpose of the announcement? Number 93. Look at the graphic. Which department will Shannon Clark manage? Number 94. What will probably happen on September 1?

해설 92. 공지의 목적을 묻는 문제이다. I just received an e-mail ~ regarding a new manager. Shannon Clark will begin working here next month라며 새로운 관리자에 관련된 이메일을 방금 받았으며, Shannon Clark가 다음 달에 이곳에서 근무를 시작할 것이라고 하였다. 따라서 정답은 (C)이다.

93. Shannon Clark가 관리할 부서를 묻는 문제이다. She[Shannon Clark] will be replacing Michael Brenner, who is retiring this month라며 Shannon Clark은 이달에 은퇴하는 Michael Brenner를 대신할 것이라고 하였으므로, Michael Brenner가 관리자로 일하던 마케팅 부서를 관리하게 될 것임을 알 수 있다. 따라서 정답은 (D)이다.

94. 9월 1일에 일어날 일을 묻는 문제이다. Janet Lee ~ has arranged a get-together on September 1라며 Janet Lee가 9월 1일에 열릴 모임을 마련했다고 하였다. 따라서 정답은 (C)이다.

문제 풀이 전략

1. 지문을 듣기 전에 반드시 질문과 보기를 먼저 읽어야 합니다.

① Part 4의 디렉션을 들려줄 때 71번부터 73번까지의 질문과 보기를 읽으면, 이후 계속해서 지문을 듣기 전에 질문과 보기를 미리 읽을 수 있습니다.

② 질문을 읽을 때에는 질문 유형을 파악한 후, 해당 유형에 따라 어느 부분을 들을지와 어떤 내용을 들을지 듣기 전략을 세웁니다. 시각 자료가 출제된 담화의 경우, 시각 자료를 함께 확인하면서 시각 자료의 종류와 그 내용을 파악합니다.

③ 보기를 읽을 때에는 각 보기를 다르게 구별해주는 어휘를 선택적으로 읽어야 합니다. 특별히 보기가 문장일 경우, 주어가 모두 다르면 주어를, 주어가 모두 같으면 동사 또는 목적어 등의 중요 어휘를 키워드로 결정합니다.

2. 지문을 들으면서 동시에 정답을 선택합니다.

① 질문과 보기를 읽으며 세운 듣기 전략을 토대로, 지문을 들으면서 동시에 각 문제의 정답을 곧바로 선택합니다.

② 지문의 음성이 끝날 때에는 세 문제의 정답 선택도 완료되어 있어야 합니다.

③ 지문의 음성이 끝난 후 관련된 3개의 질문을 읽어줄 때 다음 지문과 관련된 3개의 질문과 보기를 재빨리 읽으면서 듣기 전략을 다시 세워야 합니다.

④ 만약 지문이 다 끝났는데도 정답을 선택하지 못했다면 가장 정답인 것 같은 보기를 선택하고, 곧바로 다음 지문에 해당하는 질문과 보기를 읽기 시작하는 것이 오답률을 줄이는 현명한 방법입니다.

3. 지문의 초반은 반드시 들어야 합니다.

① 지문에서 초반에 언급된 내용 중 80% 이상이 문제로 출제되므로 지문의 초반을 반드시 들어야 합니다.

② 특별히 지문의 주제/목적 문제나 화자/청자 및 담화 장소 문제처럼 전체 지문 관련 문제에 대한 정답의 단서는 대부분 지문의 초반에 언급됩니다.

③ 초반을 듣지 못하고 놓칠 경우 더 이상 관련된 내용이 언급되지 않아 정답 선택이 어려워질 수 있으므로 주의해야 합니다.

수준별 맞춤 학습 플랜

TEST 01을 마친 후 자신의 환산 점수에 맞는 학습 플랜을 선택하고 매일매일 박스에 체크하며 공부합니다. 각 TEST를 마친 후, 다양한 자료를 활용하여 각 테스트를 꼼꼼하게 리뷰합니다.

* 각 테스트를 마친 후, 해당 테스트의 점수를 교재 앞쪽에 있는 [토익 Listening 목표 달성기]에 기록하여 자신의 점수 변화를 확인할 수 있습니다.

400점 이상
2주 완성 학습 플랜

· 2주 동안 매일 테스트 1회분을 교재 뒤의 Answer Sheet(p.229)를 활용하여 실전처럼 풀어본 후 꼼꼼하게 리뷰합니다.
· 리뷰 시, 틀렸던 문제를 다시 듣고 풀어본 후, 교재 뒤의 **스크립트**를 활용하여 들리지 않았던 부분까지 완벽히 이해합니다.
· 해커스토익(Hackers.co.kr)에서 무료로 제공되는 **지문 및 문제 해석**으로 틀린 지문과 문제의 의미를 확실하게 이해합니다.
· 해커스인강(HackersIngang.com)에서 무료로 제공되는 **단어암기장 및 단어암기 MP3**로 각 TEST의 핵심 어휘 중 모르는 어휘만 체크하여 암기합니다.

	Day 1	Day 2	Day 3	Day 4	Day 5
Week 1	□ Test 01 풀기 및 리뷰	□ Test 02 풀기 및 리뷰	□ Test 03 풀기 및 리뷰	□ Test 04 풀기 및 리뷰	□ Test 05 풀기 및 리뷰
Week 2	□ Test 06 풀기 및 리뷰	□ Test 07 풀기 및 리뷰	□ Test 08 풀기 및 리뷰	□ Test 09 풀기 및 리뷰	□ Test 10 풀기 및 리뷰

※ ≪해커스 토익 실전 1000제 3 Listening 해설집≫(별매)으로 리뷰하기
  · 자신이 틀렸던 문제와 난이도 최상 문제를 다시 한번 풀어보고 완벽하게 이해합니다.
  · 틀린 문제는 정답 및 오답 해설을 보며 오답이 왜 오답인지 그 이유까지 확실하게 파악합니다.

300~395점
3주 완성 학습 플랜

· 3주 동안 첫째 날, 둘째 날에 테스트 1회분씩을 풀어본 후 꼼꼼하게 리뷰하고, 셋째 날에는 2회분에 대한 심화 학습을 합니다.
· 리뷰 시, 틀렸던 문제를 다시 듣고 풀어본 후, 교재 뒤의 **스크립트**를 활용하여 들리지 않았던 부분까지 완벽히 이해합니다.
· 심화 학습 시, 리뷰했던 내용을 복습하고 대화/지문의 핵심 어휘를 정리하고 암기합니다.
· 해커스토익(Hackers.co.kr)에서 무료로 제공되는 **지문 및 문제 해석**으로 틀린 지문과 문제의 의미를 확실하게 이해합니다.
· 해커스인강(HackersIngang.com)에서 무료로 제공되는 **단어암기장 및 단어암기 MP3**로 각 TEST의 핵심 어휘를 암기합니다.

	Day 1	Day 2	Day 3	Day 4	Day 5
Week 1	□ Test 01 풀기 및 리뷰	□ Test 02 풀기 및 리뷰	□ Test 01&02 심화 학습	□ Test 03 풀기 및 리뷰	□ Test 04 풀기 및 리뷰
Week 2	□ Test 03&04 심화 학습	□ Test 05 풀기 및 리뷰	□ Test 06 풀기 및 리뷰	□ Test 05&06 심화 학습	□ Test 07 풀기 및 리뷰
Week 3	□ Test 08 풀기 및 리뷰	□ Test 07&08 심화 학습	□ Test 09 풀기 및 리뷰	□ Test 10 풀기 및 리뷰	□ Test 09&10 심화 학습

※ ≪해커스 토익 실전 1000제 3 Listening 해설집≫(별매)으로 리뷰하기
  · 자신이 틀렸던 문제와 난이도 중 이상의 문제를 다시 한번 풀어보고 완벽하게 이해합니다.
  · 틀린 문제는 정답 및 오답 해설을 보며 오답이 왜 오답인지 그 이유까지 확실하게 파악합니다.
  · 모든 문제마다 표시된 문제 유형을 보며 자신이 자주 틀리는 문제 유형이 무엇인지 파악하고 보완합니다.
  · 대화/지문에 자주색으로 표시된 정답의 단서를 보고 정답을 선택해보며 문제 풀이 노하우를 파악합니다.

295점 이하
4주 완성 학습 플랜

· 4주 동안 이틀]에 걸쳐 테스트 1회분을 풀고 꼼꼼하게 리뷰합니다.
· 리뷰 시, 모든 문제를 다시 듣고 풀어본 후, 교재 뒤쪽의 **스크립트**를 활용하여 들리지 않았던 부분까지 완벽하게 이해합니다.
· 해커스토익(Hackers.co.kr)에서 무료로 제공되는 **지문 및 문제 해석**으로 모든 지문과 문제의 의미를 완벽하게 이해합니다.
· 해커스인강(HackersIngang.com)에서 무료로 제공되는 **단어암기장 및 단어암기 MP3**로 각 TEST의 핵심 어휘를 암기합니다.

	Day 1	Day 2	Day 3	Day 4	Day 5
Week 1	☐ Test 01 풀기	☐ Test 01 리뷰	☐ Test 02 풀기	☐ Test 02 리뷰	☐ Test 03 풀기
Week 2	☐ Test 03 리뷰	☐ Test 04 풀기	☐ Test 04 리뷰	☐ Test 05 풀기	☐ Test 05 리뷰
Week 3	☐ Test 06 풀기	☐ Test 06 리뷰	☐ Test 07 풀기	☐ Test 07 리뷰	☐ Test 08 풀기
Week 4	☐ Test 08 리뷰	☐ Test 09 풀기	☐ Test 09 리뷰	☐ Test 10 풀기	☐ Test 10 리뷰

※ ≪**해커스 토익 실전 1000제 3 Listening 해설집**≫(별매)으로 리뷰하기
· 자신이 틀렸던 문제와 난이도 중 이상의 문제를 다시 한번 풀어보고 완벽하게 이해합니다.
· 틀린 문제는 정답 및 오답 해설을 보며 오답이 왜 오답인지 그 이유까지 확실하게 파악합니다.
· 모든 문제마다 표시된 문제 유형을 보며 자신이 자주 틀리는 문제 유형이 무엇인지 파악하고 보완합니다.
· 대화/지문에 자주색으로 표시된 정답의 단서를 보고 정답을 선택해보며 문제 풀이 노하우를 파악합니다.
· Part 3·4의 중요한 바꾸어 표현하기를 정리하고 암기합니다.

해커스와 함께라면 여러분의 목표를 더 빠르게 달성할 수 있습니다!
자신의 점수에 맞춰 아래 해커스 교재로 함께 학습하시면 더욱 빠르게 여러분이 목표한 바를 달성할 수 있습니다.

400점 이상	300~395점	295점 이하
≪해커스 토익 Listening≫	≪해커스 토익 750+ LC≫	≪해커스 토익 스타트 Listening≫

TEST 01

PART **1**
PART **2**
PART **3**
PART **4**
Self 체크 리스트

잠깐! 테스트 전 확인사항
1. 휴대 전화의 전원을 끄셨나요? □ 예
2. Answer Sheet, 연필, 지우개를 준비하셨나요? □ 예
3. MP3를 들을 준비가 되셨나요? □ 예

모든 준비가 완료되었으면 목표 점수를 떠올린 후 테스트를 시작합니다.
TEST 01을 통해 본인의 실력을 평가해 본 후, 본인에게 맞는 학습 플랜(p.20~21)으로 본 교재를 효율적으로 학습해 보세요.

🎧 TEST 01.mp3
실전용·복습용 문제풀이 MP3 무료 다운로드 및 스트리밍 바로듣기 (HackersIngang.com)
* 실제 시험장의 소음까지 재현해 낸 고사장 소음/매미 버전 MP3, 영국식·호주식 발음 집중 MP3, 고속 버전 MP3까지
  구매하면 실전에 더욱 완벽히 대비할 수 있습니다.

무료MP3 바로듣기

LISTENING TEST

In this section, you must demonstrate your ability to understand spoken English. This section is divided into four parts and will take approximately 45 minutes to complete. Do not mark the answers in your test book. Use the answer sheet that is provided separately.

PART 1

Directions: For each question, you will listen to four short statements about a picture in your test book. These statements will not be printed and will only be spoken one time. Select the statement that best describes what is happening in the picture and mark the corresponding letter (A), (B), (C), or (D) on the answer sheet.

Sample Answer

The statement that best describes the picture is (B), "The man is sitting at the desk." So, you should mark letter (B) on the answer sheet.

1.

2.

GO ON TO THE NEXT PAGE ▶

3.

4.

5.

6.

GO ON TO THE NEXT PAGE ➡

PART 2

Directions: For each question, you will listen to a statement or question followed by three possible responses spoken in English. They will not be printed and will only be spoken one time. Select the best response and mark the corresponding letter (A), (B), or (C) on your answer sheet.

7. Mark your answer on your answer sheet.

8. Mark your answer on your answer sheet.

9. Mark your answer on your answer sheet.

10. Mark your answer on your answer sheet.

11. Mark your answer on your answer sheet.

12. Mark your answer on your answer sheet.

13. Mark your answer on your answer sheet.

14. Mark your answer on your answer sheet.

15. Mark your answer on your answer sheet.

16. Mark your answer on your answer sheet.

17. Mark your answer on your answer sheet.

18. Mark your answer on your answer sheet.

19. Mark your answer on your answer sheet.

20. Mark your answer on your answer sheet.

21. Mark your answer on your answer sheet.

22. Mark your answer on your answer sheet.

23. Mark your answer on your answer sheet.

24. Mark your answer on your answer sheet.

25. Mark your answer on your answer sheet.

26. Mark your answer on your answer sheet.

27. Mark your answer on your answer sheet.

28. Mark your answer on your answer sheet.

29. Mark your answer on your answer sheet.

30. Mark your answer on your answer sheet.

31. Mark your answer on your answer sheet.

PART 3

Directions: In this part, you will listen to several conversations between two or more speakers. These conversations will not be printed and will only be spoken one time. For each conversation, you will be asked to answer three questions. Select the best response and mark the corresponding letter (A), (B), (C), or (D) on your answer sheet.

32. What problem does the man mention?
    (A) A device is malfunctioning.
    (B) A deadline is approaching.
    (C) A customer is dissatisfied.
    (D) A service is unreliable.

33. What does the woman offer to do?
    (A) Take over a task
    (B) Visit a client
    (C) Conduct a survey
    (D) Call a coworker

34. According to the man, what will happen later today?
    (A) A product discussion
    (B) A business luncheon
    (C) A sales presentation
    (D) A client meeting

35. Why is the man calling?
    (A) To place an order
    (B) To complain about a policy
    (C) To confirm a closing time
    (D) To make a reservation

36. What does the man ask about?
    (A) The availability of menu items
    (B) The cost of additional options
    (C) The location of a business
    (D) The use of a payment method

37. What will the man receive?
    (A) A cold appetizer
    (B) A free dessert
    (C) A basket of bread
    (D) A complimentary beverage

38. What event is most likely taking place?
    (A) A book signing
    (B) An exhibit opening
    (C) An art class
    (D) A lecture

39. What will Mr. Li do when he arrives?
    (A) Deliver a talk
    (B) Hold an auction
    (C) Buy some paintings
    (D) Teach some students

40. What does the woman want to do?
    (A) Buy an artwork
    (B) Read a publication
    (C) Meet an artist
    (D) Tour a facility

41. What problem does Sophie mention?
    (A) A handbook is missing.
    (B) A machine is out of order.
    (C) A meeting space is occupied.
    (D) A beverage is unavailable.

42. What does the man suggest?
    (A) Sending out a form
    (B) Searching in some compartments
    (C) Repairing a microwave
    (D) Visiting a different part of the building

43. What is mentioned about Mr. Harper?
    (A) He regularly orders items.
    (B) He was recently promoted.
    (C) He is in the break room now.
    (D) He owns a coffee farm.

GO ON TO THE NEXT PAGE

44. What most likely did the man receive from the woman?

    (A) A list of employees
    (B) A research paper
    (C) A job application
    (D) A reference letter

45. What does the woman mean when she says, "the workday has already ended"?

    (A) She is not able to stay late.
    (B) Her boss may not be available.
    (C) Her working hours have been shortened.
    (D) She has a busy schedule these days.

46. What will the man do on Monday?

    (A) Make a phone call
    (B) Send an e-mail
    (C) Revise a document
    (D) Start a training session

47. What most likely is the man's job?

    (A) Newspaper publisher
    (B) Web designer
    (C) Journalist
    (D) Sports club owner

48. What problem does the man mention?

    (A) A meeting has been rescheduled.
    (B) He does not know where an office is.
    (C) He is unable to contact an individual.
    (D) A team is underperforming.

49. According to the woman, what will happen on February 4?

    (A) An applicant will be hired.
    (B) An interview will be held.
    (C) A Web site will be updated.
    (D) A publication will be released.

50. Why are the employees dissatisfied?

    (A) They work too many hours per day.
    (B) They only get half an hour for lunch.
    (C) They have to come into the office too early.
    (D) They do not have enough days off.

51. What is mentioned about Pilsen Suppliers?

    (A) It has updated its vacation policy.
    (B) It will hire additional workers.
    (C) It will go out of business.
    (D) It recently opened a new branch.

52. What will the man consider doing next week?

    (A) Presenting an idea
    (B) Submitting a form
    (C) Sending out an e-mail
    (D) Announcing a change

53. What does the woman ask the man for?

    (A) His seating preferences
    (B) His business card
    (C) A telephone number
    (D) An invitation

54. Who most likely is Keith Harrison?

    (A) A legal practitioner
    (B) A real estate agent
    (C) A receptionist
    (D) An event planner

55. Why does the man say, "My name is quite difficult to spell"?

    (A) To indicate concern
    (B) To show understanding
    (C) To raise an objection
    (D) To point out an error

56. Where most likely will the speakers go this afternoon?

(A) To a print shop
(B) To a resort
(C) To an exhibition hall
(D) To a tourist attraction

57. What does the woman mention about a grand opening?

(A) It was held about a year ago.
(B) It included a performance.
(C) It took place at a convention center.
(D) It was attended by clients.

58. What will Joel probably do next?

(A) Rearrange an office
(B) Wait at an entrance
(C) Visit a storage area
(D) Return a phone call

59. What most likely was the focus of the special lecture?

(A) An industry outlook
(B) A business opportunity
(C) A consumer trend
(D) A technology's use

60. What does the man complain about?

(A) The number of display models
(B) The cost of tickets
(C) The length of lectures
(D) The type of activities

61. How is this year's event different from the previous one?

(A) It includes more speakers.
(B) It has fewer people in attendance.
(C) It has received less support.
(D) It has generated less media interest.

Inbox		
From	**Subject**	**Received**
David Greer	Warehouse Expansion	2:40 P.M.
Brent Hong	Late Delivery	1:20 P.M.
Lisa Porter	Workshop Details	10:15 A.M.
Mia Gomez	Report Deadline	8:45 A.M.

62. Why does the woman want to delay her departure?

(A) To review some materials
(B) To meet a deadline
(C) To visit a branch
(D) To resolve an issue

63. Look at the graphic. Whose e-mail does the woman refer to?

(A) David Greer's
(B) Brent Hong's
(C) Lisa Porter's
(D) Mia Gomez's

64. What does the man suggest the woman do?

(A) Go to a warehouse
(B) Hand over a task
(C) Postpone a meeting
(D) Speak with a client

GO ON TO THE NEXT PAGE

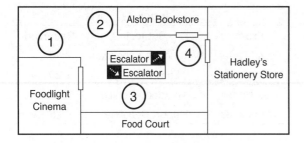

65. What does the woman mention about Gene?

(A) He has a set of tickets.
(B) He has already seen the movie.
(C) He is coming from a lower floor.
(D) He did not bring his phone along.

66. Look at the graphic. Where are the speakers standing?

(A) Location 1
(B) Location 2
(C) Location 3
(D) Location 4

67. What will the woman probably do next?

(A) Confirm a meeting location
(B) Visit an information desk
(C) Head up to a different floor
(D) Enter a stationery store

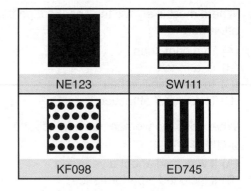

68. Who most likely is the man?

(A) A sales representative
(B) An interior designer
(C) A real estate agent
(D) A store manager

69. Look at the graphic. Which model was recently released?

(A) NE123
(B) SW111
(C) KF098
(D) ED745

70. What should the man do to place an advance order?

(A) Consult a manager
(B) Go to a Web site
(C) Submit a document
(D) Place a phone call

PART 4

Directions: In this part, you will listen to several short talks by a single speaker. These talks will not be printed and will only be spoken one time. For each talk, you will be asked to answer three questions. Select the best response and mark the corresponding letter (A), (B), (C), or (D) on your answer sheet.

71. What will the listener do later today?

(A) Submit a report
(B) Go to an airport
(C) Send out an e-mail
(D) Fill out a survey

72. What is the listener asked to do?

(A) Print a document
(B) Meet with a manager
(C) Increase a budget
(D) Talk to a client

73. What does the speaker remind the listener about?

(A) A reimbursement policy
(B) A promotion opportunity
(C) A workspace relocation
(D) A deadline extension

74. Who most likely is the speaker?

(A) A photographer
(B) A writer
(C) A director
(D) An actress

75. Why does the speaker especially thank Ms. Anderson?

(A) She worked additional hours.
(B) She edited a script.
(C) She gave some advice.
(D) She planned an event.

76. What will happen after dinner?

(A) A speech will be given.
(B) A work will be shown.
(C) A workshop will be held.
(D) An evaluation will be conducted.

77. Where most likely is the announcement taking place?

(A) In a service center
(B) In a restaurant kitchen
(C) In a storage facility
(D) In a retail outlet

78. What does the speaker mean when he says, "there is a lot of frozen food"?

(A) A product needs to be consumed.
(B) A task must be completed quickly.
(C) A delivery includes the wrong items.
(D) A worker should be told of a problem.

79. What is mentioned about Mr. Wilkins?

(A) He can be found in his office.
(B) He is planning to hire staff.
(C) He was just promoted.
(D) He asked for some equipment.

80. Who most likely are the listeners?

(A) Painters
(B) Curators
(C) Tourists
(D) Interns

81. According to the speaker, why does the tour start from the Italian Gallery?

(A) An area is being remodeled.
(B) A display has been taken down.
(C) An exhibition is being prepared.
(D) A section has been newly opened.

82. What will the listeners do after lunch?

(A) They will go to the second floor.
(B) They will attend a lecture.
(C) They will take a break.
(D) They will join a workshop.

GO ON TO THE NEXT PAGE

83. Why is the speaker calling?

(A) To report a found item
(B) To offer a financial service
(C) To address a question
(D) To confirm an appointment

84. What does the speaker imply when she says, "that option will no longer be available from next week"?

(A) Business hours will be changed.
(B) An employee will go on leave.
(C) A branch will be closed down.
(D) Security procedures will be updated.

85. What does the listener have to bring?

(A) A photocopy of a bankbook
(B) An exact amount of cash
(C) A credit card application
(D) An identification card

---

86. What is the advertisement mainly about?

(A) A chance to appear in a production
(B) An opportunity to compete in a contest
(C) An offer to subscribe to a cable service
(D) An invitation to an outdoor party

87. What does the speaker mention about the Orange Hotel?

(A) It has a large banquet room.
(B) It is a famous tourist attraction.
(C) It will be closed in June.
(D) It will be a filming location.

88. What does the speaker ask the listeners to send to Mr. Geltman?

(A) Some scenario samples
(B) Some personal details
(C) A photograph
(D) A video clip

89. What is mentioned about the lecture series?

(A) It is held at a university.
(B) It is an annual event.
(C) It has a specific theme.
(D) It started later than anticipated.

90. Who most likely is Miles Kramer?

(A) An educational researcher
(B) A novelist
(C) A graduate student
(D) A professor

91. What does the speaker suggest the listeners do?

(A) Move to the front seats
(B) Form a discussion group
(C) Purchase a publication
(D) Read the first chapter of a book

---

92. Who most likely is Stacy Addison?

(A) A consultant
(B) A realtor
(C) An investor
(D) A recruiter

93. Why does the speaker say, "she's worked on many similar projects before"?

(A) To indicate surprise
(B) To suggest a solution
(C) To express confidence
(D) To accept a suggestion

94. What will be assigned to Ms. Addison?

(A) A personal computer
(B) A workspace
(C) A deadline
(D) An employee card

Benefits	Membership Level			
	Blue	Yellow	Green	Purple
Discounts on refreshments on-board	√	√	√	√
Access to exclusive lounge		√	√	√
Free travel insurance			√	√
Priority boarding				√

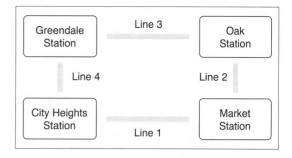

95. What did the marketing department recently do?

(A) Organized a promotion
(B) Conducted a survey
(C) Replaced a slogan
(D) Updated a policy

96. Look at the graphic. Which membership level will probably be discontinued?

(A) Blue
(B) Yellow
(C) Green
(D) Purple

97. Why did a supplier raise its prices recently?

(A) Shipping costs have risen.
(B) Workers demanded a wage increase.
(C) Ingredient prices have gone up.
(D) Consumer demand has grown stronger.

98. What is the purpose of the broadcast?

(A) To warn residents of potential danger
(B) To describe the effects of a storm
(C) To explain how a building was damaged
(D) To offer advice on how to fix the power

99. What did Mayor Roberson do this morning?

(A) Inspected a power facility
(B) Visited suburban areas
(C) Met with city workers
(D) Announced a work schedule

100. Look at the graphic. Which metro line has been closed?

(A) Line 1
(B) Line 2
(C) Line 3
(D) Line 4

Self 체크 리스트

TEST 01은 무사히 잘 마치셨죠?
이제 다음의 Self 체크 리스트를 통해 자신의 테스트 진행 내용을 점검해 볼까요?

1. 나는 테스트가 진행되는 동안 한 번도 중도에 멈추지 않았다.

   □ 예　　　　　　　□ 아니오

   아니오에 답한 경우, 이유는 무엇인가요?

2. 나는 답안지 표기까지 성실하게 모두 마무리하였다.

   □ 예　　　　　　　□ 아니오

   아니오에 답한 경우, 이유는 무엇인가요?

3. 나는 Part 2의 25문항을 푸는 동안 완전히 테스트에 집중하였다.

   □ 예　　　　　　　□ 아니오

   아니오에 답한 경우, 이유는 무엇인가요?

4. 나는 Part 3를 풀 때 음성이 들리기 전에 해당 질문과 보기를 모두 먼저 읽었다.

   □ 예　　　　　　　□ 아니오

   아니오에 답한 경우, 이유는 무엇인가요?

5. 나는 Part 4를 풀 때 음성이 들리기 전에 해당 질문과 보기를 모두 먼저 읽었다.

   □ 예　　　　　　　□ 아니오

   아니오에 답한 경우, 이유는 무엇인가요?

6. 개선해야 할 점 또는 나를 위한 충고를 적어보세요.

* 교재의 첫 장으로 돌아가서 자신이 적은 목표 점수를 확인하면서 목표에 대한 의지를 다지기 바랍니다. 개선해야 할 점은 반드시 다음 테스트에 실천해야 합니다. 그것이 가장 중요하며, 그래야만 발전할 수 있습니다.

❙TEST 02

PART **1**
PART **2**
PART **3**
PART **4**
Self 체크 리스트

잠깐! 테스트 전 확인사항
1. 휴대 전화의 전원을 끄셨나요? ☐ 예
2. Answer Sheet, 연필, 지우개를 준비하셨나요? ☐ 예
3. MP3를 들을 준비가 되셨나요? ☐ 예

모든 준비가 완료되었으면 목표 점수를 떠올린 후 테스트를 시작합니다.

무료MP3 바로듣기

🎧 TEST 02.mp3
실전용·복습용 문제풀이 MP3 무료 다운로드 및 스트리밍 바로듣기 (HackersIngang.com)
* 실제 시험장의 소음까지 재현해 낸 고사장 소음/매미 버전 MP3, 영국식·호주식 발음 집중 MP3, 고속 버전 MP3까지
구매하면 실전에 더욱 완벽히 대비할 수 있습니다.

LISTENING TEST

In this section, you must demonstrate your ability to understand spoken English. This section is divided into four parts and will take approximately 45 minutes to complete. Do not mark the answers in your test book. Use the answer sheet that is provided separately.

PART 1

Directions: For each question, you will listen to four short statements about a picture in your test book. These statements will not be printed and will only be spoken one time. Select the statement that best describes what is happening in the picture and mark the corresponding letter (A), (B), (C), or (D) on the answer sheet.

Sample Answer

The statement that best describes the picture is (B), "The man is sitting at the desk." So, you should mark letter (B) on the answer sheet.

1.

2.

GO ON TO THE NEXT PAGE ➤

3.

4.

5.

6.

GO ON TO THE NEXT PAGE ➡

PART 2

Directions: For each question, you will listen to a statement or question followed by three possible responses spoken in English. They will not be printed and will only be spoken one time. Select the best response and mark the corresponding letter (A), (B), or (C) on your answer sheet.

7. Mark your answer on your answer sheet.

8. Mark your answer on your answer sheet.

9. Mark your answer on your answer sheet.

10. Mark your answer on your answer sheet.

11. Mark your answer on your answer sheet.

12. Mark your answer on your answer sheet.

13. Mark your answer on your answer sheet.

14. Mark your answer on your answer sheet.

15. Mark your answer on your answer sheet.

16. Mark your answer on your answer sheet.

17. Mark your answer on your answer sheet.

18. Mark your answer on your answer sheet.

19. Mark your answer on your answer sheet.

20. Mark your answer on your answer sheet.

21. Mark your answer on your answer sheet.

22. Mark your answer on your answer sheet.

23. Mark your answer on your answer sheet.

24. Mark your answer on your answer sheet.

25. Mark your answer on your answer sheet.

26. Mark your answer on your answer sheet.

27. Mark your answer on your answer sheet.

28. Mark your answer on your answer sheet.

29. Mark your answer on your answer sheet.

30. Mark your answer on your answer sheet.

31. Mark your answer on your answer sheet.

PART 3

Directions: In this part, you will listen to several conversations between two or more speakers. These conversations will not be printed and will only be spoken one time. For each conversation, you will be asked to answer three questions. Select the best response and mark the corresponding letter (A), (B), (C), or (D) on your answer sheet.

32. What will the community center receive?

(A) Donations from a company
(B) Computers from local charities
(C) Funds from the government
(D) Equipment from a university

33. What are the speakers planning to do?

(A) Upgrade old devices
(B) Move to a larger building
(C) Order additional books
(D) Run an educational workshop

34. Why must the speakers review some documents?

(A) To compare some prices
(B) To identify some donors
(C) To determine some restrictions
(D) To research some venues

35. What industry does the woman work in?

(A) Hospitality
(B) Agriculture
(C) Construction
(D) Economics

36. Why did the woman contact the man?

(A) To verify a delivery time
(B) To inquire about job duties
(C) To arrange an interview
(D) To confirm a contract detail

37. What will the man most likely bring for the woman?

(A) A résumé
(B) A work sample
(C) An application form
(D) A reference letter

38. What does the man say about Detroit?

(A) It experienced bad weather.
(B) It has a newly built airport.
(C) It is only an hour away.
(D) It is hosting a major event.

39. According to the woman, why is Mr. Herman coming to the office?

(A) To train some personnel
(B) To discuss travel arrangements
(C) To make an announcement
(D) To observe a presentation

40. What will the man probably do next?

(A) Take a lunch break
(B) Begin a meeting
(C) Pass on some information
(D) Share some sales reports

41. Why does the man say "summer is approaching"?

(A) To suggest a change of schedule
(B) To ask a deadline extension
(C) To announce a seasonal event
(D) To explain a decline in sales

42. What does the woman ask about?

(A) The start of a promotion
(B) The amount of a discount
(C) The location of a business
(D) The name of a product

43. What will the man do in the coming days?

(A) Contact media outlets
(B) Order different kinds of clothing
(C) Create an advertisement
(D) Clean a section of the store

GO ON TO THE NEXT PAGE

44. Who most likely is the man?

(A) A sales associate
(B) A store manager
(C) A delivery person
(D) A maintenance worker

45. What is mentioned about the shelves?

(A) They must be installed on the door.
(B) They have already been assembled.
(C) They are too large to be brought in.
(D) They were purchased last week.

46. What does the man suggest?

(A) Displaying some signs
(B) Signing a document
(C) Delaying a task
(D) Moving some items

47. Where does the woman work?

(A) At a consultancy
(B) At a real estate company
(C) At a grocery store
(D) At a landscaping firm

48. What does the woman say her company did last summer?

(A) Took on a commercial job
(B) Expanded to other cities
(C) Relocated its headquarters
(D) Raised its prices

49. What does the woman ask for?

(A) Property locations
(B) Budget amounts
(C) Price comparisons
(D) Project details

50. What is the purpose of the woman's visit?

(A) To view some test results
(B) To schedule an appointment
(C) To get some medication
(D) To pick up a building map

51. Who most likely are the men?

(A) Pharmacists
(B) Doctors
(C) Medical researchers
(D) Clinic directors

52. What information does Daniel provide?

(A) The location for a shot
(B) The name of a business
(C) The cost of an examination
(D) The number of a room

53. Where most likely do the speakers work?

(A) At a financial institution
(B) At a cosmetics company
(C) At an advertising agency
(D) At a convention center

54. What does the man mean when he says, "Many people commented on it"?

(A) A method was a great success.
(B) A service received positive feedback.
(C) An event attracted many visitors.
(D) A venue introduced a new policy.

55. What does the man suggest?

(A) Reviewing a slideshow
(B) Relocating a booth
(C) Contacting a colleague
(D) Leaving for a function

56. Who most likely is the woman?

(A) A construction worker
(B) A restaurant owner
(C) A real estate agent
(D) An interior designer

57. What does the man want to do?

(A) Test an appliance
(B) Prepare a meal
(C) Visit another location
(D) Complete a form

58. What does the woman mention about the deposit?

(A) It will be returned after a one-week period.
(B) It may be increased in special circumstances.
(C) It must be paid with a personal check.
(D) It is due shortly after an application is accepted.

---

59. What is the conversation mainly about?

(A) The reason for evaluations
(B) The details of a negotiation
(C) The success of an investment
(D) The cost of operations

60. What is mentioned about staff?

(A) They will receive salary increases.
(B) They will learn specialized skills.
(C) They will transfer to a new division.
(D) They will undergo an assessment.

61. Why does the woman require the man's approval?

(A) She needs to conduct an analysis.
(B) She plans to post a memo.
(C) She wants to submit another offer.
(D) She wishes to agree to a deal.

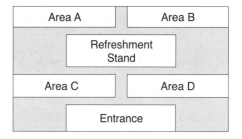

62. What type of event is happening tonight?

(A) A performance rehearsal
(B) An awards ceremony
(C) A movie screening
(D) A play opening

63. What does the woman ask the man to do?

(A) Arrange some furniture
(B) Work a late shift
(C) Hang up some frames
(D) Greet incoming guests

64. Look at the graphic. Where most likely will photos be taken?

(A) In Area A
(B) In Area B
(C) In Area C
(D) In Area D

GO ON TO THE NEXT PAGE

Dale Consultancy Reimbursement Form
Employee Name: James Vold

Reason for Expense	Amount
Airfare	$345
Osaka Hotel (3 nights)	$621
Bento Hotel Restaurant	$31
Taxi fares	$45
Shiro Airport Café	$24
TOTAL	**$1,067**

Flight	Destination	Status	Updated Arrival Time
AB701	Phoenix	On Time	9:00 A.M.
UR770	Portland	Delayed	10:30 A.M.
WX803	Cincinnati	Delayed	12:00 P.M.
ZP890	Portland	On Time	3:30 P.M.
TA900	Dallas	Delayed	6:00 P.M.

65. Look at the graphic. Which amount was not reimbursed?

(A) $345
(B) $31
(C) $45
(D) $24

66. Why does the man apologize?

(A) He sent a report to the wrong address.
(B) He failed to submit a document.
(C) He made a mistake in his calculations.
(D) He did not get permission for an expense.

67. What problem does the woman mention?

(A) A due date has been already passed.
(B) A company policy was changed.
(C) A budget amount has been reduced.
(D) A supervisor's permission is required.

68. Why is the man worried?

(A) A ticket was not printed.
(B) An airport is located far away.
(C) A flight might be missed.
(D) A terminal has been blocked off.

69. What does the man want to do?

(A) Listen to a lecture on a laptop
(B) Access the Internet
(C) Check in at a gate
(D) Inform a supervisor of an arrival time

70. Look at the graphic. Which flight will the speakers take?

(A) UR770
(B) WX803
(C) ZP890
(D) TA900

PART 4

Directions: In this part, you will listen to several short talks by a single speaker. These talks will not be printed and will only be spoken one time. For each talk, you will be asked to answer three questions. Select the best response and mark the corresponding letter (A), (B), (C), or (D) on your answer sheet.

71. What was changed recently?

   (A) The name of a company
   (B) The time of an appointment
   (C) The cost of a service
   (D) The location of a business

72. What is the listener asked to do?

   (A) Request new glasses
   (B) Contact a physician
   (C) Arrange an examination
   (D) Bring a document

73. Why should the listener show up early?

   (A) To talk with a specialist
   (B) To pay an outstanding bill
   (C) To complete some paperwork
   (D) To take a short test

74. Who most likely is the speaker?

   (A) A company president
   (B) A business consultant
   (C) A government official
   (D) A branch manager

75. What does Starbox Incorporated most likely focus on?

   (A) Computer programs
   (B) Travel packages
   (C) Television programs
   (D) Property development

76. What does the speaker imply when he says, "I was simply pursuing my hobby at the time"?

   (A) He knew that a product was imperfect.
   (B) He took a job because it interested him.
   (C) He did not want to work in the field.
   (D) He did not expect to achieve success.

77. Who is the speaker?

   (A) A research assistant
   (B) A corporate advisor
   (C) A product engineer
   (D) A Web site designer

78. What did the speaker do five years ago?

   (A) Started a new company
   (B) Created a social media platform
   (C) Oversaw a business merger
   (D) Accepted a job at an agency

79. What will happen over the next two weeks?

   (A) Discounts will be offered.
   (B) A survey will be conducted.
   (C) A campaign will be developed.
   (D) Evaluations will be performed.

80. What type of business is being advertised?

   (A) An electronics retailer
   (B) A waste disposal company
   (C) An appliance repair shop
   (D) A computer manufacturer

81. According to the speaker, what happens each month?

   (A) A device is put on sale.
   (B) An exhibit is held.
   (C) An item is given away.
   (D) A donation is made.

82. How can the listeners take part in a drawing?

   (A) By becoming a member
   (B) By making an online profile
   (C) By using a coupon
   (D) By spending a certain amount

GO ON TO THE NEXT PAGE

83. Where most likely does the speaker work?

(A) At a university
(B) At a print shop
(C) At a financial firm
(D) At an advertising agency

84. Why are volunteers needed?

(A) To plan a job fair for students
(B) To rent an informational booth
(C) To post flyers around a city
(D) To represent a business at an event

85. According to the speaker, what has already been done?

(A) A legal professional was contacted.
(B) Some handouts were prepared.
(C) Applications were collected.
(D) Some questions were answered.

---

86. What is the speaker mainly discussing?

(A) The expansion of a retail chain
(B) The introduction of a new model
(C) The elimination of a product line
(D) The promotion of a department head

87. Why does the speaker say, "Our warehouse is currently full of stock"?

(A) To express uncertainty
(B) To explain a decision
(C) To offer an apology
(D) To request suggestions

88. What will the speaker probably do next?

(A) Answer questions from staff
(B) Arrange a future meeting
(C) Hand out some clothing
(D) Introduce a floor plan

---

89. What is the purpose of the call?

(A) To cancel a payment
(B) To change a service
(C) To confirm an address
(D) To make a complaint

90. What does the speaker mean when she says, "it seems like he needs to visit my home again"?

(A) A package was not delivered.
(B) A worker was not available.
(C) A treatment was not effective.
(D) A task was not agreed upon.

91. What does the speaker want to discuss?

(A) An application process
(B) A refund policy
(C) A future appointment
(D) A discount amount

---

92. What is the topic of the seminar?

(A) Labor laws
(B) Trade regulations
(C) Investment strategies
(D) Overseas markets

93. What will most likely happen first?

(A) A case study will be reviewed.
(B) Guests will divide into groups.
(C) Programs will be handed out.
(D) A talk will be given.

94. According to the speaker, what will listeners be able to do?

(A) Work on independent exercises
(B) Inquire about their fields
(C) Take a brief break for lunch
(D) Turn in forms after the session

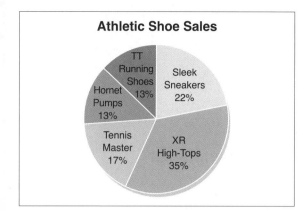

Athletic Shoe Sales

TT Running Shoes 13%
Hornet Pumps 13%
Sleek Sneakers 22%
Tennis Master 17%
XR High-Tops 35%

Animal Name	Species	Age
Mocha	Sand fox	5 months
Ginger	Jackal	10 months
Omar	Hyena	6 years
Pebble	Ostrich	28 years

95. Who most likely is the speaker?

(A) A product designer
(B) A company spokesperson
(C) A research analyst
(D) A corporate lawyer

96. What did the speaker do last week?

(A) Held an informal meeting
(B) Distributed questionnaires
(C) Responded to queries
(D) Tested merchandise

97. Look at the graphic. Which product are customers dissatisfied with?

(A) XR High-Tops
(B) Sleek Sneakers
(C) Tennis Master
(D) Hornet Pumps

98. Who most likely are the listeners?

(A) Guest lecturers
(B) Government inspectors
(C) New employees
(D) University students

99. What is mentioned about the Sahara Wildlife Reserve?

(A) It relies entirely on donations.
(B) It will be expanded this year.
(C) It offers internship opportunities.
(D) It cannot take in any more animals.

100. Look at the graphic. What will the listeners see first?

(A) A sand fox
(B) A jackal
(C) A hyena
(D) An ostrich

▌정답 음성(QR)이나 정답(p.164)을 이용해 채점하시기 바랍니다. 정답 음성에서 Boy는 (B)를, David는 (D)를 나타냅니다.
▌다음 페이지에 있는 Self 체크 리스트를 통해 자신의 문제 풀이 방식과 태도를 점검해 보세요.

Self 체크 리스트

TEST 02는 무사히 잘 마치셨죠?
이제 다음의 Self 체크 리스트를 통해 자신의 테스트 진행 내용을 점검해 볼까요?

1. 나는 테스트가 진행되는 동안 한 번도 중도에 멈추지 않았다.

   ☐ 예　　　　　　　☐ 아니오

   아니오에 답한 경우, 이유는 무엇인가요?

2. 나는 답안지 표기까지 성실하게 모두 마무리하였다.

   ☐ 예　　　　　　　☐ 아니오

   아니오에 답한 경우, 이유는 무엇인가요?

3. 나는 Part 2의 25문항을 푸는 동안 완전히 테스트에 집중하였다.

   ☐ 예　　　　　　　☐ 아니오

   아니오에 답한 경우, 이유는 무엇인가요?

4. 나는 Part 3를 풀 때 음성이 들리기 전에 해당 질문과 보기를 모두 먼저 읽었다.

   ☐ 예　　　　　　　☐ 아니오

   아니오에 답한 경우, 이유는 무엇인가요?

5. 나는 Part 4를 풀 때 음성이 들리기 전에 해당 질문과 보기를 모두 먼저 읽었다.

   ☐ 예　　　　　　　☐ 아니오

   아니오에 답한 경우, 이유는 무엇인가요?

6. 개선해야 할 점 또는 나를 위한 충고를 적어보세요.

* 교재의 첫 장으로 돌아가서 자신이 적은 목표 점수를 확인하면서 목표에 대한 의지를 다지기 바랍니다. 개선해야 할 점은 반드시 다음 테스트에 실천해야 합니다. 그것이 가장 중요하며, 그래야만 발전할 수 있습니다.

▌TEST 03

PART **1**
PART **2**
PART **3**
PART **4**
Self 체크 리스트

잠깐! 테스트 전 확인사항
1. 휴대 전화의 전원을 끄셨나요? □ 예
2. Answer Sheet, 연필, 지우개를 준비하셨나요? □ 예
3. MP3를 들을 준비가 되셨나요? □ 예

모든 준비가 완료되었으면 목표 점수를 떠올린 후 테스트를 시작합니다.

🎧 TEST 03.mp3
실전용·복습용 문제풀이 MP3 무료 다운로드 및 스트리밍 바로듣기 (HackersIngang.com)
* 실제 시험장의 소음까지 재현해 낸 고사장 소음/매미 버전 MP3, 영국식·호주식 발음 집중 MP3, 고속 버전 MP3까지
  구매하면 실전에 더욱 완벽히 대비할 수 있습니다.

무료MP3 바로듣기

LISTENING TEST

In this section, you must demonstrate your ability to understand spoken English. This section is divided into four parts and will take approximately 45 minutes to complete. Do not mark the answers in your test book. Use the answer sheet that is provided separately.

PART 1

Directions: For each question, you will listen to four short statements about a picture in your test book. These statements will not be printed and will only be spoken one time. Select the statement that best describes what is happening in the picture and mark the corresponding letter (A), (B), (C), or (D) on the answer sheet.

Sample Answer
Ⓐ ● Ⓒ Ⓓ

The statement that best describes the picture is (B), "The man is sitting at the desk." So, you should mark letter (B) on the answer sheet.

1.

2.

GO ON TO THE NEXT PAGE ➡

3.

4.

5.

6.

GO ON TO THE NEXT PAGE ➡

PART 2

Directions: For each question, you will listen to a statement or question followed by three possible responses spoken in English. They will not be printed and will only be spoken one time. Select the best response and mark the corresponding letter (A), (B), or (C) on your answer sheet.

7. Mark your answer on your answer sheet.

8. Mark your answer on your answer sheet.

9. Mark your answer on your answer sheet.

10. Mark your answer on your answer sheet.

11. Mark your answer on your answer sheet.

12. Mark your answer on your answer sheet.

13. Mark your answer on your answer sheet.

14. Mark your answer on your answer sheet.

15. Mark your answer on your answer sheet.

16. Mark your answer on your answer sheet.

17. Mark your answer on your answer sheet.

18. Mark your answer on your answer sheet.

19. Mark your answer on your answer sheet.

20. Mark your answer on your answer sheet.

21. Mark your answer on your answer sheet.

22. Mark your answer on your answer sheet.

23. Mark your answer on your answer sheet.

24. Mark your answer on your answer sheet.

25. Mark your answer on your answer sheet.

26. Mark your answer on your answer sheet.

27. Mark your answer on your answer sheet.

28. Mark your answer on your answer sheet.

29. Mark your answer on your answer sheet.

30. Mark your answer on your answer sheet.

31. Mark your answer on your answer sheet.

PART 3

Directions: In this part, you will listen to several conversations between two or more speakers. These conversations will not be printed and will only be spoken one time. For each conversation, you will be asked to answer three questions. Select the best response and mark the corresponding letter (A), (B), (C), or (D) on your answer sheet.

32. Who most likely are the speakers?
    (A) Travel agents
    (B) Event planners
    (C) Advertising executives
    (D) Environmental researchers

33. What is mentioned about the Silkwood Hotel?
    (A) It launched a new service.
    (B) It has renovated its suites.
    (C) It is hosting a conference.
    (D) It will hold a promotion.

34. What does the man ask the woman to do?
    (A) Call a company
    (B) Make a reservation
    (C) Revise a newsletter
    (D) Send an e-mail

35. Where most likely do the speakers work?
    (A) At a car rental agency
    (B) At a home electronics shop
    (C) At a furniture retailer
    (D) At a courier company

36. Why is the man worried?
    (A) More vehicles may be required.
    (B) Customers have submitted complaints.
    (C) Branches might be closed.
    (D) Total sales have dropped.

37. What does Amelia ask for?
    (A) An electronic device
    (B) A truck key
    (C) An order form
    (D) A business card

38. What is the conversation mainly about?
    (A) A company dinner
    (B) A guest list
    (C) A remodeling project
    (D) A customer survey

39. What does the woman recommend?
    (A) Speaking to a manager
    (B) Training some staff
    (C) Changing some rules
    (D) Attending a conference

40. What did the man do last week?
    (A) Sampled a food selection
    (B) Hired a new chef
    (C) Participated in an event
    (D) Modified an agenda

41. Why did the man contact the woman?
    (A) To respond to a customer survey
    (B) To recommend a vaccination
    (C) To schedule an appointment
    (D) To explain a medical procedure

42. What will the woman do on Tuesday evening?
    (A) Return from a trip
    (B) Visit a friend
    (C) Go to a doctor's office
    (D) Attend a seminar

43. Why does the woman say, "I finish work at 1 P.M."?
    (A) To point out a problem
    (B) To indicate a deadline
    (C) To agree to a proposal
    (D) To propose an alternative

GO ON TO THE NEXT PAGE

44. What is the conversation mainly about?

(A) A printing error
(B) A construction project
(C) A business pamphlet
(D) An employee transfer

45. What happened last month?

(A) Customer refunds were processed.
(B) A new location was opened.
(C) An agreement was signed.
(D) Some facilities were renovated.

46. What does the man offer to do?

(A) Distribute some brochures
(B) Inspect a building
(C) Interview a designer
(D) Contact another company

---

47. Why is the woman looking for Liew?

(A) To check that he contacted a client
(B) To confirm that he scheduled a meeting
(C) To give him a document to review
(D) To ask him to change an account password

48. What is Liew currently doing?

(A) Attending a press conference
(B) Participating in a training session
(C) Talking to a chief editor
(D) Updating some software

49. What does the man mean when he says, "It should only last another 20 minutes"?

(A) A task can be completed.
(B) A request will be approved.
(C) A room will be available.
(D) A timetable can be altered.

---

50. What is the problem?

(A) A purchase was not approved.
(B) A delivery will arrive late.
(C) A device is malfunctioning.
(D) A proposal was rejected.

51. What is scheduled to happen in the afternoon?

(A) An employee orientation
(B) An executive meeting
(C) A technology seminar
(D) A product demonstration

52. What does the man say about the IT department?

(A) It will hire additional staff.
(B) It is not currently busy.
(C) It moved to a new office.
(D) It has a new department head.

---

53. According to the woman, what do some customers want to buy?

(A) A portable charger
(B) A room furnishing
(C) A mobile phone
(D) A remote controller

54. What is the man uncertain about?

(A) Why a product is unavailable
(B) Where an item is located
(C) How much a device costs
(D) When a shipment will arrive

55. What does the woman suggest?

(A) Assigning another worker to a shift
(B) Offering customers a discount
(C) Contacting a product manufacturer
(D) Rewarding some staff members

---

56. How did the woman find out about the event at the museum?

(A) By listening to the radio
(B) By watching television
(C) By reading a magazine
(D) By talking to a friend

57. According to the man, what did the National Space Agency do?

(A) Purchased some instruments
(B) Conducted a study
(C) Designed a display
(D) Provided some items

58. What costs an extra fee?

(A) Participating in a guided tour
(B) Accessing a temporary exhibit
(C) Attending a lecture series
(D) Viewing a documentary film

59. What does the man ask the woman about?

(A) The location of merchandise
(B) Preparations for an event
(C) The progress of construction work
(D) Plans for a staff meeting

60. What problem does the woman mention?

(A) Some orders arrived late.
(B) A conference was canceled.
(C) Some equipment was damaged.
(D) A miscommunication occurred.

61. What does the man say he will do?

(A) Sweep the aisles
(B) Verify supply levels
(C) Confirm a discount amount
(D) Locate delivered packages

Brenton Sports & Leisure Complex Floor Information	
Floor 4	Rooftop pool & Snack Bar
Floor 3	Bowling alley & Ping-pong tables
Floor 2	Indoor pool & Fitness Center
Floor 1	Reception & Locker room

62. What is mentioned about Jessica?

(A) She has purchased tickets online.
(B) She has visited a complex before.
(C) She wants to borrow a car.
(D) She wants to change a schedule.

63. What will the woman most likely do on Saturday morning?

(A) Work overtime hours
(B) Attend a party
(C) Give someone a ride
(D) Help a friend move

64. Look at the graphic. Which floor will the speakers meet on?

(A) Floor 1
(B) Floor 2
(C) Floor 3
(D) Floor 4

GO ON TO THE NEXT PAGE

Bedford Dry Cleaners

Customer: Paula Steinman
Drop-off Date: May 22

Item	Service	Charge
Jean jacket	Add buttons	$5
Silk dress	Shorten	$15
Leather skirt	Clean	$20
Silk shirt	Press	$10
Total Paid		$50

65. What event will the speakers attend tomorrow night?

(A) A grand opening sale
(B) A fashion show
(C) A fund-raising event
(D) A trade fair

66. Why does the man want to switch dry cleaners?

(A) A garment was damaged.
(B) A business is going to close.
(C) A promotion has expired.
(D) A location is more convenient.

67. Look at the graphic. Which service qualifies for a discount?

(A) Adding buttons
(B) Shortening
(C) Cleaning
(D) Pressing

Hartford Public Library
New Books (August)

Field	Title	Available from
Language	*Beginner Japanese*	August 7
Home	*Storage and You*	August 7
History	*The History of London*	August 13
Travel	*A Guide to Marseilles*	August 13

68. According to the man, what has been changed?

(A) The process of returning a book
(B) The application for membership
(C) The duration of lending
(D) The policies for technology use

69. Look at the graphic. Which book will arrive in September?

(A) *Beginner Japanese*
(B) *Storage and You*
(C) *The History of London*
(D) *A Guide to Marseilles*

70. What will the man most likely do next?

(A) Update a library account
(B) Search for a publication
(C) Order a replacement book
(D) Speak with a supervisor

PART 4

Directions: In this part, you will listen to several short talks by a single speaker. These talks will not be printed and will only be spoken one time. For each talk, you will be asked to answer three questions. Select the best response and mark the corresponding letter (A), (B), (C), or (D) on your answer sheet.

71. What can employees do next week?

(A) Sign up for a contest
(B) Donate some items
(C) Make various crafts
(D) Decorate a lobby

72. Why does the speaker need some volunteers?

(A) To give out some flyers
(B) To complete some administrative tasks
(C) To advertise an upcoming fundraiser
(D) To transport some contributions

73. What should some listeners do before the end of the day?

(A) Contact a coworker
(B) Pick up a product
(C) Participate in a workshop
(D) Request a deadline extension

74. What is the speaker mainly discussing?

(A) A damaged product
(B) An overdue rental
(C) A new return policy
(D) An online reservation

75. What does the speaker recommend the listener do on the holidays?

(A) Use the side entrance of a building
(B) Call an information hotline
(C) Place an item in a container
(D) Go to the shop in the morning

76. Why should the listener act quickly?

(A) A schedule has been changed.
(B) A complaint has been made.
(C) A service will be canceled.
(D) An amount will increase.

77. Who most likely is Sally Greenly?

(A) A web designer
(B) A photographer
(C) A consultant
(D) A technician

78. According to the speaker, what will happen next month?

(A) A Web site will be launched.
(B) A conference will be held.
(C) An office will be renovated.
(D) A company will evaluate employees.

79. What does the speaker mean when he says, "there are no tables in the conference room at the moment"?

(A) Some equipment is missing.
(B) A task has been completed.
(C) Some furniture is needed.
(D) A space is available.

80. What happened yesterday?

(A) A retail facility began operations.
(B) A construction site was chosen.
(C) An economic report was released.
(D) A company merger took place.

81. What does the speaker say about the city government?

(A) It will request repayment of a debt.
(B) It will receive additional revenue.
(C) It will take control of a property.
(D) It will manage a renovation project.

82. What is mentioned about Analytic Systems?

(A) It will increase its payroll taxes.
(B) It will purchase another factory.
(C) Its relocation caused many job losses.
(D) Its closure was due to financial problems.

GO ON TO THE NEXT PAGE

83. What is the passage mainly about?

(A) A negotiation process
(B) A retirement party
(C) A training opportunity
(D) A job vacancy

84. Why does the speaker say, "We do have many competent employees at our company"?

(A) To express agreement
(B) To explain a change
(C) To reject a request
(D) To show gratitude

85. What are listeners encouraged to do?

(A) Participate in a questionnaire
(B) Talk to a regional manager
(C) Submit a document
(D) Contact a partner company

86. What is the purpose of the announcement?

(A) To promote a product
(B) To announce a regulation
(C) To describe an event
(D) To introduce a service

87. What does the speaker mention about the device?

(A) It can be used in many museums.
(B) It plays content automatically.
(C) It must be reserved in advance.
(D) It has several language settings.

88. According to the speaker, how can listeners get information about a temporary exhibition?

(A) By speaking to an employee
(B) By visiting a booth
(C) By joining a group
(D) By reading a pamphlet

89. What is being advertised?

(A) A television package
(B) An insurance policy
(C) An Internet service
(D) An electronic device

90. What do residents qualify for?

(A) A gift certificate
(B) A software upgrade
(C) A discounted rate
(D) A complimentary trial

91. What should listeners bring to the office?

(A) A copy of a receipt
(B) A credit card
(C) A registration form
(D) A piece of identification

92. What is the broadcast mainly about?

(A) A construction project
(B) A roadway accident
(C) A holiday festival
(D) A weather forecast

93. What does the speaker mean when she says, "heavy rains fell last week"?

(A) A deadline was not met.
(B) An event was not held.
(C) Some procedures were not followed.
(D) Some workers had to work overtime.

94. Who will the listeners hear from next?

(A) A professional driver
(B) A crew member
(C) A business owner
(D) A government official

Oakridge Subway Station	
Exit 10 Harbor Street	Exit 11 Field Street
Exit 12 Bridge Street	Exit 13 Oak Street

Delivery Schedule		
Date	**Company**	**Shipment Contents**
May 12	Lloyd Ferris	Dishwashers
May 13	Monroe Industries	Dryers
May 14	Abdul & Sons	Microwaves
May 15	Stone Incorporated	Refrigerators

95. Why is the speaker calling?

(A) To announce an art gallery opening
(B) To explain a membership program
(C) To notify a prize winner
(D) To request an outstanding payment

96. What does the speaker offer to do?

(A) Exchange some tickets
(B) Cancel a fee
(C) Provide a refund
(D) Reserve some seats

97. Look at the graphic. Which exit is closest to the administration office?

(A) Exit 10
(B) Exit 11
(C) Exit 12
(D) Exit 13

98. Where do the listeners work?

(A) At a retail store
(B) At a distribution center
(C) At a testing facility
(D) At a manufacturing plant

99. What does the speaker ask one of the listeners to do?

(A) Give an employee a tour
(B) Post a notice near an exit
(C) Print out a new schedule
(D) Record some notes

100. Look at the graphic. Which company has postponed its delivery?

(A) Lloyd Ferris
(B) Monroe Industries
(C) Abdul & Sons
(D) Stone Incorporated

정답 p.164 / 점수 환산표 p.167 / 스크립트 p.180 / 무료 해석 바로 보기(정답 및 정답 음성 포함)

▮정답 음성(QR)이나 정답(p.164)을 이용해 채점하시기 바랍니다. 정답 음성에서 Boy는 (B)를, David는 (D)를 나타냅니다.
▮다음 페이지에 있는 Self 체크 리스트를 통해 자신의 문제 풀이 방식과 태도를 점검해 보세요.

Self 체크 리스트

TEST 03는 무사히 잘 마치셨죠?
이제 다음의 **Self** 체크 리스트를 통해 자신의 테스트 진행 내용을 점검해 볼까요?

1. 나는 테스트가 진행되는 동안 한 번도 중도에 멈추지 않았다.

   □ 예　　　　　　　□ 아니오

   아니오에 답한 경우, 이유는 무엇인가요?

2. 나는 답안지 표기까지 성실하게 모두 마무리하였다.

   □ 예　　　　　　　□ 아니오

   아니오에 답한 경우, 이유는 무엇인가요?

3. 나는 Part 2의 25문항을 푸는 동안 완전히 테스트에 집중하였다.

   □ 예　　　　　　　□ 아니오

   아니오에 답한 경우, 이유는 무엇인가요?

4. 나는 Part 3를 풀 때 음성이 들리기 전에 해당 질문과 보기를 모두 먼저 읽었다.

   □ 예　　　　　　　□ 아니오

   아니오에 답한 경우, 이유는 무엇인가요?

5. 나는 Part 4를 풀 때 음성이 들리기 전에 해당 질문과 보기를 모두 먼저 읽었다.

   □ 예　　　　　　　□ 아니오

   아니오에 답한 경우, 이유는 무엇인가요?

6. 개선해야 할 점 또는 나를 위한 충고를 적어보세요.

* 교재의 첫 장으로 돌아가서 자신이 적은 목표 점수를 확인하면서 목표에 대한 의지를 다지기 바랍니다. 개선해야 할 점은 반드시 다음 테스트에 실천해야 합니다. 그것이 가장 중요하며, 그래야만 발전할 수 있습니다.

▮TEST 04

PART 1
PART 2
PART 3
PART 4
Self 체크 리스트

🎧 TEST 04.mp3
실전용·복습용 문제풀이 MP3 무료 다운로드 및 스트리밍 바로듣기 (HackersIngang.com)
* 실제 시험장의 소음까지 재현해 낸 고사장 소음/매미 버전 MP3, 영국식·호주식 발음 집중 MP3, 고속 버전 MP3까지
구매하면 실전에 더욱 완벽히 대비할 수 있습니다.

무료MP3 바로듣기

LISTENING TEST

In this section, you must demonstrate your ability to understand spoken English. This section is divided into four parts and will take approximately 45 minutes to complete. Do not mark the answers in your test book. Use the answer sheet that is provided separately.

PART 1

Directions: For each question, you will listen to four short statements about a picture in your test book. These statements will not be printed and will only be spoken one time. Select the statement that best describes what is happening in the picture and mark the corresponding letter (A), (B), (C), or (D) on the answer sheet.

Sample Answer
Ⓐ ● Ⓒ Ⓓ

The statement that best describes the picture is (B), "The man is sitting at the desk." So, you should mark letter (B) on the answer sheet.

1.

2.

GO ON TO THE NEXT PAGE

3.

4.

5.

6.

GO ON TO THE NEXT PAGE ➡

PART 2

Directions: For each question, you will listen to a statement or question followed by three possible responses spoken in English. They will not be printed and will only be spoken one time. Select the best response and mark the corresponding letter (A), (B), or (C) on your answer sheet.

7. Mark your answer on your answer sheet.

8. Mark your answer on your answer sheet.

9. Mark your answer on your answer sheet.

10. Mark your answer on your answer sheet.

11. Mark your answer on your answer sheet.

12. Mark your answer on your answer sheet.

13. Mark your answer on your answer sheet.

14. Mark your answer on your answer sheet.

15. Mark your answer on your answer sheet.

16. Mark your answer on your answer sheet.

17. Mark your answer on your answer sheet.

18. Mark your answer on your answer sheet.

19. Mark your answer on your answer sheet.

20. Mark your answer on your answer sheet.

21. Mark your answer on your answer sheet.

22. Mark your answer on your answer sheet.

23. Mark your answer on your answer sheet.

24. Mark your answer on your answer sheet.

25. Mark your answer on your answer sheet.

26. Mark your answer on your answer sheet.

27. Mark your answer on your answer sheet.

28. Mark your answer on your answer sheet.

29. Mark your answer on your answer sheet.

30. Mark your answer on your answer sheet.

31. Mark your answer on your answer sheet.

PART 3

Directions: In this part, you will listen to several conversations between two or more speakers. These conversations will not be printed and will only be spoken one time. For each conversation, you will be asked to answer three questions. Select the best response and mark the corresponding letter (A), (B), (C), or (D) on your answer sheet.

32. Why is the man calling?
    (A) To purchase a ticket
    (B) To hire a car service
    (C) To change a reservation
    (D) To confirm a flight time

33. Where will Ms. Ming most likely go first upon arrival?
    (A) To an office
    (B) To a train station
    (C) To a hotel
    (D) To a rental agency

34. What does the woman say she will do?
    (A) Update a timetable
    (B) Sign an agreement
    (C) Return a vehicle
    (D) Wait in an airport

35. What are the speakers mainly discussing?
    (A) Local restaurants
    (B) Food rates
    (C) Event catering
    (D) Diet programs

36. What does the woman mention about the menu?
    (A) It includes a vegetarian selection.
    (B) It was recently revised.
    (C) It indicates discounts for group orders.
    (D) It shows new drink varieties.

37. What does the woman ask the man about?
    (A) Meal prices
    (B) Venue choices
    (C) Delivery times
    (D) Beverage options

38. Who most likely is the woman?
    (A) A clinic patient
    (B) A personal assistant
    (C) A receptionist
    (D) A pharmacist

39. What does the woman ask for?
    (A) An insurance card
    (B) A driver's license
    (C) A registration form
    (D) A medicine prescription

40. According to the woman, what is a benefit of the new system?
    (A) Patients will be notified.
    (B) Records will be protected.
    (C) Information will be shared.
    (D) Software will be upgraded.

41. What is the purpose of the call?
    (A) To arrange a workshop tour
    (B) To order some decorative items
    (C) To reserve an exhibition booth
    (D) To propose a business deal

42. What does the woman offer to do?
    (A) Visit a store
    (B) Mail some samples
    (C) Reduce some prices
    (D) Hang up a frame

43. What does the man ask about?
    (A) A production capacity
    (B) The size of a workforce
    (C) A manufacturing process
    (D) The names of some assistants

GO ON TO THE NEXT PAGE

44. According to the woman, what does the supervisor want to do?

(A) Search for an architect
(B) Change a meeting time
(C) Look over some plans
(D) Evaluate some staff

45. What problem does the man mention?

(A) A task is taking too long.
(B) A new hire is going to be late.
(C) A building has been closed down.
(D) A customer has made a complaint.

46. Why does the man say, "I'll e-mail you the presentation materials in a minute"?

(A) To agree to take on an assignment
(B) To show interest in a project
(C) To accept an offer of help
(D) To express concern about a situation

---

47. What are the speakers mainly discussing?

(A) A museum closing
(B) A historical site
(C) A remodeled venue
(D) A future exhibition

48. What does Brian imply about Hall C?

(A) It is currently vacant.
(B) It will be expanded soon.
(C) It is bigger than another area.
(D) It will be used for a convention.

49. Why is the woman concerned?

(A) A project deadline is unclear.
(B) A display has too few items.
(C) A space has to be enlarged.
(D) A schedule might be tight.

---

50. What did the woman do last week?

(A) Finished taking a class
(B) Completed an accounting report
(C) Attended a ceremony
(D) Taught a business course

51. What does the man ask the woman to do?

(A) Seek out an advisor
(B) Check some messages
(C) Rearrange a schedule
(D) Respond to some questions

52. What will the man probably do after 2 P.M.?

(A) Get in touch with the woman again
(B) Distribute handouts to participants
(C) Visit an administrator's office
(D) Submit a curriculum outline

---

53. What does the woman imply when she says, "he is based in Edmonton"?

(A) Mr. Patel will arrive on schedule.
(B) Mr. Patel should book a different flight.
(C) Mr. Patel should postpone a trip.
(D) Mr. Patel will relocate to another city.

54. According to the man, who most likely is Mr. Patel?

(A) A pilot
(B) A technician
(C) An investor
(D) A manager

55. What problem does the woman mention?

(A) A meeting place is all booked.
(B) An engineer is unavailable.
(C) A deadline is approaching.
(D) A device is malfunctioning.

---

56. What does the man need assistance with?

(A) Printing out a picture
(B) Placing an order
(C) Selecting a product
(D) Locating an item

57. Where does the woman most likely work?

(A) At a furniture supplier
(B) At a paint store
(C) At a print shop
(D) At an art gallery

58. What will the woman most likely do next?

(A) Put up a sign
(B) Contact a manager
(C) Announce a sale
(D) Get some samples

59. What are the speakers mainly discussing?

(A) Marketing a new product
(B) Expanding a clothing shop
(C) Setting up a Web Site
(D) Holding a press conference

60. What does the woman recommend?

(A) Posting an advertisement
(B) Providing employee training
(C) Updating some information
(D) Hiring a professional

61. What will the woman probably do next?

(A) Read some e-mails
(B) Compare some prices
(C) Reach out to an acquaintance
(D) Stop by a store branch

Movie Schedule		
Title	Starting time	Theater No.
Made in Melbourne	6:30 P.M.	Theater 1
Around the Bend	6:45 P.M.	Theater 2
On Eddy Street	6:55 P.M.	Theater 3
Made in Melbourne	7:45 P.M.	Theater 4
Through the Flames	7:55 P.M.	Theater 5

62. What problem does the man mention?

(A) Some facilities have been damaged.
(B) Some tickets are no longer valid.
(C) A film has not been released yet.
(D) A screening has no available seats.

63. Look at the graphic. Which movie will the woman watch?

(A) *Made in Melbourne*
(B) *Around the Bend*
(C) *On Eddy Street*
(D) *Through the Flames*

64. What will the woman probably do next?

(A) Review a transaction record
(B) Request a complimentary item
(C) Download a company's application
(D) Purchase some food and beverages

GO ON TO THE NEXT PAGE

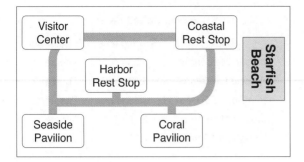

Conference Room C Schedule	
Meeting Time	Booked By
10 A.M. – 11 A.M.	Scott White
1 P.M. – 2 P.M.	Vera Gonzalez
3 P.M. – 4 P.M.	Brad Derby
4 P.M. – 5 P.M.	Janice Chung

65. Look at the graphic. Where is the observation deck located?

(A) In Seaside Pavilion
(B) In Coastal Rest Stop
(C) In Harbor Rest Stop
(D) In Coral Pavilion

66. What does the woman say about the boardwalk?

(A) It will be crowded tomorrow.
(B) It will undergo renovations.
(C) It is far from a parking lot.
(D) It was damaged by poor weather.

67. According to the woman, what has been installed on a deck recently?

(A) A coastal walk
(B) A concession stand
(C) Some picnic tables
(D) Some sightseeing devices

68. What problem does the woman mention?

(A) A meeting space is fully booked.
(B) A mark has been made on a rug.
(C) An applicant is running behind schedule.
(D) A light fixture has been damaged.

69. Look at the graphic. Who booked the room for a client meeting?

(A) Scott White
(B) Vera Gonzalez
(C) Brad Derby
(D) Janice Chung

70. What will the man probably do next?

(A) Collect some documents
(B) Contact a colleague
(C) Attend an interview
(D) Download some information

PART 4

Directions: In this part, you will listen to several short talks by a single speaker. These talks will not be printed and will only be spoken one time. For each talk, you will be asked to answer three questions. Select the best response and mark the corresponding letter (A), (B), (C), or (D) on your answer sheet.

71. Where does the speaker most likely work?

(A) At a financial institution
(B) At a recruitment firm
(C) At a sportswear retailer
(D) At a chain restaurant

72. How can some points be used?

(A) Online shopping
(B) Travel rewards
(C) Magazine subscription
(D) Extra discounts

73. What is the listener instructed to do?

(A) Call a hotline
(B) Complete an online form
(C) Reset an old code
(D) Learn about a point system

74. What is the purpose of the speech?

(A) To introduce an employee
(B) To provide instructions
(C) To open a conference
(D) To promote a new car

75. According to the speaker, what was Mr. Chao in charge of?

(A) Writing a magazine article
(B) Communicating with clients
(C) Meeting monthly sales targets
(D) Running an advertising campaign

76. What has the company done recently?

(A) Cut its production costs
(B) Opened a new branch
(C) Increased its earnings
(D) Launched a publication

77. What is the announcement mainly about?

(A) A store opening
(B) A membership upgrade
(C) A monthly sale
(D) An event promotion

78. What does the speaker say people will be excited to do?

(A) Attend a screening
(B) Sign up for a newsletter
(C) Watch a performance
(D) Meet an author

79. What does the speaker suggest listeners do?

(A) Purchase a pass
(B) Download a program
(C) Check an online schedule
(D) Bring a valid ID card

80. Who most likely is the speaker?

(A) An author
(B) A scientist
(C) An event planner
(D) A travel agent

81. What does the speaker imply when she says, "The conference is on June 15"?

(A) An appointment date must be changed.
(B) A Web site includes inaccurate information.
(C) An employee was notified of a problem.
(D) A service should be provided quickly.

82. What does the speaker ask the listener to do?

(A) Return a call
(B) Adjust a price
(C) Visit an office
(D) Reschedule a meeting

GO ON TO THE NEXT PAGE

83. Who most likely is the speaker?

(A) A political candidate
(B) A journalist
(C) A private attorney
(D) A government employee

84. What was the speaker responsible for?

(A) Overseeing an expansion
(B) Creating regulations
(C) Managing a special budget
(D) Carrying out research

85. What does the speaker say about the party?

(A) He expected more guests.
(B) He did not know about it.
(C) He planned to invite his family.
(D) He was involved in organizing it.

---

86. Where does the speaker work?

(A) At a construction firm
(B) At a manufacturing plant
(C) At a sports arena
(D) At a conference center

87. What does the speaker mean when she says, "Now it's time to discuss the project timetable"?

(A) A payment was received.
(B) A proposal is acceptable.
(C) A deadline is flexible.
(D) A correction was made.

88. What does the speaker plan to do on Thursday?

(A) Tour a facility
(B) Meet with a client
(C) Send an e-mail
(D) Take a trip

---

89. According to the speaker, what will be opening this week?

(A) A toy shop
(B) A radio station
(C) An artist workspace
(D) An apartment building

90. What is mentioned about Wentworth Warehouse?

(A) It was converted into housing.
(B) It was purchased at a discount.
(C) It was demolished recently.
(D) It was moved to another area.

91. What will listeners probably hear next?

(A) A song
(B) An advertisement
(C) A news report
(D) An interview

---

92. Where most likely do the listeners work?

(A) At an auto repair shop
(B) At a bike store
(C) At a car wash
(D) At a hardware store

93. What information should employees point out?

(A) The business's operating hours
(B) The prices for various services
(C) The code to obtain a free coupon
(D) The day when a business will open

94. What does the speaker imply when she says, "I'm not sure how many people read it"?

(A) A method may not be successful.
(B) A suggestion will not be followed.
(C) A business may be shut down.
(D) A publication will be promoted.

Landville Plaza Directory	
Floor	**Department**
1	Finance
2	Sales
3	Human Resources
4	Customer Service
5	Research and Development

Monday	Tuesday	Wednesday	Thursday	Friday
☔	☀	☔	☀	☀

95. According to the speaker, what did the listener do yesterday?

(A) Held interviews with applicants
(B) Departed for a gathering
(C) Talked to a colleague
(D) Transferred to a new division

96. What is Victoria Styles willing to do?

(A) Lead an orientation session
(B) Accept a promotion
(C) Make some travel arrangements
(D) Reach out to a customer

97. Look at the graphic. What department does Victoria Styles work in?

(A) Finance
(B) Human Resources
(C) Customer Service
(D) Research and Development

98. Why does the speaker thank the listeners?

(A) A feature was added to a product.
(B) A model received positive reviews.
(C) A report contained accurate data.
(D) A task was finished ahead of schedule.

99. Look at the graphic. When will the test most likely be conducted?

(A) On Tuesday
(B) On Wednesday
(C) On Thursday
(D) On Friday

100. What did Charlotte Cruz do this morning?

(A) Confirmed a reservation
(B) Contacted another department
(C) Inspected a site
(D) Set up some equipment

정답 p.164 / 점수 환산표 p.167 / 스크립트 p.186 / 무료 해석 바로 보기(정답 및 정답 음성 포함)

▮정답 음성(QR)이나 정답(p.164)을 이용해 채점하시기 바랍니다. 정답 음성에서 Boy는 (B)를, David는 (D)를 나타냅니다.
▮다음 페이지에 있는 Self 체크 리스트를 통해 자신의 문제 풀이 방식과 태도를 점검해 보세요.

Self 체크 리스트

TEST 04는 무사히 잘 마치셨죠?
이제 다음의 Self 체크 리스트를 통해 자신의 테스트 진행 내용을 점검해 볼까요?

1. 나는 테스트가 진행되는 동안 한 번도 중도에 멈추지 않았다.

　　□ 예　　　　　　　□ 아니오

　　아니오에 답한 경우, 이유는 무엇인가요?

2. 나는 답안지 표기까지 성실하게 모두 마무리하였다.

　　□ 예　　　　　　　□ 아니오

　　아니오에 답한 경우, 이유는 무엇인가요?

3. 나는 Part 2의 25문항을 푸는 동안 완전히 테스트에 집중하였다.

　　□ 예　　　　　　　□ 아니오

　　아니오에 답한 경우, 이유는 무엇인가요?

4. 나는 Part 3를 풀 때 음성이 들리기 전에 해당 질문과 보기를 모두 먼저 읽었다.

　　□ 예　　　　　　　□ 아니오

　　아니오에 답한 경우, 이유는 무엇인가요?

5. 나는 Part 4를 풀 때 음성이 들리기 전에 해당 질문과 보기를 모두 먼저 읽었다.

　　□ 예　　　　　　　□ 아니오

　　아니오에 답한 경우, 이유는 무엇인가요?

6. 개선해야 할 점 또는 나를 위한 충고를 적어보세요.

* 교재의 첫 장으로 돌아가서 자신이 적은 목표 점수를 확인하면서 목표에 대한 의지를 다지기 바랍니다. 개선해야 할 점은 반드시 다음 테스트에 실천해야 합니다. 그것이 가장 중요하며, 그래야만 발전할 수 있습니다.

TEST 05

잠깐! 테스트 전 확인사항

1. 휴대 전화의 전원을 끄셨나요? □ 예
2. Answer Sheet, 연필, 지우개를 준비하셨나요? □ 예
3. MP3를 들을 준비가 되셨나요? □ 예

모든 준비가 완료되었으면 목표 점수를 떠올린 후 테스트를 시작합니다.

🎧 TEST 05.mp3

실전용·복습용 문제풀이 MP3 무료 다운로드 및 스트리밍 바로듣기 (HackersIngang.com)
* 실제 시험장의 소음까지 재현해 낸 고사장 소음/매미 버전 MP3, 영국식·호주식 발음 집중 MP3, 고속 버전 MP3까지
  구매하면 실전에 더욱 완벽히 대비할 수 있습니다.

무료MP3 바로듣기

LISTENING TEST

In this section, you must demonstrate your ability to understand spoken English. This section is divided into four parts and will take approximately 45 minutes to complete. Do not mark the answers in your test book. Use the answer sheet that is provided separately.

PART 1

Directions: For each question, you will listen to four short statements about a picture in your test book. These statements will not be printed and will only be spoken one time. Select the statement that best describes what is happening in the picture and mark the corresponding letter (A), (B), (C), or (D) on the answer sheet.

Sample Answer

The statement that best describes the picture is (B), "The man is sitting at the desk." So, you should mark letter (B) on the answer sheet.

1.

2.

GO ON TO THE NEXT PAGE

3.

4.

5.

6.

GO ON TO THE NEXT PAGE

PART 2

Directions: For each question, you will listen to a statement or question followed by three possible responses spoken in English. They will not be printed and will only be spoken one time. Select the best response and mark the corresponding letter (A), (B), or (C) on your answer sheet.

7. Mark your answer on your answer sheet.

8. Mark your answer on your answer sheet.

9. Mark your answer on your answer sheet.

10. Mark your answer on your answer sheet.

11. Mark your answer on your answer sheet.

12. Mark your answer on your answer sheet.

13. Mark your answer on your answer sheet.

14. Mark your answer on your answer sheet.

15. Mark your answer on your answer sheet.

16. Mark your answer on your answer sheet.

17. Mark your answer on your answer sheet.

18. Mark your answer on your answer sheet.

19. Mark your answer on your answer sheet.

20. Mark your answer on your answer sheet.

21. Mark your answer on your answer sheet.

22. Mark your answer on your answer sheet.

23. Mark your answer on your answer sheet.

24. Mark your answer on your answer sheet.

25. Mark your answer on your answer sheet.

26. Mark your answer on your answer sheet.

27. Mark your answer on your answer sheet.

28. Mark your answer on your answer sheet.

29. Mark your answer on your answer sheet.

30. Mark your answer on your answer sheet.

31. Mark your answer on your answer sheet.

PART 3

Directions: In this part, you will listen to several conversations between two or more speakers. These conversations will not be printed and will only be spoken one time. For each conversation, you will be asked to answer three questions. Select the best response and mark the corresponding letter (A), (B), (C), or (D) on your answer sheet.

32. What is the conversation mainly about?

(A) A new telephone system
(B) A technical issue
(C) A departmental meeting
(D) A building renovation

33. What is Mr. Bradford's team doing?

(A) Fixing an Intranet system
(B) Bringing in more materials
(C) Repairing some telephone lines
(D) Establishing a wireless connection

34. What does the woman suggest?

(A) Working on a different floor
(B) Unplugging a machine from the wall
(C) Notifying customers about an error
(D) Purchasing a piece of equipment

35. What does the man's family plan to do?

(A) Book a table at a restaurant
(B) Find some accommodations
(C) Travel to another country
(D) Visit a tourist attraction

36. What is provided for free to guests?

(A) Meals
(B) Internet access
(C) Transportation
(D) Guidebooks

37. Why does the woman ask the man to wait?

(A) She needs to help someone else.
(B) She needs to verify something.
(C) She wants to provide a brochure.
(D) She wants to print passes to a site.

38. Where most likely do the speakers work?

(A) At a bookstore
(B) At a bakery
(C) At a pharmacy
(D) At a supermarket

39. What does the woman imply when she says, "We were featured in a local magazine"?

(A) A publication was purchased.
(B) An article was positive.
(C) A report was accurate.
(D) A subscription was renewed.

40. What does Alex suggest?

(A) Updating a schedule
(B) Distributing flyers
(C) Conducting a survey
(D) Offering discounts

41. What are the speakers mainly discussing?

(A) A press conference
(B) An architect position
(C) A photo shoot
(D) A magazine subscription

42. What does the woman propose?

(A) Meeting at a construction site
(B) Rescheduling an appointment
(C) Contacting a theater owner
(D) Revising an article

43. What does the man say the woman can do?

(A) Return to a venue at a later date
(B) Bring a copy of a publication
(C) Exhibit some images at a gallery
(D) Print out some blueprints

GO ON TO THE NEXT PAGE

44. According to the woman, what happened last Tuesday?

(A) A professional contract expired.
(B) A shipment of goods arrived.
(C) A complaint was submitted online.
(D) A customer exchanged an item.

45. How does the man want to deal with the problem?

(A) By renewing an agreement
(B) By demanding a full refund
(C) By starting a new business relationship
(D) By asking for a membership discount

46. What does the woman request the man do?

(A) Display some signs
(B) Organize a storage area
(C) Edit a service catalog
(D) Deliver some merchandise

47. Who most likely is the woman?

(A) An event organizer
(B) A tailor
(C) An engineer
(D) An interior designer

48. According to the woman, what will affect the price the most?

(A) Size
(B) Design
(C) Materials
(D) Accessories

49. What will the woman probably do next?

(A) Take some measurements
(B) Order a fabric
(C) Complete a transaction
(D) Request some adjustments

50. Where do the speakers most likely work?

(A) At a financial institution
(B) At a staffing agency
(C) At an office supply store
(D) At a graphic design firm

51. What did Tim and Laura do this morning?

(A) Met with a potential client
(B) Attended a staff meeting
(C) Made travel arrangements
(D) Conducted job interviews

52. What do Tim and Laura recommend?

(A) Reviewing a contract
(B) Visiting some companies
(C) Explaining some benefits
(D) Changing a process

53. Who most likely are the speakers?

(A) Security guards
(B) Secretaries
(C) Performers
(D) Photographers

54. Why does the man say, "it's not cloudy at all today"?

(A) To express satisfaction
(B) To indicate uncertainty
(C) To disagree with a suggestion
(D) To respond to a question

55. What will the speakers probably do next?

(A) Drive to a destination
(B) Contact a taxi service
(C) Review a schedule
(D) Find a parking spot

56. What problem does the woman mention?

(A) She forgot to update an application.
(B) A machine stopped functioning.
(C) She is unfamiliar with a program.
(D) An inventory level is too low.

57. What does the man suggest?

(A) Referring to a handbook
(B) E-mailing some colleagues
(C) Consulting with an advisor
(D) Copying some manuals

58. According to the man, what should the woman talk to the manager about?

(A) Acquiring additional computer parts
(B) Customizing some new software
(C) Errors in an important file
(D) Complications with a messaging system

59. Why is the woman calling?

(A) To change some billing information
(B) To ask about a charge
(C) To complain about a product
(D) To cancel a membership account

60. What did the man recently do?

(A) Updated a Web page
(B) Sent out a notification
(C) Hired an instructor
(D) Renewed a policy

61. What does the man offer to do?

(A) Provide a discount
(B) Print a document
(C) Refund a fee
(D) Confirm a purchase

Eastside Cable				
	Service			
	Premium Sports Channels	Game Downloads	Premium Movie Channels	Video Recording
Package A	✓		✓	✓
Package B		✓		✓
Package C	✓	✓	✓	

62. What did the man forget?

(A) An activation code
(B) A product pamphlet
(C) A fee payment
(D) A visit time

63. Look at the graphic. Which service is the man most interested in?

(A) Premium Sports Channels
(B) Game Downloads
(C) Premium Movie Channels
(D) Video Recording

64. According to the woman, what is the man unable to receive?

(A) A gift with purchase
(B) A company brochure
(C) A piece of equipment
(D) A reduced price

GO ON TO THE NEXT PAGE

Perez Office Table

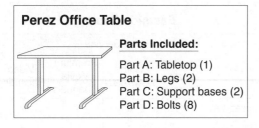

Parts Included:

Part A: Tabletop (1)
Part B: Legs (2)
Part C: Support bases (2)
Part D: Bolts (8)

65. Where does the conversation most likely take place?

(A) In a meeting room
(B) In an employee lounge
(C) In a furniture store
(D) In a warehouse

66. Look at the graphic. Which part is missing?

(A) Part A
(B) Part B
(C) Part C
(D) Part D

67. What will the man probably do during his lunch break?

(A) Call a business
(B) Move some tables
(C) Look over a manual
(D) Find additional tools

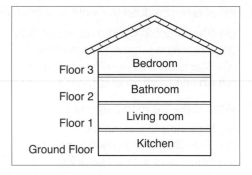

68. Why is the man late?

(A) He was stuck in traffic.
(B) He met with a client.
(C) He was not feeling well.
(D) He misplaced an item.

69. Look at the graphic. On which floor will some supplies be stored?

(A) Ground Floor
(B) Floor 1
(C) Floor 2
(D) Floor 3

70. According to the woman, what will be delivered this afternoon?

(A) Some furniture
(B) Some computer components
(C) An appliance
(D) A culinary tool

PART 4

Directions: In this part, you will listen to several short talks by a single speaker. These talks will not be printed and will only be spoken one time. For each talk, you will be asked to answer three questions. Select the best response and mark the corresponding letter (A), (B), (C), or (D) on your answer sheet.

71. Who most likely is the speaker?

(A) A delivery person
(B) A tow truck driver
(C) A hospital employee
(D) A city worker

72. What does the speaker remind the listeners to do?

(A) Use marked entrances and exits
(B) Consult with medical officials
(C) Contact emergency personnel
(D) Avoid parking in certain zones

73. According to the speaker, what should the listeners look for?

(A) Detour signs
(B) Colored lines
(C) Lighted displays
(D) Traffic cones

74. What problem does the speaker mention?

(A) A trip has been delayed.
(B) A project has been canceled.
(C) A client made a complaint.
(D) A coworker missed an appointment.

75. What does the speaker imply when she says, "You helped create the application for them last year"?

(A) A deadline will be met.
(B) A task will not be difficult.
(C) A product will be purchased.
(D) A program was popular.

76. What does the speaker suggest the listener do?

(A) Reschedule a meeting
(B) Speak with an assistant
(C) Check a schedule
(D) E-mail a file

77. According to the speaker, what will happen in August?

(A) Some computers will be purchased.
(B) A division will be expanded.
(C) A building will be renovated.
(D) Some workers will be trained.

78. What is located on the fourth floor?

(A) Temporary workstations
(B) Executive offices
(C) Construction tools
(D) New conference rooms

79. What will most likely be done toward the end of this month?

(A) Desks will be set up.
(B) Equipment will be moved.
(C) Staff will go on leave.
(D) Painters will finish a job.

80. Where most likely does the speaker work?

(A) At a real estate firm
(B) At a retail outlet
(C) At a travel agency
(D) At a delivery company

81. What does the speaker instruct the listener to do?

(A) Provide an electronic signature
(B) Return a parcel
(C) Visit a facility
(D) Confirm an address

82. What does the speaker say might happen after seven days?

(A) A message will be sent out.
(B) A request will be processed.
(C) A tracking number will expire.
(D) A package will be shipped back.

GO ON TO THE NEXT PAGE

83. According to the speaker, who is Betty O'Rourke?

(A) A local celebrity
(B) A mechanical engineer
(C) A corporate leader
(D) A city mayor

84. What is mentioned about Renew Incorporated?

(A) It lost a recent bid.
(B) It will set up equipment.
(C) It will lead a marketing effort.
(D) It switched to solar energy.

85. What does the speaker imply when she says, "people should not worry"?

(A) Increases will be minor.
(B) Bills will be accurate.
(C) Customers will be notified.
(D) Errors will be avoided.

---

86. What type of business most likely is Digital Solutions?

(A) An online retailer
(B) A software developer
(C) A graphic design company
(D) A recording studio

87. Why has the firm's stock value risen?

(A) Its product has been very successful.
(B) Its operations have moved overseas.
(C) It was awarded a major contract.
(D) It has teamed up with another business.

88. What does the speaker say will happen next month?

(A) A device will be distributed to stores.
(B) A merger will be formalized.
(C) An application will be released.
(D) A cell phone will be reviewed.

---

89. What did the speaker do this morning?

(A) Attended a workshop
(B) Approved a design
(C) Read an e-mail
(D) Sent a message

90. What does the speaker mean when he says, "That leaves us the break room"?

(A) A suggestion has been accepted.
(B) A room must be prepared.
(C) A change must be made.
(D) A proposal has been considered.

91. According to the speaker, what is at the reception desk?

(A) A survey
(B) A training manual
(C) A sign-up sheet
(D) A program

---

92. Why is the speaker calling?

(A) To ask about an incorrect invoice
(B) To change an earlier order
(C) To thank a company for its services
(D) To get information about a speaker

93. What does Music Central need?

(A) Extra microphones
(B) A partial refund
(C) Additional speakers
(D) An extended warranty

94. What is the listener asked to do this afternoon?

(A) Send a revised statement
(B) Print a company catalog
(C) Fill out a registration form
(D) Ship a sample product

Survey Results	
Air Conditioner	34%
Air Purifier	26%
Electric Fan	22%
Space Heater	18%

95. Why is Greg Henderson unavailable?

(A) He is participating in a focus group.
(B) He is attending a design conference.
(C) He is visiting a production plant.
(D) He is inspecting a research facility.

96. Look at the graphic. What type of device is the Flow S60?

(A) An air conditioner
(B) An air purifier
(C) An electric fan
(D) A space heater

97. What will the speaker distribute?

(A) Manuals
(B) Application forms
(C) Promotional brochures
(D) Questionnaires

Bean Bus Tour

Departure	Boston Common
Stop 1	Newbury Street
Stop 2	Boston Harbor
Stop 3	Old State House
Stop 4	Bunker Hill

98. What does the speaker mention about the information booth?

(A) It opened five years ago.
(B) It will begin selling souvenirs.
(C) It has few employees.
(D) It is located in a hotel.

99. Which month will the company offer a discount?

(A) April
(B) May
(C) June
(D) July

100. Look at the graphic. Which stop will be temporarily inaccessible?

(A) Stop 1
(B) Stop 2
(C) Stop 3
(D) Stop 4

정답 p.165 / 점수 환산표 p.167 / 스크립트 p.192 / 무료 해석 바로 보기(정답 및 정답 음성 포함)

▌정답 음성(QR)이나 정답(p.165)을 이용해 채점하시기 바랍니다. 정답 음성에서 Boy는 (B)를, David는 (D)를 나타냅니다.
▌다음 페이지에 있는 Self 체크 리스트를 통해 자신의 문제 풀이 방식과 태도를 점검해 보세요.

Self 체크 리스트

TEST 05는 무사히 잘 마치셨죠?
이제 다음의 Self 체크 리스트를 통해 자신의 테스트 진행 내용을 점검해 볼까요?

1. 나는 테스트가 진행되는 동안 한 번도 중도에 멈추지 않았다.

   □ 예 　　　　　　　□ 아니오

   아니오에 답한 경우, 이유는 무엇인가요?

2. 나는 답안지 표기까지 성실하게 모두 마무리하였다.

   □ 예 　　　　　　　□ 아니오

   아니오에 답한 경우, 이유는 무엇인가요?

3. 나는 Part 2의 25문항을 푸는 동안 완전히 테스트에 집중하였다.

   □ 예 　　　　　　　□ 아니오

   아니오에 답한 경우, 이유는 무엇인가요?

4. 나는 Part 3를 풀 때 음성이 들리기 전에 해당 질문과 보기를 모두 먼저 읽었다.

   □ 예 　　　　　　　□ 아니오

   아니오에 답한 경우, 이유는 무엇인가요?

5. 나는 Part 4를 풀 때 음성이 들리기 전에 해당 질문과 보기를 모두 먼저 읽었다.

   □ 예 　　　　　　　□ 아니오

   아니오에 답한 경우, 이유는 무엇인가요?

6. 개선해야 할 점 또는 나를 위한 충고를 적어보세요.

* 교재의 첫 장으로 돌아가서 자신이 적은 목표 점수를 확인하면서 목표에 대한 의지를 다지기 바랍니다. 개선해야 할 점은 반드시 다음 테스트에 실천해야 합니다. 그것이 가장 중요하며, 그래야만 발전할 수 있습니다.

▌TEST 06

PART 1
PART 2
PART 3
PART 4
Self 체크 리스트

잠깐! 테스트 전 확인사항

1. 휴대 전화의 전원을 끄셨나요? □ 예
2. Answer Sheet, 연필, 지우개를 준비하셨나요? □ 예
3. MP3를 들을 준비가 되셨나요? □ 예

모든 준비가 완료되었으면 목표 점수를 떠올린 후 테스트를 시작합니다.

🎧 TEST 06.mp3

실전용·복습용 문제풀이 MP3 무료 다운로드 및 스트리밍 바로듣기 (HackersIngang.com)
* 실제 시험장의 소음까지 재현해 낸 고사장 소음/매미 버전 MP3, 영국식·호주식 발음 집중 MP3, 고속 버전 MP3까지
  구매하면 실전에 더욱 완벽히 대비할 수 있습니다.

무료MP3 바로듣기

LISTENING TEST

In this section, you must demonstrate your ability to understand spoken English. This section is divided into four parts and will take approximately 45 minutes to complete. Do not mark the answers in your test book. Use the answer sheet that is provided separately.

PART 1

Directions: For each question, you will listen to four short statements about a picture in your test book. These statements will not be printed and will only be spoken one time. Select the statement that best describes what is happening in the picture and mark the corresponding letter (A), (B), (C), or (D) on the answer sheet.

Sample Answer
Ⓐ ● Ⓒ Ⓓ

The statement that best describes the picture is (B), "The man is sitting at the desk." So, you should mark letter (B) on the answer sheet.

1.

2.

GO ON TO THE NEXT PAGE

3.

4.

5.

6.

GO ON TO THE NEXT PAGE

PART 2

Directions: For each question, you will listen to a statement or question followed by three possible responses spoken in English. They will not be printed and will only be spoken one time. Select the best response and mark the corresponding letter (A), (B), or (C) on your answer sheet.

7. Mark your answer on your answer sheet.

8. Mark your answer on your answer sheet.

9. Mark your answer on your answer sheet.

10. Mark your answer on your answer sheet.

11. Mark your answer on your answer sheet.

12. Mark your answer on your answer sheet.

13. Mark your answer on your answer sheet.

14. Mark your answer on your answer sheet.

15. Mark your answer on your answer sheet.

16. Mark your answer on your answer sheet.

17. Mark your answer on your answer sheet.

18. Mark your answer on your answer sheet.

19. Mark your answer on your answer sheet.

20. Mark your answer on your answer sheet.

21. Mark your answer on your answer sheet.

22. Mark your answer on your answer sheet.

23. Mark your answer on your answer sheet.

24. Mark your answer on your answer sheet.

25. Mark your answer on your answer sheet.

26. Mark your answer on your answer sheet.

27. Mark your answer on your answer sheet.

28. Mark your answer on your answer sheet.

29. Mark your answer on your answer sheet.

30. Mark your answer on your answer sheet.

31. Mark your answer on your answer sheet.

PART 3

Directions: In this part, you will listen to several conversations between two or more speakers. These conversations will not be printed and will only be spoken one time. For each conversation, you will be asked to answer three questions. Select the best response and mark the corresponding letter (A), (B), (C), or (D) on your answer sheet.

32. Who most likely is the man?

(A) A store clerk
(B) A ticket seller
(C) A taxi driver
(D) A travel guide

33. According to the man, why is traffic heavy now?

(A) Repair work is being done.
(B) A parade is being held.
(C) Rush hour has begun.
(D) A sports event has ended.

34. Why is the woman going to a store today?

(A) To participate in a job interview
(B) To cover a shift for a coworker
(C) To return a damaged product
(D) To take advantage of an offer

35. What does the man ask the woman for?

(A) A computer password
(B) A product review
(C) A performance assessment
(D) A project schedule

36. Why does the man have to check the woman's work in advance?

(A) To meet a new deadline
(B) To fulfill a manager's request
(C) To evaluate her performance
(D) To ensure there are no issues

37. What does the man imply when he says, "There are only multiple-choice questions"?

(A) He worries about the difficulty of a task.
(B) He thinks a task will not take long.
(C) He believes a test should be changed.
(D) He wants a task to be done online.

38. Where most likely is the conversation taking place?

(A) In a parking garage
(B) At a public park
(C) At a sports stadium
(D) In a repair shop

39. What does the man say about a bike rack?

(A) It is the only place to put bicycles.
(B) It is easy to find.
(C) It is usually full with bicycles.
(D) It is surrounded by benches.

40. Why does the man suggest using a lock?

(A) Visitors can borrow a lock free of charge.
(B) A safety regulation is strictly enforced.
(C) Security at a site is inadequate.
(D) A facility will close soon.

41. What does the woman want to order?

(A) Some chemical solutions
(B) Some work apparel
(C) Some laboratory devices
(D) Some office tables

42. Why does the man apologize?

(A) A product is unavailable.
(B) A payment was not made.
(C) A shipment will arrive late.
(D) A model has not been released.

43. Why does the man recommend YK160?

(A) It is available in several versions.
(B) It is the most discounted model.
(C) It is similar to another item.
(D) It is made of improved materials.

GO ON TO THE NEXT PAGE

해커스 토익 실전 1000제 3 Listening

44. What industry do the speakers most likely work in?

(A) Manufacturing
(B) Retail
(C) Shipping
(D) Marketing

45. Why is Kyle worried?

(A) Costs have risen recently.
(B) A facility is at full capacity.
(C) Items will expire soon.
(D) A display is ineffective.

46. What does the woman offer to do?

(A) Train some staff members
(B) Move some furniture
(C) Repair some equipment
(D) Design some advertisements

47. Where does the woman most likely work?

(A) At a public library
(B) At an advertising agency
(C) At a grocery store
(D) At a private law firm

48. What is the man unable to do?

(A) Sign a contract
(B) Begin a job immediately
(C) Leave for a trip
(D) Revise a schedule later

49. What does the woman ask the man to do?

(A) Review some regulations
(B) Answer some questions
(C) Photocopy a document
(D) Contact a manager

50. What problem does the woman mention?

(A) An office is too small.
(B) An instruction manual is missing.
(C) A desk is not the right size.
(D) A Web site is not working.

51. What does the man offer to do?

(A) Find some information online
(B) Send a repairperson with a part
(C) Order some models from a factory
(D) Visit a manager of another branch

52. What type of information does the man need?

(A) A delivery address
(B) A product code
(C) A date of purchase
(D) An order number

53. Why does the woman make a call?

(A) To sign up a new client
(B) To sell a financial product
(C) To respond to a question
(D) To talk about an online application

54. What problem does the man mention?

(A) He forgot his password.
(B) He was charged a fee.
(C) He lost his credit card.
(D) He received a wrong item.

55. What will the man probably do next?

(A) Check an account balance
(B) Change a password
(C) Register for a service
(D) Participate in a survey

56. What is the conversation mainly about?

(A) An update for investors
(B) An agenda for a conference
(C) A script for a presentation
(D) An article for a newsletter

57. What has the man finished doing?

(A) Organizing upcoming negotiations
(B) Summarizing some information
(C) Responding to some criticism
(D) Printing out some documents

58. Why does the woman say, "The Edgar Telecom project"?

(A) To provide an example
(B) To explain a decision
(C) To identify a problem
(D) To suggest a change

59. What are the speakers mainly discussing?

(A) A coworker's retirement
(B) A holiday party
(C) A recent vacation
(D) A company's anniversary

60. What does the woman suggest?

(A) Arranging a vacation
(B) Organizing an event
(C) Expanding a team
(D) Providing a day off

61. What does Greg agree to do?

(A) Assess a proposal
(B) Ask for contributions
(C) Send a letter
(D) Buy a greeting card

Claim Check	
Name	Janet Graham
Number of Items	1
Item Type	Bag
Date Left	April 7
Date of Pickup	April 7

62. Where most likely is the conversation taking place?

(A) In an airport
(B) In a tourism office
(C) In a train station
(D) In a hotel

63. What will the woman do until 3 P.M.?

(A) Visit a bank
(B) Unpack some products
(C) Tour a facility
(D) Browse in some stores

64. Look at the graphic. Which piece of information needs to be changed?

(A) Number of Items
(B) Item Type
(C) Date Left
(D) Date of Pickup

GO ON TO THE NEXT PAGE

Our Competitors	Feature of Reward Program
Grant's Deli	points for writing online reviews
The Sandwich Crew	points for attending events
Waterfield Eats	points for ordering set meals
Urban Picnic	points for using a mobile app

65. What are the speakers mainly discussing?

(A) The agenda for a department gathering
(B) The replacement of a promotional method
(C) The outcome of an advertising campaign
(D) The decision to buy programs for employees

66. Look at the graphic. Which business does the woman refer to?

(A) Grant's Deli
(B) The Sandwich Crew
(C) Waterfield Eats
(D) Urban Picnic

67. What will the company most likely gain in the future?

(A) Positive coverage on television
(B) Detailed information about customers
(C) Tax benefits from the government
(D) Patents for some new technology

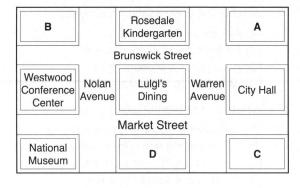

68. Who most likely is the woman?

(A) A restaurant worker
(B) A government official
(C) A call center employee
(D) A tour group leader

69. Look at the graphic. Where is the business that the man wants to visit?

(A) In Building A
(B) In Building B
(C) In Building C
(D) In Building D

70. What does the man need to do until 2 P.M.?

(A) Submit a product review
(B) Attend a training session
(C) Make a reservation
(D) Meet with a client

Directions: In this part, you will listen to several short talks by a single speaker. These talks will not be printed and will only be spoken one time. For each talk, you will be asked to answer three questions. Select the best response and mark the corresponding letter (A), (B), (C), or (D) on your answer sheet.

71. What type of business is being advertised?

(A) A travel agency
(B) A software developer
(C) A translation service
(D) A language tutoring center

72. What service does Commslink provide?

(A) Sitting in on meetings
(B) Grading papers in 24 hours
(C) Providing one-on-one instruction
(D) Introducing potential clients

73. What can people find on the company's Web site?

(A) A map of branch locations
(B) A list of service fees
(C) Feedback from past clients
(D) Names of company executives

74. What will take place on Saturday?

(A) A holiday party
(B) An athletic event
(C) A training workshop
(D) A business conference

75. What does the speaker say Cindy is doing?

(A) Placing an order
(B) Contacting a volunteer
(C) Booking a venue
(D) Evaluating an employee

76. What has Redwood Department Store agreed to provide?

(A) Receipts
(B) Discounts
(C) Refunds
(D) Vouchers

77. Who most likely is Ms. Falken?

(A) A legal consultant
(B) A financial advisor
(C) A secretary
(D) A data specialist

78. What does the speaker imply when he says, "I'm sure you all remember"?

(A) Some passwords were memorized.
(B) An issue was serious.
(C) An employee was introduced before.
(D) Some instructions were repeated.

79. What does the speaker suggest that the listeners write down?

(A) An extension number
(B) An employee's name
(C) A company's address
(D) A meeting time

80. Who most likely is the speaker?

(A) An artist
(B) A gallery owner
(C) A festival organizer
(D) An art instructor

81. What problem does the speaker mention?

(A) A building was damaged.
(B) A document was misplaced.
(C) An item is too large.
(D) A space is too crowded.

82. What does the speaker predict?

(A) A series of works will arrive.
(B) A show will receive good reviews.
(C) A painting will be finished next week.
(D) An event will have record attendance.

GO ON TO THE NEXT PAGE

83. Why does the speaker say, "we have your safety in mind"?

(A) To show the importance of a program
(B) To give a reminder about a danger
(C) To offer a reason for a decision
(D) To stress the need to follow a rule

84. What does the speaker say about the routes to the mountain base?

(A) They begin at the cable-car station.
(B) They are currently being repaired.
(C) They are closed when it gets dark.
(D) They take the same amount of time.

85. Who should go to the information desk?

(A) People who lost a possession
(B) People who want to exchange a ticket
(C) People who need help walking
(D) People who are first-time visitors

---

86. According to the speaker, how did Scion Incorporated expand?

(A) By developing a new product
(B) By enhancing marketing
(C) By utilizing social media
(D) By buying a competitor

87. What does Mitchell Horner intend to do next week?

(A) Register a business
(B) Start a position
(C) Attend a meeting
(D) Give an interview

88. What does the speaker say she will do?

(A) Give an explanation
(B) Download a program
(C) Introduce a guest
(D) Call a representative

---

89. Why is the speaker calling?

(A) To ask for a portfolio
(B) To explain a task
(C) To set up an interview
(D) To announce a decision

90. According to the speaker, what distinguishes the listener from others?

(A) She has excellent technical abilities.
(B) She has received awards for her achievement.
(C) She has worked in the industry for decades.
(D) She has been highly recommended by another firm.

91. Why does the speaker say, "Our school year begins in June"?

(A) To explain a promotion strategy
(B) To indicate a start date
(C) To answer a scheduling question
(D) To specify an application deadline

---

92. What did the listener recently do?

(A) Moved to a new residence
(B) Started his subscription
(C) Wrote an article for a magazine
(D) Ordered some back issues

93. According to the speaker, what can the listener read from the magazine?

(A) Techniques to repair a car
(B) Past racing competitions
(C) Safety regulations for drivers
(D) Prices of brand-new vehicles

94. According to the speaker, what must the listener do to access online content?

(A) Update a password
(B) Contact an employee
(C) Create an account
(D) Make a payment

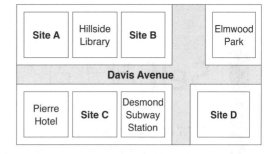

User Options
(1) Record
(2) Invite
(3) Mute
(4) Chat

95. What is the purpose of the workshop?

(A) To explain company policies
(B) To provide investment advice
(C) To promote information security
(D) To present job-search strategies

96. Why is Ms. Welch unable to participate in the session today?

(A) She is working on another assignment.
(B) She has taken some personal leave.
(C) She has relocated to a new office.
(D) She is experiencing a technical issue.

97. Look at the graphic. Which option will be removed?

(A) Option (1)
(B) Option (2)
(C) Option (3)
(D) Option (4)

Site A	Hillside Library	Site B		Elmwood Park
Davis Avenue				
Pierre Hotel	Site C	Desmond Subway Station		Site D

98. Who most likely are the listeners?

(A) Tour group members
(B) Camp attendees
(C) Language academy students
(D) City officials

99. Look at the graphic. Where is Kingsway Mall located?

(A) Site A
(B) Site B
(C) Site C
(D) Site D

100. What does the speaker mention about the restaurant?

(A) It has many customers on weekends.
(B) It stays open late in the evenings.
(C) It offers affordable lunch specials.
(D) It hosts a variety of special events.

정답 p.165 / 점수 환산표 p.167 / 스크립트 p.198 / 무료 해석 바로 보기(정답 및 정답 음성 포함)

▌정답 음성(QR)이나 정답(p.165)을 이용해 채점하시기 바랍니다. 정답 음성에서 Boy는 (B)를, David는 (D)를 나타냅니다.
▌다음 페이지에 있는 Self 체크 리스트를 통해 자신의 문제 풀이 방식과 태도를 점검해 보세요.

Self 체크 리스트

TEST 06는 무사히 잘 마치셨죠?
이제 다음의 Self 체크 리스트를 통해 자신의 테스트 진행 내용을 점검해 볼까요?

1. 나는 테스트가 진행되는 동안 한 번도 중도에 멈추지 않았다.

   □ 예　　　　　　　　□ 아니오

   아니오에 답한 경우, 이유는 무엇인가요?

2. 나는 답안지 표기까지 성실하게 모두 마무리하였다.

   □ 예　　　　　　　　□ 아니오

   아니오에 답한 경우, 이유는 무엇인가요?

3. 나는 Part 2의 25문항을 푸는 동안 완전히 테스트에 집중하였다.

   □ 예　　　　　　　　□ 아니오

   아니오에 답한 경우, 이유는 무엇인가요?

4. 나는 Part 3를 풀 때 음성이 들리기 전에 해당 질문과 보기를 모두 먼저 읽었다.

   □ 예　　　　　　　　□ 아니오

   아니오에 답한 경우, 이유는 무엇인가요?

5. 나는 Part 4를 풀 때 음성이 들리기 전에 해당 질문과 보기를 모두 먼저 읽었다.

   □ 예　　　　　　　　□ 아니오

   아니오에 답한 경우, 이유는 무엇인가요?

6. 개선해야 할 점 또는 나를 위한 충고를 적어보세요.

* 교재의 첫 장으로 돌아가서 자신이 적은 목표 점수를 확인하면서 목표에 대한 의지를 다지기 바랍니다. 개선해야 할 점은 반드시 다음 테스트에
　실천해야 합니다. 그것이 가장 중요하며, 그래야만 발전할 수 있습니다.

▎TEST 07

PART 1
PART 2
PART 3
PART 4
Self 체크 리스트

잠깐! 테스트 전 확인사항
1. 휴대 전화의 전원을 끄셨나요? □ 예
2. Answer Sheet, 연필, 지우개를 준비하셨나요? □ 예
3. MP3를 들을 준비가 되셨나요? □ 예

모든 준비가 완료되었으면 목표 점수를 떠올린 후 테스트를 시작합니다.

🎧 TEST 07.mp3
실전용·복습용 문제풀이 MP3 무료 다운로드 및 스트리밍 바로듣기 (HackersIngang.com)
* 실제 시험장의 소음까지 재현해 낸 고사장 소음/매미 버전 MP3, 영국식·호주식 발음 집중 MP3, 고속 버전 MP3까지
  구매하면 실전에 더욱 완벽히 대비할 수 있습니다.

무료MP3 바로듣기

LISTENING TEST

In this section, you must demonstrate your ability to understand spoken English. This section is divided into four parts and will take approximately 45 minutes to complete. Do not mark the answers in your test book. Use the answer sheet that is provided separately.

PART 1

Directions: For each question, you will listen to four short statements about a picture in your test book. These statements will not be printed and will only be spoken one time. Select the statement that best describes what is happening in the picture and mark the corresponding letter (A), (B), (C), or (D) on the answer sheet.

Sample Answer

The statement that best describes the picture is (B), "The man is sitting at the desk." So, you should mark letter (B) on the answer sheet.

1.

2.

GO ON TO THE NEXT PAGE ➡

3.

4.

5.

6.

PART 2

Directions: For each question, you will listen to a statement or question followed by three possible responses spoken in English. They will not be printed and will only be spoken one time. Select the best response and mark the corresponding letter (A), (B), or (C) on your answer sheet.

7. Mark your answer on your answer sheet.

8. Mark your answer on your answer sheet.

9. Mark your answer on your answer sheet.

10. Mark your answer on your answer sheet.

11. Mark your answer on your answer sheet.

12. Mark your answer on your answer sheet.

13. Mark your answer on your answer sheet.

14. Mark your answer on your answer sheet.

15. Mark your answer on your answer sheet.

16. Mark your answer on your answer sheet.

17. Mark your answer on your answer sheet.

18. Mark your answer on your answer sheet.

19. Mark your answer on your answer sheet.

20. Mark your answer on your answer sheet.

21. Mark your answer on your answer sheet.

22. Mark your answer on your answer sheet.

23. Mark your answer on your answer sheet.

24. Mark your answer on your answer sheet.

25. Mark your answer on your answer sheet.

26. Mark your answer on your answer sheet.

27. Mark your answer on your answer sheet.

28. Mark your answer on your answer sheet.

29. Mark your answer on your answer sheet.

30. Mark your answer on your answer sheet.

31. Mark your answer on your answer sheet.

PART 3

Directions: In this part, you will listen to several conversations between two or more speakers. These conversations will not be printed and will only be spoken one time. For each conversation, you will be asked to answer three questions. Select the best response and mark the corresponding letter (A), (B), (C), or (D) on your answer sheet.

32. Who most likely are the speakers?

  (A) Park rangers
  (B) Construction workers
  (C) Florists
  (D) Landscapers

33. What does the man want to do first?

  (A) Prepare the ground for plants
  (B) Fill in holes with dirt
  (C) Go on an early lunch break
  (D) Clean out the back of a truck

34. What problem does the man mention?

  (A) A cart was left behind.
  (B) A bush cannot be removed.
  (C) A glove was damaged.
  (D) A shovel is not large enough.

35. What is the woman trying to find?

  (A) A spray cleaner
  (B) A power drill
  (C) Some artwork
  (D) Some hooks

36. Why does the woman reject an offer?

  (A) She is being assisted by other staff.
  (B) She is not interested in a promotion.
  (C) She knows where some items are stocked.
  (D) She knows why a product is sold out.

37. According to the man, how can the woman get more information?

  (A) By downloading an application
  (B) By picking up a shop directory
  (C) By seeking out employees
  (D) By using a device

38. Where most likely are the speakers?

  (A) In a retail store
  (B) In a store room
  (C) In a printing office
  (D) In a community center

39. What does the woman need to do before her shift?

  (A) Check a shift schedule
  (B) Sign up for training
  (C) Restart a device
  (D) Order some supplies

40. How can the woman obtain more information?

  (A) By speaking to a supervisor
  (B) By downloading a manual
  (C) By reviewing some instructions
  (D) By looking at a posted notice

41. Who most likely are the speakers?

  (A) Professional musicians
  (B) Event planners
  (C) Company board members
  (D) Financial consultants

42. Why does the woman say, "I got an e-mail this morning"?

  (A) To express confusion
  (B) To report an error
  (C) To ask for assistance
  (D) To give assurance

43. What is mentioned about a budget?

  (A) It covered all the essential expenses.
  (B) It is going to be increased soon.
  (C) It will be announced to a team.
  (D) It should be spent on catering.

GO ON TO THE NEXT PAGE

44. Who most likely is the woman?

(A) A repairperson
(B) A salesperson
(C) A janitor
(D) A maintenance worker

45. According to the woman, what is a feature of the product?

(A) It can move itself.
(B) It can be cleaned easily.
(C) It is environmentally friendly.
(D) It comes in various sizes.

46. What will most likely happen next?

(A) A floor will be blocked off.
(B) A store will be restocked.
(C) A device will be used.
(D) An item will be put on sale.

47. What is the problem?

(A) A lobby is crowded.
(B) A drink has been spilled.
(C) A hotel has no vacancies.
(D) A room is too small.

48. What solution does the woman suggest?

(A) Talking to a personnel member
(B) Canceling hotel reservations
(C) Finding some other chairs
(D) Modifying an itinerary

49. Why will the woman be unable to use the swimming pool?

(A) A check-in process was delayed.
(B) A performance has been scheduled.
(C) The facility is being remodeled.
(D) The water is being tested.

50. According to the man, why does the woman require some information?

(A) To prepare a notification
(B) To propose an idea to a supervisor
(C) To respond to client inquires
(D) To complete a questionnaire

51. What does the man say riders can do online?

(A) Sign up for a newsletter
(B) Request fare reductions
(C) Read about subway routes
(D) Add money to a card

52. What did the woman forget about?

(A) A new fee
(B) A special giveaway
(C) A temporary closure
(D) A station remodel

53. What is mentioned about Mr. Marquez?

(A) He requested a transfer.
(B) He moved to a new position.
(C) He hired a consultant.
(D) He organized a staff activity.

54. What will most likely happen on November third?

(A) Some invitations will be mailed out.
(B) Some employees will listen to a lecture.
(C) A safety procedure will be implemented.
(D) A director will announce a fundraiser date.

55. What is the man concerned about?

(A) A failed inspection
(B) A frequent complaint
(C) A scheduling conflict
(D) An unsuccessful workshop

56. What is the woman planning to do next week?

(A) Entertain some visitors
(B) Book a table at a restaurant
(C) Organize a tour of a factory
(D) Travel to Japan for work

57. What does the man recommend the woman do?

(A) Ask about a down payment
(B) Contact an agent in advance
(C) Place a meal order
(D) Arrange for a boat ride

58. What does the man mention about some local businesses?

(A) They specialize in cruise packages.
(B) They offer reasonably priced rentals.
(C) They will send some representatives.
(D) They will provide area guidebooks.

---

59. According to the woman, what is located at the end of a hallway?

(A) A conference room
(B) A storage closet
(C) An emergency staircase
(D) A building elevator

60. What does the man mean when he says, "I'm experiencing some pain in my wrist"?

(A) He needs to contact a doctor.
(B) He cannot help with a task.
(C) He needs to go on a break.
(D) He cannot come to work tomorrow.

61. What does the woman suggest?

(A) Taking some leave
(B) Visiting a clinic
(C) Confirming some information
(D) Rescheduling an appointment

Room 101	Lobby	Room 102
Conference Room	Room 103	Room 104

62. Who most likely is the man?

(A) An architect
(B) A repairperson
(C) A building janitor
(D) A graphic designer

63. Why does the woman apologize?

(A) She forgot to make a reservation.
(B) She provided incorrect information.
(C) She missed a phone call.
(D) She was late for an appointment.

64. Look at the graphic. Which room will the man visit?

(A) Room 101
(B) Room 102
(C) Room 103
(D) Room 104

GO ON TO THE NEXT PAGE ➤

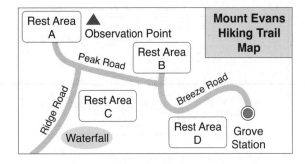

From	Subject	Date
Ken Powers	Thanks for Your Order	August 6
Ken Powers	RE: Complaint about Order #4991	August 12
Raymond Liu	RE: Coupon Specifications	August 13
Linda Wright	Question about Taxi Cost	August 15

65. What does the woman offer to do?

(A) Borrow some hiking gear
(B) Take pictures of a landscape
(C) Purchase some refreshments
(D) Contact a station official

66. According to the woman, what happened last week?

(A) A path was officially opened.
(B) A picnic area was used for an event.
(C) A hike had to be postponed.
(D) A storm created poor conditions.

67. Look at the graphic. Where does the woman suggest taking a break?

(A) At Rest Area A
(B) At Rest Area B
(C) At Rest Area C
(D) At Rest Area D

68. What does the man imply about the jackets?

(A) They will be featured in a publication.
(B) They will be kept at an art studio.
(C) They were paid for with a gift card.
(D) They were imported from overseas.

69. Look at the graphic. When did the woman receive a discount coupon?

(A) On August 6
(B) On August 12
(C) On August 13
(D) On August 15

70. According to the woman, what happened earlier today?

(A) A consultation with a photographer
(B) A launch for a clothing line
(C) A show for fashion designers
(D) A gathering with the media

PART 4

Directions: In this part, you will listen to several short talks by a single speaker. These talks will not be printed and will only be spoken one time. For each talk, you will be asked to answer three questions. Select the best response and mark the corresponding letter (A), (B), (C), or (D) on your answer sheet.

71. Why is the speaker calling?

(A) To request a payment
(B) To answer a question
(C) To ask for additional shirts
(D) To report a problem

72. What will most likely happen on Friday?

(A) An order will be sent.
(B) Staff members will receive training.
(C) A project will get underway.
(D) T-shirt designs will be changed.

73. What does the speaker offer to do?

(A) Contact a designer
(B) Exchange a product
(C) Reduce a charge
(D) Provide a work sample

---

74. Where do the listeners most likely work?

(A) At a research facility
(B) At a medical clinic
(C) At a service center
(D) At a staffing agency

75. Why does the speaker say, "we don't know who has an appointment tomorrow"?

(A) To complain about an event program
(B) To indicate the need for more staff
(C) To emphasize the urgency of a task
(D) To address a recent question

76. What does the speaker mention about Janet Lee?

(A) She is currently on leave.
(B) She has contacted some customers.
(C) She will distribute a document.
(D) She was recently promoted.

---

77. Who most likely is the speaker?

(A) An accountant
(B) A researcher
(C) A lawyer
(D) A realtor

78. What does the speaker imply when she says, "most people don't want to stay long"?

(A) A request may not be granted.
(B) A deadline should be moved.
(C) A fee will not be reduced.
(D) An appointment will be rescheduled.

79. What does the speaker ask the listener to do?

(A) Return a call
(B) Visit an office
(C) Complete a form
(D) Send an e-mail

---

80. According to the speaker, what type of event did the CEO arrange?

(A) An industry convention
(B) A company orientation
(C) A fund-raising dinner
(D) A corporate retreat

81. What are the listeners expected to do over the next few days?

(A) Watch some instructional videos
(B) Participate in group activities
(C) Discuss potential trip destinations
(D) Share updates with a board member

82. Why must the listeners meet at 4 P.M.?

(A) To pose for a photograph
(B) To take a tour of a resort
(C) To make decisions about an event
(D) To listen to a talk from an executive

GO ON TO THE NEXT PAGE

83. What did the city council do?

(A) Voted to change a tax code
(B) Updated an outdated policy
(C) Decided to demolish a building
(D) Held a debate on safety standards

84. Who is John Hamilton?

(A) A government official
(B) A historian
(C) An architect
(D) A park employee

85. What will happen on Friday?

(A) A plan will be announced.
(B) An inspection will take place.
(C) A meeting will be held.
(D) A facility will open.

---

86. What is the topic of the talk?

(A) Real estate developments
(B) Renovation projects
(C) Interior design ideas
(D) City zoning laws

87. What is the speaker passing out?

(A) Membership cards
(B) Information booklets
(C) Images of a structure
(D) Maps of an area

88. What is mentioned about Burlington Associates?

(A) It is currently seeking new workers.
(B) It has moved to a new location.
(C) It was founded a decade ago.
(D) It is having a busy year.

---

89. What task have the listeners been assigned?

(A) Developing an event for local tourists
(B) Determining how to target foreign visitors
(C) Creating a new attraction
(D) Planning an international fund-raiser

90. What does the speaker say about the snow sculptures?

(A) They are at risk of melting.
(B) They take a long time to construct.
(C) They are popular among attendees.
(D) They were previously featured in flyers.

91. What will the listeners do in 30 minutes?

(A) Take a break
(B) Listen to a speech
(C) Watch a presentation
(D) Discuss some ideas

---

92. Who most likely are the listeners?

(A) Personnel managers
(B) Sales representatives
(C) Administrative assistants
(D) Customer service agents

93. What will most likely happen next?

(A) A demonstration will be given.
(B) A manual will be handed out.
(C) Job duties will be explained.
(D) Evaluations will be conducted.

94. Why does the speaker say, "You may be surprised by the results"?

(A) To suggest that a product is popular
(B) To point out the disadvantages of a plan
(C) To indicate that a method is effective
(D) To show the accuracy of some data

Broadcast Schedule

Wednesday Afternoons (April)	
12:00-2:00	*Health Check*
2:00-2:20	Traffic Report
2:20-3:30	*Culture Break*
3:30-5:00	*Investment Strategies*
5:00-5:10	Weather Update
5:10-6:00	*Gourmet Cooking*

EZ Auto Rentals

Customer: Janis Lyle
Receipt #: 84758

Vehicle Rental:	£125.00
Fuel:	£45.00
Collision Insurance:	£75.00
Navigation System:	£25.00
Total:	£270.00

95. What does the speaker mention about Jeff Wallace?

(A) He has hosted other radio programs.
(B) He travels often for his job.
(C) He was the owner of a company.
(D) He is planning to retire soon.

96. According to the speaker, what might some callers receive?

(A) A bus pass
(B) A hotel voucher
(C) An airline ticket
(D) A guidebook

97. Look at the graphic. Which show will be replaced?

(A) *Health Check*
(B) *Culture Break*
(C) *Investment Strategies*
(D) *Gourmet Cooking*

98. What did the speaker do last week?

(A) Visited some relatives
(B) Met with a customer
(C) Attended a convention
(D) Toured an overseas branch

99. Look at the graphic. How much will the woman be refunded?

(A) £125.00
(B) £45.00
(C) £75.00
(D) £25.00

100. What does the speaker request be sent to her?

(A) Promotional materials
(B) A customer satisfaction survey
(C) Insurance documents
(D) An updated invoice

Self 체크 리스트

TEST 07은 무사히 잘 마치셨죠?
이제 다음의 Self 체크 리스트를 통해 자신의 테스트 진행 내용을 점검해 볼까요?

1. 나는 테스트가 진행되는 동안 한 번도 중도에 멈추지 않았다.

   □ 예   □ 아니오

   아니오에 답한 경우, 이유는 무엇인가요?

2. 나는 답안지 표기까지 성실하게 모두 마무리하였다.

   □ 예   □ 아니오

   아니오에 답한 경우, 이유는 무엇인가요?

3. 나는 Part 2의 25문항을 푸는 동안 완전히 테스트에 집중하였다.

   □ 예   □ 아니오

   아니오에 답한 경우, 이유는 무엇인가요?

4. 나는 Part 3를 풀 때 음성이 들리기 전에 해당 질문과 보기를 모두 먼저 읽었다.

   □ 예   □ 아니오

   아니오에 답한 경우, 이유는 무엇인가요?

5. 나는 Part 4를 풀 때 음성이 들리기 전에 해당 질문과 보기를 모두 먼저 읽었다.

   □ 예   □ 아니오

   아니오에 답한 경우, 이유는 무엇인가요?

6. 개선해야 할 점 또는 나를 위한 충고를 적어보세요.

* 교재의 첫 장으로 돌아가서 자신이 적은 목표 점수를 확인하면서 목표에 대한 의지를 다지기 바랍니다. 개선해야 할 점은 반드시 다음 테스트에
실천해야 합니다. 그것이 가장 중요하며, 그래야만 발전할 수 있습니다.

TEST 08

PART **1**
PART **2**
PART **3**
PART **4**
Self 체크 리스트

잠깐! 테스트 전 확인사항
1. 휴대 전화의 전원을 끄셨나요? □ 예
2. Answer Sheet, 연필, 지우개를 준비하셨나요? □ 예
3. MP3를 들을 준비가 되셨나요? □ 예

모든 준비가 완료되었으면 목표 점수를 떠올린 후 테스트를 시작합니다.

🎧 TEST 08.mp3
실전용·복습용 문제풀이 MP3 무료 다운로드 및 스트리밍 바로듣기 (HackersIngang.com)
* 실제 시험장의 소음까지 재현해 낸 고사장 소음/매미 버전 MP3, 영국식·호주식 발음 집중 MP3, 고속 버전 MP3까지
  구매하면 실전에 더욱 완벽히 대비할 수 있습니다.

무료MP3 바로듣기

LISTENING TEST

In this section, you must demonstrate your ability to understand spoken English. This section is divided into four parts and will take approximately 45 minutes to complete. Do not mark the answers in your test book. Use the answer sheet that is provided separately.

PART 1

Directions: For each question, you will listen to four short statements about a picture in your test book. These statements will not be printed and will only be spoken one time. Select the statement that best describes what is happening in the picture and mark the corresponding letter (A), (B), (C), or (D) on the answer sheet.

Sample Answer

The statement that best describes the picture is (B), "The man is sitting at the desk." So, you should mark letter (B) on the answer sheet.

1.

2.

GO ON TO THE NEXT PAGE ➤

3.

4.

5.

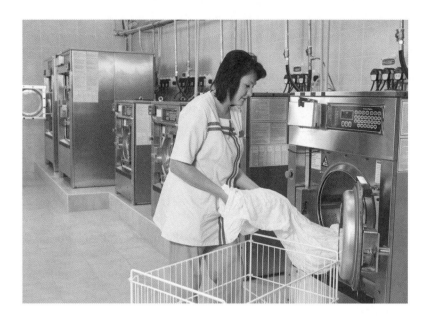

6.

GO ON TO THE NEXT PAGE ➡

PART 2

Directions: For each question, you will listen to a statement or question followed by three possible responses spoken in English. They will not be printed and will only be spoken one time. Select the best response and mark the corresponding letter (A), (B), or (C) on your answer sheet.

7. Mark your answer on your answer sheet.

8. Mark your answer on your answer sheet.

9. Mark your answer on your answer sheet.

10. Mark your answer on your answer sheet.

11. Mark your answer on your answer sheet.

12. Mark your answer on your answer sheet.

13. Mark your answer on your answer sheet.

14. Mark your answer on your answer sheet.

15. Mark your answer on your answer sheet.

16. Mark your answer on your answer sheet.

17. Mark your answer on your answer sheet.

18. Mark your answer on your answer sheet.

19. Mark your answer on your answer sheet.

20. Mark your answer on your answer sheet.

21. Mark your answer on your answer sheet.

22. Mark your answer on your answer sheet.

23. Mark your answer on your answer sheet.

24. Mark your answer on your answer sheet.

25. Mark your answer on your answer sheet.

26. Mark your answer on your answer sheet.

27. Mark your answer on your answer sheet.

28. Mark your answer on your answer sheet.

29. Mark your answer on your answer sheet.

30. Mark your answer on your answer sheet.

31. Mark your answer on your answer sheet.

PART 3

Directions: In this part, you will listen to several conversations between two or more speakers. These conversations will not be printed and will only be spoken one time. For each conversation, you will be asked to answer three questions. Select the best response and mark the corresponding letter (A), (B), (C), or (D) on your answer sheet.

32. What task has the woman been assigned?

(A) Planning an event
(B) Revising an annual report
(C) Arranging rides for staff
(D) Promoting a competition

33. What does the man request the woman do?

(A) Lead a team-building exercise
(B) Consider a different date
(C) Speak to a department head
(D) Announce the results of a match

34. What does the man offer to do?

(A) Get passes for a game
(B) Write down some directions
(C) Search for a local business
(D) Message some colleagues

35. Who most likely is the man?

(A) A film editor
(B) A television program host
(C) A box office attendant
(D) A movie critic

36. What does the woman ask the man about?

(A) The name of an actor
(B) The availability of a showing
(C) The length of a performance
(D) The price of a ticket

37. What does the man say about Andy Baker?

(A) He will meet with investors.
(B) He attended a cinema opening.
(C) He will respond to some inquiries.
(D) He released a production last year.

38. Who most likely is the man?

(A) A car rental agent
(B) A truck driver
(C) A vehicle salesperson
(D) A travel specialist

39. Why does the woman say, "But we only have a $400 budget for this"?

(A) To indicate a problem
(B) To confirm an amount
(C) To decline an offer
(D) To complain about prices

40. What will the woman most likely do next?

(A) Take a driving test
(B) Fill out some documents
(C) Review a price quote
(D) Go to a parking lot

41. What are the speakers mainly discussing?

(A) A coworker's vacation
(B) A corporate regulation
(C) An overseas investment
(D) A supervisor's promotion

42. What does the woman ask the man about?

(A) The reason for a change
(B) The duration of a trip
(C) The cost of a renovation
(D) The size of a warehouse

43. What did the woman do last week?

(A) Talked with a manager
(B) Applied for a transfer
(C) Edited a policy manual
(D) Submitted a written complaint

GO ON TO THE NEXT PAGE

44. Where does the conversation probably take place?

(A) At a department store
(B) At a library
(C) At an accounting office
(D) At a bookstore

45. What suggestion does the man make?

(A) Contacting an organization again
(B) Borrowing a specific book
(C) Going to another area
(D) Ordering a replacement card

46. What information does the man need?

(A) An account holder's name
(B) A publication title
(C) An e-mail address
(D) An identification number

47. Why did the man call the woman?

(A) To provide payment details
(B) To reserve some merchandise
(C) To inquire about a piece of gear
(D) To learn about an upcoming launch

48. What does the woman mention about racquet grips?

(A) They are currently out of stock.
(B) They are made with quality materials.
(C) They come in various types.
(D) They have been used by sports stars.

49. What will the man probably do this afternoon?

(A) Attend a tennis class
(B) Browse some items
(C) Call a sales associate
(D) Return some racquets

50. What problem does the woman describe?

(A) She visited the incorrect office.
(B) She lost a financial document.
(C) She does not have a day planner.
(D) She is late for a consultation.

51. What does the woman allow the man to do?

(A) Participate in a conference call
(B) Remove equipment from an office
(C) Send notes to an advisor
(D) Review her personal belongings

52. What detail does the man provide?

(A) A meeting location
(B) A reservation time
(C) A client's name
(D) A coworker's address

53. What task has the woman been assigned?

(A) Preparing some marketing materials
(B) Giving a presentation at a conference
(C) Making some travel arrangements
(D) Providing transportation to an airport

54. Why does the woman say, "Mr. Hoffman mentioned a team meeting scheduled for May 22"?

(A) To change a schedule
(B) To reject a request
(C) To introduce a plan
(D) To ask for clarification

55. What does the man say he will do?

(A) Discuss an issue with a colleague
(B) Postpone a staff meeting
(C) Bring fewer belongings
(D) Locate an event venue

56. What most likely will take place later today?

(A) A business luncheon
(B) A workshop
(C) A picnic
(D) A cycling trip

57. What problem does the woman mention?

(A) A receipt was misplaced.
(B) An item was thrown out.
(C) Some equipment is damaged.
(D) Some food is spoiled.

58. What will the woman probably do?

(A) Move into a new apartment
(B) Join a cycling club
(C) Visit a grocery store
(D) Change a pick-up time

59. What did the man do recently?

(A) Conducted a tour
(B) Gave a speech
(C) Attended a conference
(D) Visited a venue

60. What is mentioned about the air-conditioning?

(A) It is too small to cool the room.
(B) It has a problem in need of repair.
(C) It cannot be set at a cooler temperature.
(D) It will require paying an extra charge to use it.

61. What does the man ask Jordy to do?

(A) Contact a maintenance manager
(B) Set up a device
(C) Cancel a reservation
(D) Find an address

Langley Community Center Lecture Schedule (September 4-7)	
Day	Topic
Monday	Home Decorating
Tuesday	Gardening
Wednesday	Nutrition
Thursday	Social Media

62. Why is the woman unavailable this week?

(A) She plans to meet some friends.
(B) She has to visit her cousins.
(C) She must lead a company workshop.
(D) She will go on a business trip.

63. What does the man offer to do?

(A) Repair equipment
(B) Purchase a ticket
(C) Provide transportation
(D) Confirm a reservation

64. Look at the graphic. Which day will the speakers most likely attend a lecture?

(A) Monday
(B) Tuesday
(C) Wednesday
(D) Thursday

GO ON TO THE NEXT PAGE

Desmond Electronics Floor Directory	
Floor 5	Marketing Department
Floor 4	Research Department
Floor 3	Administrative Department
Floor 2	Sales Department
Floor 1	Reception

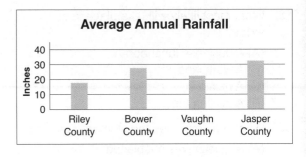

Average Annual Rainfall

65. What is the purpose of the man's visit?

(A) He is delivering a package.
(B) He is signing an employment contract.
(C) He is setting up office equipment.
(D) He is attending an interview.

66. Look at the graphic. Which department does Mr. Grayson most likely belong to?

(A) Marketing
(B) Research
(C) Administrative
(D) Sales

67. What does the woman suggest?

(A) Checking an office address
(B) Parking in a different location
(C) Calling a company representative
(D) Coming back at a later time

68. What does the man ask the woman about?

(A) Why an analysis was performed
(B) When construction will begin
(C) Whether an assessment is finished
(D) If an amusement park has opened

69. What was the woman responsible for?

(A) Conducting an examination
(B) Selecting a meeting place
(C) Printing a map of a region
(D) Securing a business contract

70. Look at the graphic. Which county has been recommended?

(A) Riley County
(B) Bower County
(C) Vaughn County
(D) Jasper County

PART 4

Directions: In this part, you will listen to several short talks by a single speaker. These talks will not be printed and will only be spoken one time. For each talk, you will be asked to answer three questions. Select the best response and mark the corresponding letter (A), (B), (C), or (D) on your answer sheet.

71. Where does the listener probably work?
    (A) At a travel agency
    (B) At a media company
    (C) At a financial firm
    (D) At a law office

72. What will the speaker do on Monday?
    (A) Prepare a report
    (B) Go to the airport
    (C) Attend a convention
    (D) Give a presentation

73. What information does the speaker ask for?
    (A) Restaurant recommendations
    (B) Clients' names
    (C) A meeting agenda
    (D) An order number

74. At what event is the speech being given?
    (A) A service center opening
    (B) A product launch party
    (C) A monthly shareholders meeting
    (D) A company anniversary celebration

75. Why does the speaker praise Patricia Sanderson?
    (A) She altered a logo design.
    (B) She designed a popular Web site.
    (C) She suggested a device feature.
    (D) She signed an important client.

76. What will most likely happen next?
    (A) An employee will be introduced.
    (B) A device will be demonstrated.
    (C) A speech will be given.
    (D) A video will be played.

77. Why does the speaker say, "There are many students studying at universities in this state"?
    (A) To confirm a change in policy
    (B) To introduce a new service
    (C) To describe a recent trend
    (D) To explain a rise in sales

78. What does the speaker suggest?
    (A) Extending a promotion
    (B) Conducting a survey
    (C) Offering a new benefit
    (D) Introducing a free trial

79. Why will a meeting be held tomorrow?
    (A) To create a focus group
    (B) To discuss some strategies
    (C) To test a sample product
    (D) To analyze some figures

80. Where most likely are the listeners?
    (A) At a construction site
    (B) At a medical clinic
    (C) At a manufacturing plant
    (D) At a car dealership

81. According to the speaker, what has been changed?
    (A) The price of some merchandise
    (B) The order of a tour
    (C) The type of machines used
    (D) The operational hours of a facility

82. What are listeners instructed to do?
    (A) Avoid touching equipment
    (B) Read an instruction manual
    (C) Wear protective gear
    (D) Enroll in a class

GO ON TO THE NEXT PAGE

83. According to the speaker, what should the listeners do first?

(A) Request some identification
(B) Deposit a check
(C) Count some money
(D) Provide a form

84. What does the speaker imply when he says, "you should just call a supervisor"?

(A) A bank account cannot be accessed by a customer.
(B) A device must be retrieved by a technician.
(C) A record must be verified by a manager.
(D) An error cannot be handled by a trainee.

85. What should listeners do at the end of a shift?

(A) Go through a back door
(B) Refill some containers
(C) Put away some cash
(D) Lock a drawer

---

86. What is the advertisement mainly about?

(A) A radio program
(B) An awards ceremony
(C) An acting audition
(D) A musical contest

87. What does the speaker say about the judges?

(A) They will be former contestants.
(B) They will choose the final winner.
(C) They will be changed each week.
(D) They will consider viewer feedback.

88. What does the speaker say is available on the Web site?

(A) An audio recording
(B) A venue list
(C) A performance schedule
(D) A film trailer

---

89. What is mentioned about the previous speakers?

(A) They worked for major publications.
(B) They graduated from James College.
(C) They gave stimulating lectures.
(D) They received writing prizes.

90. What will the speaker talk about?

(A) The importance of reading
(B) The influence of literature
(C) The value of higher education
(D) The effects of legal reform

91. Who is Jack Coyle?

(A) An author
(B) A college lecturer
(C) A public official
(D) A lawyer

---

92. What field does the speaker work in?

(A) Advertising
(B) Marketing
(C) Education
(D) City planning

93. How did the speaker find out about Mr. Davidson?

(A) By reading an article
(B) By watching footage
(C) By attending one of his lectures
(D) By speaking to a colleague

94. Why does the speaker say, "My class ends at the beginning of December"?

(A) To specify when she can start a project
(B) To confirm the date an event will finish on
(C) To indicate when a talk must be given by
(D) To stress the need to reschedule an activity

Changing Rooms			
Aisle 1	Aisle 2	Aisle 3	Aisle 4
	Main Entrance	Checkout Area	

STEP 1	Meet with clients
↓	
STEP 2	Discuss plan with team leader
↓	
STEP 3	Draft blueprints
↓	
STEP 4	Modify plans based on feedback
↓	
STEP 5	Submit for approval

95. Who is the speaker most likely addressing?

(A) Store customers
(B) Marketing consultants
(C) Shop employees
(D) Construction workers

96. Look at the graphic. Where has the display been set up?

(A) In Aisle 1
(B) In Aisle 2
(C) In Aisle 3
(D) In Aisle 4

97. According to the speaker, what will be announced tomorrow?

(A) The dates of a renovation project
(B) The name of a design firm
(C) The details of a sportswear production
(D) The location of a new branch

98. What happened last month?

(A) A permit application was rejected.
(B) A structure was inspected.
(C) A project was started.
(D) A sports arena was completed.

99. Why is a change being made?

(A) To reduce some expenses
(B) To reflect client requests
(C) To improve communication
(D) To accommodate time constraints

100. Look at the graphic. Which step was removed from a work process?

(A) Meet with clients
(B) Discuss plan with team leader
(C) Modify plans based on feedback
(D) Submit for approval

정답 p.165 / 점수 환산표 p.167 / 스크립트 p.210 / 무료 해석 바로 보기(정답 및 정답 음성 포함)

▌정답 음성(QR)이나 정답(p.165)을 이용해 채점하시기 바랍니다. 정답 음성에서 Boy는 (B)를, David는 (D)를 나타냅니다.
▌다음 페이지에 있는 Self 체크 리스트를 통해 자신의 문제 풀이 방식과 태도를 점검해 보세요.

Self 체크 리스트

TEST 08은 무사히 잘 마치셨죠?
이제 다음의 Self 체크 리스트를 통해 자신의 테스트 진행 내용을 점검해 볼까요?

1. 나는 테스트가 진행되는 동안 한 번도 중도에 멈추지 않았다.

   □ 예   □ 아니오

   아니오에 답한 경우, 이유는 무엇인가요?

2. 나는 답안지 표기까지 성실하게 모두 마무리하였다.

   □ 예   □ 아니오

   아니오에 답한 경우, 이유는 무엇인가요?

3. 나는 Part 2의 25문항을 푸는 동안 완전히 테스트에 집중하였다.

   □ 예   □ 아니오

   아니오에 답한 경우, 이유는 무엇인가요?

4. 나는 Part 3를 풀 때 음성이 들리기 전에 해당 질문과 보기를 모두 먼저 읽었다.

   □ 예   □ 아니오

   아니오에 답한 경우, 이유는 무엇인가요?

5. 나는 Part 4를 풀 때 음성이 들리기 전에 해당 질문과 보기를 모두 먼저 읽었다.

   □ 예   □ 아니오

   아니오에 답한 경우, 이유는 무엇인가요?

6. 개선해야 할 점 또는 나를 위한 충고를 적어보세요.

* 교재의 첫 장으로 돌아가서 자신이 적은 목표 점수를 확인하면서 목표에 대한 의지를 다지기 바랍니다. 개선해야 할 점은 반드시 다음 테스트에
  실천해야 합니다. 그것이 가장 중요하며, 그래야만 발전할 수 있습니다.

▍TEST 09

잠깐! 테스트 전 확인사항

1. 휴대 전화의 전원을 끄셨나요? □ 예
2. Answer Sheet, 연필, 지우개를 준비하셨나요? □ 예
3. MP3를 들을 준비가 되셨나요? □ 예

모든 준비가 완료되었으면 목표 점수를 떠올린 후 테스트를 시작합니다.

 🎧 TEST 09.mp3

실전용·복습용 문제풀이 MP3 무료 다운로드 및 스트리밍 바로듣기 (HackersIngang.com)

* 실제 시험장의 소음까지 재현해 낸 고사장 소음/매미 버전 MP3, 영국식·호주식 발음 집중 MP3, 고속 버전 MP3까지
구매하면 실전에 더욱 완벽히 대비할 수 있습니다.

무료MP3 바로듣기

LISTENING TEST

In this section, you must demonstrate your ability to understand spoken English. This section is divided into four parts and will take approximately 45 minutes to complete. Do not mark the answers in your test book. Use the answer sheet that is provided separately.

PART 1

Directions: For each question, you will listen to four short statements about a picture in your test book. These statements will not be printed and will only be spoken one time. Select the statement that best describes what is happening in the picture and mark the corresponding letter (A), (B), (C), or (D) on the answer sheet.

Sample Answer

The statement that best describes the picture is (B), "The man is sitting at the desk." So, you should mark letter (B) on the answer sheet.

1.

2.

GO ON TO THE NEXT PAGE ➞

3.

4.

5.

6.

GO ON TO THE NEXT PAGE

PART 2

Directions: For each question, you will listen to a statement or question followed by three possible responses spoken in English. They will not be printed and will only be spoken one time. Select the best response and mark the corresponding letter (A), (B), or (C) on your answer sheet.

7. Mark your answer on your answer sheet.

8. Mark your answer on your answer sheet.

9. Mark your answer on your answer sheet.

10. Mark your answer on your answer sheet.

11. Mark your answer on your answer sheet.

12. Mark your answer on your answer sheet.

13. Mark your answer on your answer sheet.

14. Mark your answer on your answer sheet.

15. Mark your answer on your answer sheet.

16. Mark your answer on your answer sheet.

17. Mark your answer on your answer sheet.

18. Mark your answer on your answer sheet.

19. Mark your answer on your answer sheet.

20. Mark your answer on your answer sheet.

21. Mark your answer on your answer sheet.

22. Mark your answer on your answer sheet.

23. Mark your answer on your answer sheet.

24. Mark your answer on your answer sheet.

25. Mark your answer on your answer sheet.

26. Mark your answer on your answer sheet.

27. Mark your answer on your answer sheet.

28. Mark your answer on your answer sheet.

29. Mark your answer on your answer sheet.

30. Mark your answer on your answer sheet.

31. Mark your answer on your answer sheet.

PART 3

Directions: In this part, you will listen to several conversations between two or more speakers. These conversations will not be printed and will only be spoken one time. For each conversation, you will be asked to answer three questions. Select the best response and mark the corresponding letter (A), (B), (C), or (D) on your answer sheet.

32. Why is Malinda unable to stay until 5 P.M.?

(A) She is not feeling very well.
(B) She must get a family member.
(C) She has to drop off some supplies.
(D) She will go to a school function.

33. What does the man agree to do?

(A) Call a receptionist
(B) Interview an applicant
(C) Show people around a gym
(D) Fill in for a colleague

34. According to the woman, where did the man previously work?

(A) At a fitness center
(B) At an advertising firm
(C) At a construction company
(D) At a recruitment agency

35. Where do the speakers most likely work?

(A) At a concert hall
(B) At a clothing retail outlet
(C) At a record store
(D) At an electronics repair shop

36. What does the man recommend?

(A) Selling merchandise online
(B) Contacting local performers
(C) Organizing jazz concerts
(D) Giving away prizes

37. According to the woman, what do some customers want?

(A) Artists' signatures
(B) Musical instruments
(C) Limited edition posters
(D) New albums

38. Where most likely does the conversation take place?

(A) At a bus terminal
(B) At a park
(C) At a garage
(D) At a car dealership

39. What does the woman say about her husband?

(A) He forgot to print a document.
(B) He wants to buy a monthly pass.
(C) He is employed by a nearby business.
(D) He is running some errands.

40. What should the woman do when she leaves?

(A) Make a payment
(B) Speak with an attendant
(C) Ask for a ticket
(D) Confirm an appointment

41. What type of event does the man have to attend?

(A) A branch opening
(B) A training seminar
(C) A charity fundraiser
(D) An industry expo

42. What does the woman need help with?

(A) Managing a team meeting
(B) Setting a budget for expenses
(C) Coming up with saving ideas
(D) Calculating numbers for accounting

43. Why does the man say, "I'll take a later flight, then"?

(A) To accept an upgrade
(B) To turn down a proposal
(C) To confirm a departure time
(D) To agree to a request

GO ON TO THE NEXT PAGE

44. What is the conversation mainly about?

(A) Hiring a personal chef
(B) Postponing a luncheon
(C) Eating at an on-site facility
(D) Extending a break period

45. According to the woman, why has there been a change?

(A) To respond to worker comments
(B) To improve safety measures
(C) To reduce company expenses
(D) To accommodate staff schedules

46. When will the man most likely join the woman?

(A) When a restaurant opens
(B) When a work trip ends
(C) When a menu is changed
(D) When a task is completed

---

47. Who most likely is the man?

(A) A factory worker
(B) A marketing manager
(C) A salesperson
(D) A technician

48. Why does the man say, "The new Gentro model will be released next quarter"?

(A) To suggest that a part be replaced
(B) To explain why a component is unavailable
(C) To introduce a new product feature
(D) To notify of a special promotion plan

49. What will the man most likely do next?

(A) Adjust some settings
(B) Check an expiry date
(C) Repair a battery
(D) Install some software

---

50. Why is the man calling?

(A) To reserve an item
(B) To cancel an account
(C) To request an extension
(D) To make a complaint

51. According to the woman, what did the library do last month?

(A) Launched a Web site
(B) Changed a notification procedure
(C) Increased fines for overdue materials
(D) Ordered new books

52. What does the woman say she can do?

(A) Return a book
(B) Pass on a message
(C) Send an e-mail
(D) Waive a charge

---

53. What was held on Monday?

(A) An employee orientation
(B) A job interview
(C) A staff meeting
(D) A training session

54. What is mentioned about Sheryl Johnson?

(A) She lacks relevant experience.
(B) She will provide a work sample.
(C) She has requested a transfer.
(D) She will lead a seminar.

55. What will the woman probably do next?

(A) Visit another company
(B) Contact an applicant
(C) Discuss a matter with a superior
(D) Place résumés in a filing cabinet

---

56. Where is the conversation most likely taking place?

(A) At a performance venue
(B) At an amusement park
(C) At a science museum
(D) At a shopping mall

57. According to Amy, What is being celebrated this month?

(A) The expansion of a company
(B) The promotion of an employee
(C) The anniversary of a business
(D) The construction of a facility

58. Why was the man unaware of an event?

(A) He is not on a mailing list.
(B) He could not attend a conference.
(C) He did not notice a schedule.
(D) He was given inaccurate information.

59. Who most likely is the man?

(A) A craftsman
(B) A personal assistant
(C) A salesperson
(D) A fashion designer

60. What problem does the woman mention?

(A) An order arrived late.
(B) A stock room is messy.
(C) A price tag is incorrect.
(D) A product is damaged.

61. What does the woman ask the man to do?

(A) Supply a receipt
(B) Wrap a purchase
(C) Repair an item
(D) Provide a discount

Subscriber Numbers

62. What happened in May?

(A) A subscription fee was increased.
(B) A choice of offerings was broadened.
(C) An annual report was released.
(D) Some funds were borrowed.

63. Look at the graphic. Which country was the streaming service first launched in?

(A) Brazil
(B) Canada
(C) Germany
(D) Japan

64. What does the man suggest?

(A) Contacting an advertiser
(B) Attending a meeting
(C) Reviewing some data
(D) Composing a message

GO ON TO THE NEXT PAGE

Employee Name	Extension Number
Monica Pearce	9087
Josh Han	1099
Valarie Dupree	4419
Will Garcia	7893

65. What will the man do tonight?

(A) Upgrade computer software
(B) Assist with a move
(C) Get in touch with a client
(D) Participate in a meeting

66. What problem does the man mention?

(A) A goal was missed.
(B) A list is incomplete.
(C) A directory is inaccessible.
(D) A desk can no longer be used.

67. Look at the graphic. Who works in the marketing department?

(A) Monica Pearce
(B) Josh Han
(C) Valarie Dupree
(D) Will Garcia

Angle Apparel	
Receipt #: 456297	
Item	**Price**
Sportswear hat	$14.99
Red Line jacket	$18.99
Coolman sandals	$22.99
Ace jeans	$39.99

68. What did the woman do yesterday?

(A) Placed an online order
(B) Visited a store
(C) Gave someone a present
(D) Called a local branch

69. Look at the graphic. What amount is inaccurate?

(A) $14.99
(B) $18.99
(C) $22.99
(D) $39.99

70. What will the woman receive with the refund?

(A) A complimentary product
(B) A ticket for a sports game
(C) A prepaid card
(D) An extra discount

PART 4

Directions: In this part, you will listen to several short talks by a single speaker. These talks will not be printed and will only be spoken one time. For each talk, you will be asked to answer three questions. Select the best response and mark the corresponding letter (A), (B), (C), or (D) on your answer sheet.

71. Who is the speaker?

(A) A flight attendant
(B) A ticket agent
(C) An airline pilot
(D) A security guard

72. When will Flight 876 reach its destination?

(A) At 5:10 P.M.
(B) At 5:20 P.M.
(C) At 5:30 P.M.
(D) At 5:40 P.M.

73. What does the speaker suggest listeners do?

(A) Complete a document
(B) Choose an in-flight meal
(C) Report to an information desk
(D) Confirm a flight time

---

74. What is being advertised?

(A) A residential cleaning service
(B) An eco-friendly product line
(C) A new supermarket chain
(D) An innovative home appliance

75. What is supposed to happen in March?

(A) A marketing campaign will start.
(B) Samples will be given to customers.
(C) A product will be available in retail stores.
(D) Existing models will be replaced.

76. According to the speaker, what can listeners do online?

(A) Download a special coupon
(B) Find a store location
(C) Ask for a refund
(D) Make a purchase

77. What type of business does the speaker work for?

(A) An accommodation facility
(B) A catering company
(C) A law firm
(D) A real estate agency

78. Why does the speaker say, "But over 75 guests will be attending this event"?

(A) To approve a request
(B) To confirm a plan
(C) To indicate a problem
(D) To show excitement

79. What does the speaker ask the listener to do?

(A) Print a revised contract
(B) Call a party planner
(C) Provide an attendee list
(D) Visit an event venue

---

80. What is the announcement mainly about?

(A) A new discovery
(B) Severe weather condition
(C) Traffic information
(D) An athletic competition

81. What are listeners advised to do?

(A) Avoid exercise
(B) Park in designated areas
(C) Report health problems
(D) Contact an official

82. What does the speaker say is available on the Web site?

(A) Traffic updates
(B) Medical information
(C) Air quality data
(D) Nutrition tips

GO ON TO THE NEXT PAGE

83. What type of business is being advertised?

(A) An advertising firm
(B) An educational institution
(C) A financial company
(D) A recruitment agency

84. According to the speaker, why is the company highly ranked in a survey?

(A) Its services are inexpensive.
(B) Its managers are experienced.
(C) Its products are reliable.
(D) Its employees are trustworthy.

85. Why should the listeners contact the hotline?

(A) To verify a payment
(B) To arrange a consultation
(C) To cancel a service
(D) To participate in a survey

86. What did the speaker do last week?

(A) Hired some performers
(B) Attended a concert
(C) Purchased some tickets
(D) Participated in a contest

87. Why does the speaker say, "this is supposedly her final tour"?

(A) To notify of a cancellation
(B) To evaluate a performance
(C) To persuade the listener
(D) To specify a time limit

88. What does the speaker ask the listener to do?

(A) Provide transportation
(B) Locate a venue
(C) Confirm information
(D) Make a payment

89. What is the main purpose of the talk?

(A) To explain a company regulation
(B) To introduce a software product
(C) To discuss an insurance plan
(D) To promote a Web site

90. According to the speaker, what can managers do?

(A) Receive customer feedback
(B) Approve program updates
(C) Change staff assignments
(D) Track employee performance

91. What will most likely happen next?

(A) A video will be played.
(B) A demonstration will be given.
(C) A supervisor will be introduced.
(D) A questionnaire will be distributed.

92. Which department does the speaker most likely work for?

(A) Product development
(B) Marketing
(C) Finance
(D) Advertising

93. What problem does the speaker mention?

(A) A product is not entirely safe.
(B) An item is not selling well.
(C) An advertisement was criticized.
(D) A budget was exceeded.

94. What does the speaker imply when he says, "fragrance-free products are popular these days"?

(A) A survey will be conducted.
(B) A request has to be approved.
(C) A display must be rearranged.
(D) A plan needs to be changed.

Staircase	Booth A	Booth B
Ground Floor Bathroom	Booth C	Booth D
		Information Desk

Bretford Incorporated - Interview Dates

Monday, May 2	Marketing Department
Tuesday, May 3	Design Department
Wednesday, May 4	Sales Department
Thursday, May 5	Accounting Department
Friday, May 6	*No Interviews Scheduled*

95. What is mentioned about the event?

(A) It has participants from many countries.
(B) It occurs in the same city every year.
(C) It is sponsored by local organizations.
(D) It will end later than expected.

96. Look at the graphic. Which booth is Matthew Walsh using?

(A) Booth A
(B) Booth B
(C) Booth C
(D) Booth D

97. According to the speaker, what can listeners do at the information desk?

(A) Pick up a brochure
(B) Buy a ticket
(C) Enter a contest
(D) Register for a class

98. Look at the graphic. Which department is the woman applying to?

(A) Marketing
(B) Design
(C) Sales
(D) Accounting

99. What does the speaker ask the listener to do?

(A) Provide a job description
(B) Check on a delivery
(C) Change a schedule
(D) Expedite a process

100. What did the speaker do on Wednesday?

(A) Replied to an e-mail
(B) Submitted a sample
(C) Visited a family member
(D) Filled out an application

정답 p.166 / 점수 환산표 p.167 / 스크립트 p.216 / 무료 해석 바로 보기(정답 및 정답 음성 포함)

▌정답 음성(QR)이나 정답(p.166)을 이용해 채점하시기 바랍니다. 정답 음성에서 Boy는 (B)를, David는 (D)를 나타냅니다.
▌다음 페이지에 있는 Self 체크 리스트를 통해 자신의 문제 풀이 방식과 태도를 점검해 보세요.

Self 체크 리스트

TEST 09은 무사히 잘 마치셨죠?
이제 다음의 Self 체크 리스트를 통해 자신의 테스트 진행 내용을 점검해 볼까요?

1. 나는 테스트가 진행되는 동안 한 번도 중도에 멈추지 않았다.

   ☐ 예   ☐ 아니오

   아니오에 답한 경우, 이유는 무엇인가요?

2. 나는 답안지 표기까지 성실하게 모두 마무리하였다.

   ☐ 예   ☐ 아니오

   아니오에 답한 경우, 이유는 무엇인가요?

3. 나는 Part 2의 25문항을 푸는 동안 완전히 테스트에 집중하였다.

   ☐ 예   ☐ 아니오

   아니오에 답한 경우, 이유는 무엇인가요?

4. 나는 Part 3를 풀 때 음성이 들리기 전에 해당 질문과 보기를 모두 먼저 읽었다.

   ☐ 예   ☐ 아니오

   아니오에 답한 경우, 이유는 무엇인가요?

5. 나는 Part 4를 풀 때 음성이 들리기 전에 해당 질문과 보기를 모두 먼저 읽었다.

   ☐ 예   ☐ 아니오

   아니오에 답한 경우, 이유는 무엇인가요?

6. 개선해야 할 점 또는 나를 위한 충고를 적어보세요.

* 교재의 첫 장으로 돌아가서 자신이 적은 목표 점수를 확인하면서 목표에 대한 의지를 다지기 바랍니다. 개선해야 할 점은 반드시 다음 테스트에
  실천해야 합니다. 그것이 가장 중요하며, 그래야만 발전할 수 있습니다.

▮ TEST 10

PART 1
PART 2
PART 3
PART 4
Self 체크 리스트

잠깐! 테스트 전 확인사항
1. 휴대 전화의 전원을 끄셨나요? □ 예
2. Answer Sheet, 연필, 지우개를 준비하셨나요? □ 예
3. MP3를 들을 준비가 되셨나요? □ 예

모든 준비가 완료되었으면 목표 점수를 떠올린 후 테스트를 시작합니다.

🎧 TEST 10.mp3
실전용·복습용 문제풀이 MP3 무료 다운로드 및 스트리밍 바로듣기 (HackersIngang.com)
* 실제 시험장의 소음까지 재현해 낸 고사장 소음/매미 버전 MP3, 영국식·호주식 발음 집중 MP3, 고속 버전 MP3까지
  구매하면 실전에 더욱 완벽히 대비할 수 있습니다.

무료MP3 바로듣기

LISTENING TEST

In this section, you must demonstrate your ability to understand spoken English. This section is divided into four parts and will take approximately 45 minutes to complete. Do not mark the answers in your test book. Use the answer sheet that is provided separately.

PART 1

Directions: For each question, you will listen to four short statements about a picture in your test book. These statements will not be printed and will only be spoken one time. Select the statement that best describes what is happening in the picture and mark the corresponding letter (A), (B), (C), or (D) on the answer sheet.

Sample Answer

The statement that best describes the picture is (B), "The man is sitting at the desk." So, you should mark letter (B) on the answer sheet.

1.

2.

GO ON TO THE NEXT PAGE ➤

3.

4.

5.

6.

GO ON TO THE NEXT PAGE ➔

TEST 01 02 03 04 05 06 07 08 09 **10**

해커스 토익 실전 1000제 3 Listening

PART 2

Directions: For each question, you will listen to a statement or question followed by three possible responses spoken in English. They will not be printed and will only be spoken one time. Select the best response and mark the corresponding letter (A), (B), or (C) on your answer sheet.

7. Mark your answer on your answer sheet.

8. Mark your answer on your answer sheet.

9. Mark your answer on your answer sheet.

10. Mark your answer on your answer sheet.

11. Mark your answer on your answer sheet.

12. Mark your answer on your answer sheet.

13. Mark your answer on your answer sheet.

14. Mark your answer on your answer sheet.

15. Mark your answer on your answer sheet.

16. Mark your answer on your answer sheet.

17. Mark your answer on your answer sheet.

18. Mark your answer on your answer sheet.

19. Mark your answer on your answer sheet.

20. Mark your answer on your answer sheet.

21. Mark your answer on your answer sheet.

22. Mark your answer on your answer sheet.

23. Mark your answer on your answer sheet.

24. Mark your answer on your answer sheet.

25. Mark your answer on your answer sheet.

26. Mark your answer on your answer sheet.

27. Mark your answer on your answer sheet.

28. Mark your answer on your answer sheet.

29. Mark your answer on your answer sheet.

30. Mark your answer on your answer sheet.

31. Mark your answer on your answer sheet.

PART 3

Directions: In this part, you will listen to several conversations between two or more speakers. These conversations will not be printed and will only be spoken one time. For each conversation, you will be asked to answer three questions. Select the best response and mark the corresponding letter (A), (B), (C), or (D) on your answer sheet.

32. Where most likely is the conversation taking place?

    (A) At a government office
    (B) At a manufacturing plant
    (C) At an accommodation facility
    (D) At a convention center

33. According to the man, what did the speakers discuss this morning?

    (A) Schedule changes
    (B) Machinery prices
    (C) Building renovations
    (D) Malfunctioning equipment

34. What problem does the woman mention?

    (A) There is not much preparation time.
    (B) An evaluation went poorly.
    (C) There are not enough employees.
    (D) A regulation has been altered.

35. How did the woman learn about a product?

    (A) By visiting a Web site
    (B) By watching television
    (C) By reading a brochure
    (D) By talking to an acquaintance

36. What does the man imply when he says, "The LS model is almost four years old at this point"?

    (A) An item has been discounted.
    (B) A device cannot be repaired.
    (C) A brand is not very popular.
    (D) A product is no longer in stock.

37. What will the man probably do next?

    (A) Inspect a gadget
    (B) Demonstrate an appliance
    (C) Process a payment
    (D) Print a receipt

38. What does the man ask the woman to do?

    (A) Scan some documents
    (B) Postpone a departure date
    (C) Come up with an agenda
    (D) Complete some reports

39. Why is the woman going out of town?

    (A) To attend a shareholders' meeting
    (B) To sign a sales contract
    (C) To speak at a team seminar
    (D) To participate in a celebration

40. According to the woman, what is Catherine Dawkins willing to do?

    (A) Switch divisions
    (B) Work additional hours
    (C) Lead an accounting team
    (D) Increase a budget

41. What did the man do two weeks ago?

    (A) Returned a book to a store
    (B) Sent a package overseas
    (C) Bought an item
    (D) Enrolled in a course

42. What does the woman say the man failed to provide?

    (A) A book title
    (B) A recipient name
    (C) An e-mail address
    (D) A unit number

43. What does the woman recommend?

    (A) Talking to a property manager
    (B) Using another courier service
    (C) Correcting some billing information
    (D) Placing an order through a Web site

GO ON TO THE NEXT PAGE

44. What are the speakers mainly discussing?

(A) Upcoming meetings
(B) A menu design
(C) Schedule updates
(D) New uniforms

45. What did the man do last week?

(A) Damaged a clothing item
(B) Removed some stains
(C) Put items in a storage space
(D) Ordered some extra pens

46. What does the man ask the woman about?

(A) The reason for a decision
(B) The date of a change
(C) The location of an event
(D) The need for authorization

---

47. What is the woman in charge of?

(A) Hiring new architects
(B) Correcting an e-mail error
(C) Planning a meeting
(D) Gathering some files

48. Why will more time be allowed for Helen?

(A) She lives far away from a building.
(B) She has not finished a design.
(C) She will be showing a visitor around.
(D) She needs more time for a
    presentation.

49. What will the woman most likely do next?

(A) Photocopy some printouts
(B) Revise an agenda
(C) Reserve a conference room
(D) Take a lunch break

---

50. Where most likely is the conversation taking place?

(A) In a doctor's office
(B) In a bookstore
(C) In a warehouse
(D) In a pharmacy

51. What information does Alex require from the woman?

(A) The name of a product
(B) The time of an appointment
(C) The availability of an item
(D) The severity of a condition

52. What will the woman probably do this afternoon?

(A) Try a free sample
(B) Read a pamphlet
(C) Consult a doctor
(D) Get some exercise

---

53. What are the speakers mainly discussing?

(A) International travel plans
(B) Foreign language lessons
(C) An overseas branch opening
(D) An educational publication

54. What information does Jenny provide?

(A) The costs of enrollment
(B) The number of students
(C) The start date of a course
(D) The material list for a class

55. What is the man eligible to receive?

(A) A special fee reduction
(B) A free online lecture
(C) A membership upgrade
(D) A complimentary handout

---

56. What problem does the woman describe?

(A) She is late for a meeting.
(B) She cannot find an office.
(C) She may not meet a deadline.
(D) She forgot to bring a report.

57. What does the man offer to do?

(A) Send an electronic copy
(B) Check an e-mail account
(C) Reschedule a conference
(D) Edit a document

58. What does the man imply when he says, "Brad is using the scanner"?

(A) A device is functioning as expected.
(B) A coworker will be able to do an assignment.
(C) A task cannot be performed immediately.
(D) A worker can fix some equipment later.

59. Why does the man call the woman?

(A) To follow up on an agreement
(B) To discuss unpaid charges
(C) To describe service coverage
(D) To encourage an expansion

60. What does the woman say about the legal team?

(A) It has been downsized.
(B) It is checking a document.
(C) It has acquired a license.
(D) It is being evaluated.

61. Why does the man congratulate the woman?

(A) A firm has received an award.
(B) A safety inspection was passed.
(C) A distributor has been contracted.
(D) A product has attracted attention.

Pain Relief Medication	Price Per Box	Price Per Pill
UltraMed	$3.50	10¢
NoAche	$4.50	8¢
HealFast	$5.50	12¢
SootheNow	$7.50	9¢

62. What did the man already do?

(A) Cleared products from the shelves
(B) Contacted a drug manufacturer
(C) Assisted some customers
(D) Reviewed stock levels

63. Why is cough medicine in short supply?

(A) An illness is common at the moment.
(B) A delivery has not arrived on schedule.
(C) A firm has stopped producing goods.
(D) A new brand was recently released.

64. Look at the graphic. Which item will the man order?

(A) UltraMed
(B) NoAche
(C) HealFast
(D) SootheNow

GO ON TO THE NEXT PAGE

Building A		Triton Theater	
	Building B	Building C	
Waverly Park		Building D	

Maria Street | Flora Road | Truro Avenue | Fresco Road | Riviera Street

Nutrition Facts

Serving Size: 10 pretzels
Servings per Pack: 3

Ingredient	Amount per Serving
Sugar	6g
Carbohydrates	32g
Fat	22g
Cholesterol	20mg

65. What industry does the man most likely work in?

(A) Education
(B) Travel
(C) Art
(D) Legal

66. Look at the graphic. Where most likely does the woman want to go?

(A) To Building A
(B) To Building B
(C) To Building C
(D) To Building D

67. What does the man offer to do?

(A) Provide contact information
(B) Make some reservations
(C) Get a map of a downtown area
(D) Telephone a local gallery

68. Where is the conversation most likely taking place?

(A) At a restaurant
(B) At an office building
(C) At a convenience store
(D) At an airport

69. Look at the graphic. Which ingredient amount is too high for the man?

(A) 6g
(B) 32g
(C) 22g
(D) 20mg

70. What does the man say he will do?

(A) Pick another snack
(B) Wait for a meal
(C) Read a product label
(D) Inquire about a lunch menu

PART 4

Directions: In this part, you will listen to several short talks by a single speaker. These talks will not be printed and will only be spoken one time. For each talk, you will be asked to answer three questions. Select the best response and mark the corresponding letter (A), (B), (C), or (D) on your answer sheet.

71. Where most likely are the listeners?

(A) At a museum
(B) At an art school
(C) At a public library
(D) At a painting studio

72. According to the speaker, what is unusual about *The Flames of Clouds*?

(A) Its size
(B) Its use of color
(C) Its date of origin
(D) Its name

73. What will listeners most likely do next?

(A) Read about some artwork
(B) Visit a gift shop
(C) Watch a brief video
(D) Go to another gallery

74. What type of business is being advertised?

(A) An online retailer
(B) A catering company
(C) A food outlet
(D) A department store

75. According to the speaker, what distinguishes the company from its competitors?

(A) Reasonable prices
(B) Unlimited toppings
(C) Unique flavors
(D) Natural ingredients

76. Why should listeners visit the business's social media page?

(A) Some deals are available.
(B) A newsletter was published.
(C) A menu can be downloaded.
(D) Some reviews have been posted.

77. What industry does Mark Larson most likely work in?

(A) Fashion
(B) Entertainment
(C) Transportation
(D) Marketing

78. What does the speaker imply when he says, "the main building is scheduled to be painted"?

(A) A facility has changed its operating hours.
(B) Some workers will need to be hired.
(C) Some materials have been delivered.
(D) An event will be temporarily relocated.

79. According to the speaker, what will Mr. Larson discuss?

(A) Recruitment strategies
(B) Training procedures
(C) Advertising techniques
(D) Communication methods

80. What is Dr. Mattson's area of expertise?

(A) Economics
(B) Journalism
(C) Statistics
(D) Ecology

81. According to the speaker, what was released on Monday?

(A) An academic publication
(B) A podcast series
(C) A policy review
(D) A list of keynote speakers

82. What is mentioned about Dr. Mattson?

(A) He will address some criticisms.
(B) He will take calls from listeners.
(C) He will talk about a course curriculum.
(D) He will submit a research proposal.

GO ON TO THE NEXT PAGE

83. Where do the listeners most likely work?

(A) At an educational institution
(B) At a cosmetics firm
(C) At an advertising company
(D) At an electronics manufacturer

84. Why does the speaker say, "I don't want to turn anyone away, though"?

(A) She will provide a solution.
(B) She will reconsider a decision.
(C) She will approve a plan.
(D) She will reject a request.

85. What will Beth Meyers most likely do?

(A) Try out some products
(B) Organize an activity
(C) Attend a meeting
(D) Contact applicants

---

86. What is Ivan Schwartz's occupation?

(A) Consultant
(B) Travel agent
(C) Programmer
(D) Instructor

87. According to the speaker, what will Ivan Schwartz do?

(A) Install some equipment
(B) Oversee an ongoing project
(C) Create a computer application
(D) Learn about new software

88. What are listeners asked to do?

(A) Undergo some training
(B) Welcome a colleague
(C) Set up an office for a manager
(D) Prepare for a business trip

---

89. Why was Gilbert Avenue closed?

(A) A vehicle accident occurred.
(B) A structure was built.
(C) A building was damaged.
(D) A public event took place.

90. What does the speaker mean when she says, "the championship football game will begin at noon"?

(A) Tickets are not available anymore.
(B) Players will arrive soon.
(C) Traffic conditions will change.
(D) Parking is not permitted downtown.

91. According to the speaker, what will listeners probably hear after a break?

(A) A report
(B) A game broadcast
(C) An advertisement
(D) A match review

---

92. What is the purpose of the report?

(A) To describe promotional efforts
(B) To discuss an upcoming election
(C) To explain tour restrictions
(D) To outline a construction project

93. According to the speaker, what does Shenzhen possess?

(A) A world-renowned shopping complex
(B) Favorable tax rates
(C) An international airport
(D) Numerous vacant retail spaces

94. What do officials think about Shenzhen?

(A) It currently has a high population.
(B) It is experiencing increases in tourism.
(C) It can achieve further economic success.
(D) It is a safe place for travelers from abroad.

Subscription Renewal Form

Subscription Period	Fee	Selection
6 months	$30	
12 months	$50	
18 months	$70	✓
24 months	$100	

Model	Price
JY34	$95
SR88	$85
WT45	$75
HK21	$65

95. What does the speaker plan to do in December?

(A) Update her mailing address
(B) Make a subscription payment
(C) Submit a magazine article
(D) Travel overseas for work

96. Look at the graphic. How much does the subscription the speaker is interested in cost?

(A) $30
(B) $50
(C) $70
(D) $100

97. What does the speaker request?

(A) A partial refund
(B) A contract extension
(C) An account closure
(D) An e-mail confirmation

98. What did the speaker do earlier today?

(A) Reviewed a report
(B) Spoke with an executive
(C) Sent out a memo
(D) Corrected a budget

99. Look at the graphic. Which model is not selling well?

(A) JY34
(B) SR88
(C) WT45
(D) HK21

100. What will the speaker most likely talk about next?

(A) The impact of a personnel change
(B) The benefit of a production method
(C) The cost of a marketing campaign
(D) The amount of anticipated savings

해커스 토익 실전 1000제 3 Listening

정답 p.166 / 점수 환산표 p.167 / 스크립트 p.222 / 무료 해석 바로 보기(정답 및 정답 음성 포함)

▌정답 음성(QR)이나 정답(p.166)을 이용해 채점하시기 바랍니다. 정답 음성에서 Boy는 (B)를, David는 (D)를 나타냅니다.
▌다음 페이지에 있는 Self 체크 리스트를 통해 자신의 문제 풀이 방식과 태도를 점검해 보세요.

Self 체크 리스트

TEST 10은 무사히 잘 마치셨죠?
이제 다음의 Self 체크 리스트를 통해 자신의 테스트 진행 내용을 점검해 볼까요?

1. 나는 테스트가 진행되는 동안 한 번도 중도에 멈추지 않았다.

  □ 예　　　　　　　　□ 아니오

  아니오에 답한 경우, 이유는 무엇인가요?

2. 나는 답안지 표기까지 성실하게 모두 마무리하였다.

  □ 예　　　　　　　　□ 아니오

  아니오에 답한 경우, 이유는 무엇인가요?

3. 나는 Part 2의 25문항을 푸는 동안 완전히 테스트에 집중하였다.

  □ 예　　　　　　　　□ 아니오

  아니오에 답한 경우, 이유는 무엇인가요?

4. 나는 Part 3를 풀 때 음성이 들리기 전에 해당 질문과 보기를 모두 먼저 읽었다.

  □ 예　　　　　　　　□ 아니오

  아니오에 답한 경우, 이유는 무엇인가요?

5. 나는 Part 4를 풀 때 음성이 들리기 전에 해당 질문과 보기를 모두 먼저 읽었다.

  □ 예　　　　　　　　□ 아니오

  아니오에 답한 경우, 이유는 무엇인가요?

6. 개선해야 할 점 또는 나를 위한 충고를 적어보세요.

* 교재의 첫 장으로 돌아가서 자신이 적은 목표 점수를 확인하면서 목표에 대한 의지를 다지기 바랍니다. 개선해야 할 점은 반드시 다음 테스트에 실천해야 합니다. 그것이 가장 중요하며, 그래야만 발전할 수 있습니다.

정답
점수 환산표
스크립트
Answer Sheet

■TEST 01

1 (B)	2 (C)	3 (C)	4 (B)	5 (D)
6 (C)	7 (A)	8 (B)	9 (A)	10 (C)
11 (C)	12 (B)	13 (B)	14 (C)	15 (C)
16 (B)	17 (B)	18 (A)	19 (C)	20 (C)
21 (A)	22 (C)	23 (A)	24 (C)	25 (A)
26 (B)	27 (C)	28 (B)	29 (B)	30 (A)
31 (C)	32 (B)	33 (A)	34 (D)	35 (D)
36 (A)	37 (D)	38 (B)	39 (A)	40 (C)
41 (D)	42 (D)	43 (A)	44 (C)	45 (B)
46 (A)	47 (C)	48 (C)	49 (D)	50 (D)
51 (A)	52 (A)	53 (D)	54 (A)	55 (B)
56 (C)	57 (A)	58 (C)	59 (A)	60 (A)
61 (A)	62 (D)	63 (B)	64 (B)	65 (A)
66 (D)	67 (C)	68 (B)	69 (B)	70 (C)
71 (B)	72 (B)	73 (C)	74 (C)	75 (A)
76 (B)	77 (C)	78 (B)	79 (D)	80 (D)
81 (A)	82 (A)	83 (A)	84 (A)	85 (D)
86 (A)	87 (D)	88 (B)	89 (C)	90 (B)
91 (A)	92 (A)	93 (C)	94 (B)	95 (B)
96 (A)	97 (C)	98 (B)	99 (D)	100 (D)

■TEST 02

1 (D)	2 (C)	3 (A)	4 (C)	5 (D)
6 (B)	7 (C)	8 (B)	9 (B)	10 (B)
11 (A)	12 (B)	13 (C)	14 (B)	15 (B)
16 (A)	17 (A)	18 (C)	19 (A)	20 (C)
21 (C)	22 (C)	23 (A)	24 (B)	25 (C)
26 (C)	27 (C)	28 (C)	29 (A)	30 (B)
31 (A)	32 (C)	33 (A)	34 (C)	35 (C)
36 (C)	37 (B)	38 (A)	39 (D)	40 (C)
41 (D)	42 (A)	43 (A)	44 (C)	45 (D)
46 (D)	47 (D)	48 (A)	49 (D)	50 (C)
51 (A)	52 (A)	53 (B)	54 (A)	55 (A)
56 (C)	57 (D)	58 (D)	59 (B)	60 (D)
61 (C)	62 (D)	63 (D)	64 (C)	65 (D)
66 (B)	67 (D)	68 (C)	69 (B)	70 (A)
71 (D)	72 (C)	73 (C)	74 (A)	75 (A)
76 (D)	77 (B)	78 (A)	79 (D)	80 (A)
81 (C)	82 (C)	83 (C)	84 (D)	85 (B)
86 (C)	87 (B)	88 (D)	89 (D)	90 (C)
91 (C)	92 (B)	93 (D)	94 (B)	95 (C)
96 (B)	97 (B)	98 (B)	99 (B)	100 (A)

■TEST 03

1 (A)	2 (C)	3 (B)	4 (D)	5 (D)
6 (B)	7 (B)	8 (C)	9 (A)	10 (C)
11 (C)	12 (B)	13 (B)	14 (C)	15 (A)
16 (B)	17 (C)	18 (B)	19 (B)	20 (C)
21 (B)	22 (B)	23 (A)	24 (B)	25 (C)
26 (A)	27 (C)	28 (B)	29 (A)	30 (A)
31 (A)	32 (B)	33 (D)	34 (D)	35 (C)
36 (A)	37 (A)	38 (D)	39 (B)	40 (C)
41 (C)	42 (A)	43 (C)	44 (C)	45 (D)
46 (D)	47 (C)	48 (B)	49 (A)	50 (C)
51 (B)	52 (B)	53 (C)	54 (B)	55 (A)
56 (A)	57 (D)	58 (B)	59 (B)	60 (C)
61 (B)	62 (B)	63 (C)	64 (D)	65 (C)
66 (B)	67 (C)	68 (C)	69 (C)	70 (B)
71 (B)	72 (D)	73 (A)	74 (B)	75 (C)
76 (D)	77 (B)	78 (A)	79 (D)	80 (A)
81 (B)	82 (C)	83 (D)	84 (A)	85 (C)
86 (D)	87 (B)	88 (D)	89 (C)	90 (D)
91 (D)	92 (A)	93 (A)	94 (C)	95 (C)
96 (A)	97 (A)	98 (B)	99 (A)	100 (C)

■TEST 04

1 (B)	2 (A)	3 (B)	4 (D)	5 (B)
6 (A)	7 (C)	8 (B)	9 (A)	10 (B)
11 (C)	12 (B)	13 (B)	14 (A)	15 (A)
16 (B)	17 (B)	18 (B)	19 (A)	20 (A)
21 (A)	22 (A)	23 (C)	24 (C)	25 (C)
26 (A)	27 (C)	28 (A)	29 (C)	30 (A)
31 (B)	32 (A)	33 (C)	34 (A)	35 (C)
36 (A)	37 (D)	38 (C)	39 (A)	40 (C)
41 (D)	42 (A)	43 (A)	44 (C)	45 (A)
46 (C)	47 (D)	48 (C)	49 (D)	50 (A)
51 (D)	52 (A)	53 (A)	54 (C)	55 (D)
56 (C)	57 (A)	58 (D)	59 (C)	60 (D)
61 (C)	62 (A)	63 (B)	64 (B)	65 (B)
66 (A)	67 (D)	68 (B)	69 (C)	70 (A)
71 (A)	72 (B)	73 (B)	74 (A)	75 (D)
76 (C)	77 (D)	78 (D)	79 (B)	80 (B)
81 (D)	82 (A)	83 (D)	84 (B)	85 (B)
86 (A)	87 (B)	88 (D)	89 (C)	90 (A)
91 (D)	92 (C)	93 (A)	94 (A)	95 (C)
96 (A)	97 (D)	98 (D)	99 (C)	100 (B)

TEST 05

1 (C)	2 (D)	3 (C)	4 (D)	5 (A)
6 (C)	7 (C)	8 (C)	9 (B)	10 (C)
11 (B)	12 (C)	13 (A)	14 (B)	15 (A)
16 (B)	17 (B)	18 (C)	19 (C)	20 (A)
21 (B)	22 (C)	23 (A)	24 (B)	25 (A)
26 (C)	27 (B)	28 (B)	29 (B)	30 (C)
31 (A)	32 (B)	33 (C)	34 (A)	35 (D)
36 (C)	37 (B)	38 (D)	39 (B)	40 (D)
41 (C)	42 (A)	43 (A)	44 (B)	45 (C)
46 (A)	47 (B)	48 (C)	49 (A)	50 (B)
51 (A)	52 (C)	53 (D)	54 (C)	55 (A)
56 (C)	57 (A)	58 (D)	59 (B)	60 (B)
61 (A)	62 (D)	63 (B)	64 (D)	65 (A)
66 (C)	67 (A)	68 (A)	69 (B)	70 (C)
71 (C)	72 (D)	73 (B)	74 (A)	75 (B)
76 (B)	77 (C)	78 (A)	79 (B)	80 (D)
81 (C)	82 (D)	83 (C)	84 (B)	85 (A)
86 (B)	87 (A)	88 (C)	89 (D)	90 (C)
91 (C)	92 (B)	93 (C)	94 (A)	95 (C)
96 (B)	97 (A)	98 (D)	99 (B)	100 (C)

TEST 06

1 (B)	2 (C)	3 (A)	4 (B)	5 (C)
6 (B)	7 (B)	8 (A)	9 (A)	10 (C)
11 (A)	12 (A)	13 (A)	14 (B)	15 (B)
16 (B)	17 (C)	18 (A)	19 (B)	20 (B)
21 (C)	22 (A)	23 (B)	24 (C)	25 (A)
26 (B)	27 (B)	28 (C)	29 (A)	30 (C)
31 (B)	32 (C)	33 (A)	34 (D)	35 (C)
36 (D)	37 (B)	38 (B)	39 (A)	40 (C)
41 (B)	42 (A)	43 (C)	44 (B)	45 (C)
46 (D)	47 (B)	48 (B)	49 (A)	50 (C)
51 (B)	52 (D)	53 (C)	54 (B)	55 (C)
56 (A)	57 (B)	58 (A)	59 (A)	60 (B)
61 (B)	62 (D)	63 (D)	64 (A)	65 (C)
66 (D)	67 (B)	68 (C)	69 (A)	70 (B)
71 (C)	72 (A)	73 (C)	74 (B)	75 (A)
76 (B)	77 (D)	78 (B)	79 (A)	80 (B)
81 (C)	82 (D)	83 (C)	84 (D)	85 (C)
86 (D)	87 (B)	88 (A)	89 (D)	90 (A)
91 (B)	92 (A)	93 (B)	94 (C)	95 (B)
96 (D)	97 (A)	98 (A)	99 (B)	100 (A)

TEST 07

1 (C)	2 (B)	3 (A)	4 (D)	5 (C)
6 (D)	7 (A)	8 (B)	9 (C)	10 (B)
11 (A)	12 (A)	13 (B)	14 (C)	15 (C)
16 (A)	17 (A)	18 (B)	19 (C)	20 (C)
21 (B)	22 (A)	23 (B)	24 (A)	25 (B)
26 (A)	27 (C)	28 (B)	29 (A)	30 (B)
31 (B)	32 (D)	33 (A)	34 (A)	35 (D)
36 (C)	37 (D)	38 (A)	39 (C)	40 (C)
41 (B)	42 (D)	43 (A)	44 (B)	45 (A)
46 (C)	47 (B)	48 (A)	49 (B)	50 (A)
51 (D)	52 (C)	53 (B)	54 (B)	55 (C)
56 (A)	57 (D)	58 (B)	59 (D)	60 (B)
61 (A)	62 (A)	63 (C)	64 (C)	65 (C)
66 (D)	67 (B)	68 (A)	69 (B)	70 (D)
71 (D)	72 (A)	73 (C)	74 (B)	75 (C)
76 (C)	77 (D)	78 (A)	79 (A)	80 (D)
81 (B)	82 (A)	83 (C)	84 (A)	85 (C)
86 (A)	87 (B)	88 (D)	89 (B)	90 (C)
91 (A)	92 (D)	93 (A)	94 (C)	95 (C)
96 (C)	97 (B)	98 (B)	99 (D)	100 (A)

TEST 08

1 (C)	2 (B)	3 (D)	4 (D)	5 (A)
6 (B)	7 (C)	8 (B)	9 (B)	10 (B)
11 (C)	12 (B)	13 (B)	14 (C)	15 (A)
16 (C)	17 (B)	18 (C)	19 (A)	20 (B)
21 (B)	22 (C)	23 (A)	24 (C)	25 (C)
26 (B)	27 (C)	28 (A)	29 (B)	30 (B)
31 (B)	32 (A)	33 (B)	34 (D)	35 (C)
36 (B)	37 (C)	38 (A)	39 (A)	40 (B)
41 (B)	42 (A)	43 (A)	44 (B)	45 (C)
46 (D)	47 (C)	48 (C)	49 (B)	50 (C)
51 (D)	52 (A)	53 (C)	54 (B)	55 (C)
56 (C)	57 (D)	58 (C)	59 (D)	60 (C)
61 (A)	62 (A)	63 (C)	64 (B)	65 (A)
66 (B)	67 (B)	68 (C)	69 (A)	70 (C)
71 (C)	72 (D)	73 (A)	74 (B)	75 (C)
76 (D)	77 (D)	78 (A)	79 (B)	80 (C)
81 (B)	82 (A)	83 (D)	84 (D)	85 (C)
86 (D)	87 (C)	88 (B)	89 (C)	90 (B)
91 (A)	92 (C)	93 (B)	94 (C)	95 (C)
96 (B)	97 (A)	98 (C)	99 (D)	100 (B)

TEST 09

1 (B)	2 (A)	3 (B)	4 (A)	5 (D)
6 (C)	7 (A)	8 (C)	9 (C)	10 (C)
11 (B)	12 (C)	13 (B)	14 (A)	15 (A)
16 (B)	17 (B)	18 (C)	19 (A)	20 (B)
21 (C)	22 (A)	23 (C)	24 (C)	25 (B)
26 (A)	27 (B)	28 (B)	29 (C)	30 (A)
31 (C)	32 (B)	33 (D)	34 (B)	35 (C)
36 (B)	37 (A)	38 (C)	39 (C)	40 (A)
41 (D)	42 (C)	43 (D)	44 (C)	45 (A)
46 (D)	47 (D)	48 (A)	49 (A)	50 (D)
51 (B)	52 (D)	53 (B)	54 (A)	55 (C)
56 (B)	57 (C)	58 (C)	59 (C)	60 (D)
61 (B)	62 (B)	63 (C)	64 (C)	65 (B)
66 (B)	67 (A)	68 (B)	69 (C)	70 (A)
71 (C)	72 (B)	73 (A)	74 (B)	75 (C)
76 (D)	77 (C)	78 (C)	79 (D)	80 (B)
81 (A)	82 (B)	83 (C)	84 (D)	85 (B)
86 (D)	87 (C)	88 (A)	89 (B)	90 (D)
91 (B)	92 (A)	93 (A)	94 (D)	95 (A)
96 (A)	97 (D)	98 (B)	99 (C)	100 (B)

TEST 10

1 (C)	2 (B)	3 (A)	4 (C)	5 (B)
6 (C)	7 (C)	8 (B)	9 (A)	10 (A)
11 (A)	12 (C)	13 (C)	14 (B)	15 (C)
16 (C)	17 (B)	18 (C)	19 (C)	20 (A)
21 (C)	22 (C)	23 (A)	24 (B)	25 (C)
26 (B)	27 (A)	28 (C)	29 (C)	30 (A)
31 (C)	32 (B)	33 (D)	34 (A)	35 (D)
36 (D)	37 (B)	38 (D)	39 (D)	40 (B)
41 (C)	42 (D)	43 (A)	44 (D)	45 (A)
46 (B)	47 (C)	48 (D)	49 (B)	50 (D)
51 (D)	52 (C)	53 (B)	54 (C)	55 (A)
56 (D)	57 (A)	58 (C)	59 (A)	60 (B)
61 (D)	62 (D)	63 (A)	64 (B)	65 (B)
66 (C)	67 (A)	68 (D)	69 (C)	70 (B)
71 (A)	72 (B)	73 (D)	74 (C)	75 (B)
76 (A)	77 (A)	78 (D)	79 (A)	80 (D)
81 (A)	82 (A)	83 (B)	84 (A)	85 (D)
86 (C)	87 (D)	88 (B)	89 (B)	90 (C)
91 (A)	92 (A)	93 (B)	94 (C)	95 (D)
96 (B)	97 (A)	98 (B)	99 (B)	100 (C)

* 아래 점수 환산표로 자신의 토익 리스닝 점수를 예상해봅니다.

정답 수	리스닝 점수	정답 수	리스닝 점수	정답 수	리스닝 점수
100	495	66	305	32	135
99	495	65	300	31	130
98	495	64	295	30	125
97	495	63	290	29	120
96	490	62	285	28	115
95	485	61	280	27	110
94	480	60	275	26	105
93	475	59	270	25	100
92	470	58	265	24	95
91	465	57	260	23	90
90	460	56	255	22	85
89	455	55	250	21	80
88	450	54	245	20	75
87	445	53	240	19	70
86	435	52	235	18	65
85	430	51	230	17	60
84	425	50	225	16	55
83	415	49	220	15	50
82	410	48	215	14	45
81	400	47	210	13	40
80	395	46	205	12	35
79	390	45	200	11	30
78	385	44	195	10	25
77	375	43	190	9	20
76	370	42	185	8	15
75	365	41	180	7	10
74	355	40	175	6	5
73	350	39	170	5	5
72	340	38	165	4	5
71	335	37	160	3	5
70	330	36	155	2	5
69	325	35	150	1	5
68	315	34	145	0	5
67	310	33	140		

※ 점수 환산표는 해커스토익 사이트 유저 데이터를 근거로 제작되었으며, 주기적으로 업데이트되고 있습니다. 해커스토익 사이트(Hackers.co.kr)에서 최신 경향을 반영하여 업데이트된 점수환산기를 이용하실 수 있습니다. (토익 > 토익게시판 > 토익점수환산기)

PART 1

1 🔊 미국식 발음

   (A) The woman is waiting at a counter.
   (B) The woman is standing near a sign.
   (C) The woman is getting on a bus.
   (D) The woman is adjusting her bag.

2 🔊 호주식 발음

   (A) A parade is moving down a street.
   (B) A crowd is listening to a band play.
   (C) Some people are strolling down a walkway.
   (D) Some musical instruments are being set up.

3 🔊 영국식 발음

   (A) A jacket has been placed on a seat.
   (B) Some clothes are folded on a shelf.
   (C) One of the women is examining a garment.
   (D) One of the women is looking out a window.

4 🔊 캐나다식 발음

   (A) People are lining up in a parking lot.
   (B) Trees have been planted along a path.
   (C) Vehicles are waiting at a traffic light.
   (D) Bicycles have been parked next to a street lamp.

5 🔊 미국식 발음

   (A) The men are sitting in a conference room.
   (B) One of the men is writing on a whiteboard.
   (C) The men are installing some equipment.
   (D) One of the men is resting an arm on a desk.

6 🔊 캐나다식 발음

   (A) Some boats are floating on the lake.
   (B) A net is hanging from a bridge.
   (C) A fishing rod is leaning on a wooden pole.
   (D) Some items are being unloaded onto a dock.

PART 2

7 🔊 캐나다식 발음 → 미국식 발음

   What do we need to prepare for next week's workshop?
   (A) I've made us a checklist.

   (B) The shop is around the corner.
   (C) I found it very informative.

8 🔊 영국식 발음 → 캐나다식 발음

   A catering company will plan the menu for the party.
   (A) I'm not sure there will be enough food.
   (B) Oh, that'll help us out a lot.
   (C) He's a good hand at cooking.

9 🔊 캐나다식 발음 → 미국식 발음

   How often do you have to travel for work?
   (A) At least twice a month.
   (B) Usually to Tokyo or Shanghai.
   (C) It's a lot of work.

10 🔊 호주식 발음 → 영국식 발음

   Is Sally's Sweets open on the weekend?
   (A) It's too sweet for my taste.
   (B) Just close it when you're done.
   (C) Let's call and ask.

11 🔊 캐나다식 발음 → 미국식 발음

   Would you mind showing me how to use the new copy machine?
   (A) That's my favorite show, too.
   (B) I'll send you the copy now.
   (C) Give me just a minute.

12 🔊 미국식 발음 → 호주식 발음

   Didn't you study architecture while you were at university?
   (A) Yes, it has beautiful buildings.
   (B) It's always been one of my interests.
   (C) Actually, he recently changed his major.

13 🔊 영국식 발음 → 호주식 발음

   Which of these computers is most suitable for playing video games?
   (A) I prefer role-playing games.
   (B) This one has the best processor.
   (C) You need to update the software.

14 🔊 캐나다식 발음 → 미국식 발음

   The meeting will be held in Room A902 at 1 P.M.
   (A) We met at the publishing conference.
   (B) It was really beneficial.
   (C) I'll be there.

15 🔊 영국식 발음 → 캐나다식 발음

   You attended Pearl Blossom's concert last night, didn't you?
   (A) I'll try to attend the seminar.
   (B) No, they postponed their new album.
   (C) I couldn't get a ticket.

16. 미국식 발음 → 호주식 발음

Who is responsible for updating the guest list for the awards ceremony?
(A) Each person can bring one guest.
(B) You'll have to ask someone else about that.
(C) Honestly, I don't think it was rewarding.

17. 캐나다식 발음 → 영국식 발음

Will you be traveling during your summer vacation or will you be staying in town?
(A) Not until later in July.
(B) I'm planning on going to Rome.
(C) It's a small town.

18. 호주식 발음 → 영국식 발음

Why didn't Naomi take the job she was offered?
(A) The pay wasn't enough for her.
(B) The offer was generous.
(C) She will make another job post.

19. 영국식 발음 → 호주식 발음

We should have some staff work late during the holiday season.
(A) They did an amazing job.
(B) We work on a higher floor.
(C) I don't think that's necessary.

20. 캐나다식 발음 → 영국식 발음

When did the baker open his new bakery?
(A) It's on Second Avenue.
(B) He specializes in wedding cakes.
(C) Sometime last month.

21. 호주식 발음 → 미국식 발음

Which model of our new phone series is the most popular?
(A) The least expensive one.
(B) You made an excellent choice.
(C) Over 30 million units.

22. 캐나다식 발음 → 영국식 발음

The new sick day policy goes into effect next week, right?
(A) It will affect all employees.
(B) I'm going to see a doctor after work.
(C) That's the plan.

23. 미국식 발음 → 영국식 발음

Why did you decide to purchase an electric car?
(A) They're better for the environment.
(B) I think it was last month.
(C) I'm having a hard time picking the right vehicle.

24. 호주식 발음 → 미국식 발음

Are you going to apply for the department manager position?
(A) Your application was received.
(B) Well, you'd better speak to the manager.
(C) I don't think I'm qualified.

25. 미국식 발음 → 캐나다식 발음

Would you prefer to go out for dinner, or should we make something?
(A) I'm not really hungry tonight.
(B) Oh, I'm a vegetarian.
(C) The nearest restaurant is closed.

26. 영국식 발음 → 호주식 발음

What's the password for the hotel's Wi-Fi network?
(A) The hotel offers free Internet in all rooms.
(B) It's on the back of your key card.
(C) Try changing your phone's settings.

27. 캐나다식 발음 → 미국식 발음

Where is the retreat going to take place?
(A) The team can bond.
(B) We're going to have a picnic.
(C) It hasn't been decided.

28. 호주식 발음 → 영국식 발음

How should I announce the promotional event to our customers?
(A) At least two weeks in advance.
(B) Let's advertise it on social media.
(C) Here's your free gift.

29. 미국식 발음 → 호주식 발음

You can still work at our trade show booth tomorrow, can't you?
(A) That seems like a fair trade.
(B) Don't worry. Nothing's changed.
(C) Can you show me the report later?

30. 영국식 발음 → 캐나다식 발음

Wasn't the new *Hunt Quest* movie really exciting?
(A) I haven't seen it yet.
(B) Sure, let's go find it.
(C) Yes, it will be released today.

31. 미국식 발음 → 호주식 발음

Could you double-check these sales figures, please?
(A) Sales should improve soon.
(B) Thanks for doing that.
(C) I'm not good with numbers.

PART 3

Questions 32-34 refer to the following conversation.

[3u] 미국식 발음 → 캐나다식 발음

W: Hi, Brandon. I'm so glad to be back at work. I feel much better now.

M: Welcome back. Well, Carrie called in sick today, so now I'm wondering what I should do with the marketing report she was working on. It is supposed to be done by tomorrow morning.

W: Oh, no. Would you like me to work on it instead of her?

M: That would be a big help. I have to prepare for the meeting with the new client, Ms. Chae. She will come by the office later today.

W: OK. I'm going to look over the report and let you know if I have any questions about it.

Questions 35-37 refer to the following conversation.

[3u] 호주식 발음 → 영국식 발음

M: Hi, I'm calling to see if I can book a table for eight at 6:00 P.M. My choir group is going to finish practice around then, and we thought we'd go for a nice meal afterwards.

W: Sure. Would you prefer to be seated inside or outside?

M: We'd prefer to sit inside. I think it's supposed to get cold later today. Oh, before I forget . . . Do you have vegetarian options?

W: We offer a number of meatless dishes. And I should also mention that because you have over five people in your group, you will be served a free bottle of wine with your meal.

Questions 38-40 refer to the following conversation.

[3u] 캐나다식 발음 → 영국식 발음

M: Diane, I'm so glad you could make it to the first day of the exhibit!

W: Thank you. I've read so much about Richard Li's work, so I had to come and see it. Are all the paintings on the second floor?

M: Yes. All the paintings are upstairs. Oh, please don't forget to pick up a booklet from the entrance. Mr. Li himself has not arrived yet, but I expect he will be here shortly. He's giving a speech about what he was trying to accomplish with this exhibit.

W: That sounds wonderful. Hopefully, I can speak with Mr. Li in person at some point tonight.

Questions 41-43 refer to the following conversation with three speakers.

[3u] 미국식 발음 → 캐나다식 발음 → 영국식 발음

W1: Excuse me. I just visited the break room and noticed that we're out of instant coffee.

M: No big deal, Sophie. For now, you can go down to the ninth floor and ask for a packet from someone in the maintenance department.

W2: Um, has anyone explained our system for restocking the break room to you, Sophie?

W1: Not yet.

M: It's pretty simple. There's a form on top of the microwave. If you notice that something's running low—instant coffee or coffee filters, for example—mark how many are needed.

W2: Right. Our office manager, Mr. Harper, checks the form once a month and then buys what is needed.

Questions 44-46 refer to the following conversation.

[3u] 영국식 발음 → 호주식 발음

W: Hello. Danya Wentz speaking.

M: Hi, Ms. Wentz. This is Harold Gatti from the Dorset Science Institute. We found your résumé and cover letter very impressive. At this stage, we just need a reference from your current employer.

W: Sure. I'll send you my supervisor's contact information by e-mail. But were you thinking of getting in touch with him today?

M: Yes, actually. Is there a problem?

W: Um . . . the workday has already ended.

M: Oh. I forgot that you're in a different time zone. It's alright—I'll talk to him on Monday.

Questions 47-49 refer to the following conversation.

[3u] 미국식 발음 → 호주식 발음

W: Max, do you think you'll have your article on the San Diego Bucks ready by February 2?

M: Absolutely. I'm almost finished with it. I just need to interview the basketball club owner and integrate his quotes into the piece.

W: Why haven't you done that already?

M: I haven't been able to reach him yet, but I'm going to keep trying. Next week, I'm going to visit his office.

W: OK. We were hoping to run your story in our February 4 issue. If you can't get an interview with him by the deadline, we will have to include your article in our next issue.

M: That's fine. Like I said, I'll keep trying.

Questions 50-52 refer to the following conversation.

[3u] 미국식 발음 → 캐나다식 발음

W: A lot of the workers at our company are requesting more vacation days. They feel that having just 10 days off isn't enough.

M: Yes, I suppose that's true. Most companies offer significantly more vacation time.

W: I think we should give workers 15 days' vacation time. One of our competitors, Pilsen Suppliers, decided to do that a few weeks ago.

M: You have a good point . . . Maybe we should increase the amount of leave our employees get. I'll think about making a proposal to the other managers at our meeting next week.

Questions 53-55 refer to the following conversation.

3》 캐나다식 발음 → 영국식 발음

W: Hi. Welcome to our annual Black Tie Gala. May I see your invitation, please?

M: I don't have one, actually. But I should be on the guest list. My last name's Brandt. B-R-A-N-D-T.

W: Let me take a look. Hmm . . . I'm afraid I don't see it here.

M: That can't be right. My lawyer, Keith Harrison, said he added me. He's one of the sponsors of the event.

W: Well, there's a Brunt listed—Brian Brunt. Would that be you?

M: Probably, yes. My name is quite difficult to spell.

W: I'm glad everything worked out then. You are seated at Table 14, right next to the stage.

Questions 56-58 refer to the following conversation with three speakers.

3》 미국식 발음 → 캐나다식 발음 → 호주식 발음

W: Since we'll be participating in the tourism expo this afternoon, why don't we take some brochures to hand out at the convention center? It would be good publicity for our resort.

M1: But haven't we run out of those?

M2: Actually, I found a whole box of them in the supply room.

W: Those must be left over from our grand opening at this time last year . . . Then, Joel, could you take out a couple of stacks?

M2: I can do that in about 30 minutes, but I need to call back our client Mr. Harris first.

M1: I'll contact Mr. Harris for you, Joel.

M2: Oh, I appreciate that. I'll head down to the supply room then.

Questions 59-61 refer to the following conversation.

3》 미국식 발음 → 호주식 발음

W: How are you enjoying the conference so far?

M: I think it's going fine. I went to a special lecture about what will happen in the automotive sector over the next several years. The instructor seemed to know a great deal about it. My only complaint is that there are so few car prototypes on display.

W: Well, they definitely had more interesting cars in the lobby last year. That's because the conference didn't receive quite as much funding this time around.

M: Yeah, that's understandable. Hopefully, the conference next year will feature more of them.

Questions 62-64 refer to the following conversation and e-mail inbox.

3》 호주식 발음 → 미국식 발음

M: Stella, you leave for Cardiff tomorrow, right? I have a few things I want to discuss before you visit our branch there.

W: Actually, I'm going to postpone my departure until Friday.

M: Really? Why's that?

W: There's a problem with one of our largest client's orders. I'm meeting with our warehouse manager tomorrow morning to deal with it. I was notified by e-mail that the shipment is two weeks overdue.

M: Hmm . . . I don't want you to push back your visit to Cardiff if you can avoid it. Why don't you get Janice in the sales department to deal with the client's problem?

W: OK. I'll call her now and explain the situation.

Questions 65-67 refer to the following conversation and floor plan.

3》 캐나다식 발음 → 미국식 발음

M: This is getting tiring—we've been standing here for half an hour. I thought Gene said he'd arrive at 4:30.

W: Yeah. Our movie starts just 10 minutes from now, and he's the one with the tickets.

M: Do you think he might be waiting somewhere else in the mall?

W: I doubt it. We were pretty clear about the meeting point—right in front of Hadley's Stationery Store.

M: Wait! I just remembered that the stationery store has another level. Maybe Gene's waiting on the fourth floor.

W: I'll go and check. You stay here on the third floor in case he shows up.

M: OK. I won't move from this spot.

Questions 68-70 refer to the following conversation and catalog.

3》 호주식 발음 → 영국식 발음

M: Excuse me . . . I need to buy some tiles for a client's home that I'm remodeling.

W: You'll find those in Aisle 7.

M: Actually, I was just there, but I didn't see what I was looking for. Um, a company called Pearson recently released a model with horizontal stripes.

W: Unfortunately, those are currently out of stock. But

we're expecting more to arrive next week. If you'd like to place an advance order, you can fill out a request form at the customer service desk.

M: Hmm . . . Let me call my client to ask her what her preference is. I'll let her know what you've told me.

PART 4

Questions 71-73 refer to the following telephone message.

[음] 영국식 발음

Ryan, it's Paula Martin, the accounting manager. Sorry to bother you. I know you are getting ready to head to the airport this afternoon. I have a question about the budget report for your department that you e-mailed me. Could you stop by my office quickly? I'd like to ask you about it before you go to Tokyo. Your trip will be so busy, and I don't want you to worry about this while there. Oh, and remember, I'm now working on the fifth floor, not the third. Thanks!

Questions 74-76 refer to the following speech.

[음] 미국식 발음

I'm so happy everyone could be here to celebrate the completion of the documentary *School of Life*. As the director, I cannot be more proud of the work we have done. You all made a great production team, and this movie could not have been made without you. I'd like to give special thanks to the film's editor, Margot Anderson, for putting in some overtime to make the changes I requested. I just watched the final version, and I think it is fantastic. After dinner, we will assemble in the ballroom so you can see the finished product.

Questions 77-79 refer to the following announcement.

[음] 캐나다식 발음

Attention, all warehouse workers. An unusually large shipment has just arrived, and it needs to be unloaded into the storeroom 12. You know, it's a warm day, and, uh . . . there is a lot of frozen food. Unless you are working on an urgent assignment right now, please head straight to Loading Dock 7. When you get there, the supervisor of that section . . . um, David Wilkins will let you know what to do. In addition, if there are any empty carts in your current area, please bring them with you. Mr. Wilkins mentioned that they were running short of them, and he wants to retrieve as many of them as possible.

Questions 80-82 refer to the following talk.

[음] 호주식 발음

OK . . . My name is Dwight Farley, and I'll be giving you a tour today. As interns, you will need to be familiar with the museum's layout and the specific paintings on display here. Usually, I start the tour in the main lobby. However, it is undergoing some renovations right now. I will show you that area next week when the work has been finished. Instead, we will start in the Italian Gallery and make our way around the first floor. Then, we will break for a 30-minute lunch at Mario's Pizzeria across the street. In the afternoon, we will finish the tour on the second floor. Let's begin!

Questions 83-85 refer to the following telephone message.

[음] 영국식 발음

Hi, this is a message for Victor Abrams. My name is Cathy Harris, and I'm calling from Maypole Bank. We discovered your bank card in one of our ATMs yesterday. What we do in cases like this is keep the card at our information desk. You can stop by and pick it up on any workday between 9:00 A.M. and 5:00 P.M. However, if you are considering coming in the afternoon on a Friday, uh . . . that option will no longer be available from next week. Please also note that you should bring a piece of government-issued ID. Call me back if you have any questions.

Questions 86-88 refer to the following advertisement.

[음] 미국식 발음

Are you interested in being on the most popular television show in the country? *Blue Sunset*, a comedy series on Channel 7, is looking for hundreds of people to be extras in party scenes. No acting experience is required. We just need a large group to be in the shots. Filming will take place in the Orange Hotel in Miami between June 13 and 16. If you are interested, please just send an e-mail with your name, age, and phone number to our casting coordinator, Joe Geltman, by June 10. Don't miss this exciting opportunity to be in a top-rated TV show!

Questions 89-91 refer to the following talk.

[음] 호주식 발음

First of all, I'd like to thank Mary Williams for inviting me to speak today. Since this lecture series will focus on fiction and society, I have chosen to speak about Miles Kramer's classic work *The University Student*. This novel highlights some of the issues within the educational system that existed about 50 years ago. If you haven't read it, don't worry. I will be focusing on small sections of the book and reading them out loud. If you are having trouble hearing me clearly, you should move closer to the front. There are plenty of seats in the first row still.

Questions 92-94 refer to the following introduction.

[3ᵞ] 캐나다식 발음

Everyone, could you please stop what you're doing and listen up? This is Stacy Addison from Westgate Consultancy Services. She'll be working with us over the next three weeks on the Gulf Ridge property development. Ms. Addison will put together a cost analysis that includes our expenditures on materials, labor, and equipment. I am confident that her report will help us increase profits . . . she's worked on many similar projects before. Please take some time to introduce yourself to her today. She will be working in the conference room this week until she is assigned an office.

Questions 95-97 refer to the following excerpt from a meeting and chart.

[3ᵞ] 호주식 발음

Next, I'd like to discuss our airline's rewards system. The marketing department just completed a customer survey. It turns out that 25 percent of those who fly with us for the first time choose our airline because of our mileage program. So, we're not going to make many changes to our membership scheme. However, we're going to stop offering discounts on in-flight snacks and drinks. The reason is quite simple. The company that supplies these to us has raised its prices recently to cover the higher cost of obtaining raw ingredients.

Questions 98-100 refer to the following broadcast and subway map.

[3ᵞ] 영국식 발음

And now for local news. The typhoon that passed through the region yesterday caused extensive damage across the city. Many neighborhoods are still without power. At 10 A.M. today, Mayor Roberson stated that it would take city workers two more days to restore electricity to the downtown area and four more days to get power to the suburbs. If you are commuting to work this morning, please note that the metro system is not fully functional. In particular, the line that runs from Greendale Station to City Heights Station has been closed due to flooding. Furthermore, there has been water damage to the lower levels of Market Station. Stay tuned for further updates.

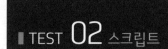

TEST 02 스크립트

* 무료 해석은 해커스토익(Hackers.co.kr)에서
다운로드 받을 수 있습니다.

* ∩R 코드로
바로가기

PART 1

1 🔊 캐나다식 발음

(A) She is decorating a bookshelf.
(B) She is replacing a light bulb.
(C) She is covering a sofa in plastic.
(D) She is taking a lamp out of a box.

2 🔊 영국식 발음

(A) They are buying train tickets.
(B) They are emptying their backpacks.
(C) They are facing the windows.
(D) They are pushing against a door.

3 🔊 캐나다식 발음

(A) Items have been placed in a case.
(B) Merchandise is being labeled.
(C) Dishes have been piled on the floor.
(D) Food is being prepared for service.

4 🔊 미국식 발음

(A) Some shoppers are exchanging bags.
(B) Some shoppers are pointing at a pillar.
(C) Some shoppers are passing a display.
(D) Some shoppers are trying on clothing.

5 🔊 호주식 발음

(A) A man is lifting a bowl off the ground.
(B) A vendor is filling containers.
(C) Vases are being stacked in a corner.
(D) Some pottery is being made by hand.

6 🔊 영국식 발음

(A) Some people are lining up outside a restaurant.
(B) Furniture has been arranged on the sidewalk.
(C) Curtains are covering some windows.
(D) Some men are installing an awning.

PART 2

7 🔊 캐나다식 발음 → 미국식 발음

When will the clients arrive?
(A) They most likely will.
(B) The building lobby.
(C) No later than 3 o'clock.

8 🔊 영국식 발음 → 호주식 발음

Which of these shirts do you think I should buy?
(A) You should wrap them.
(B) My preference is the brown one.
(C) Yes, it's the perfect size.

9 🔊 미국식 발음 → 캐나다식 발음

Will my transportation costs be reimbursed?
(A) We stopped in Venice.
(B) If you hand in the receipts.
(C) I'll look in my purse.

10 🔊 호주식 발음 → 영국식 발음

Do you know who was named the new lead engineer?
(A) I can't recall the restaurant's name.
(B) Someone was recruited from outside the firm.
(C) Mr. Vans placed the order.

11 🔊 캐나다식 발음 → 미국식 발음

Where did the delivery person leave the package?
(A) Check with the receptionist.
(B) It arrived about 10 minutes ago.
(C) You can just leave it on my desk.

12 🔊 호주식 발음 → 영국식 발음

How did you get tickets for the sold-out concert?
(A) Our seats are very close to the stage.
(B) My company is the event's sponsor.
(C) The band will be performing on Friday.

13 🔊 미국식 발음 → 캐나다식 발음

Who volunteered for our community service event?
(A) Thanks for offering your time.
(B) The event was a major success.
(C) Why don't you ask our boss about that?

14 🔊 호주식 발음 → 영국식 발음

A taxi is coming for me at 7 A.M.
(A) Sure, taxes are due on April 15th.
(B) You'll have to be up very early, then.
(C) Sometime this morning.

15 🔊 미국식 발음 → 호주식 발음

Who's responsible for promoting the technology expo?
(A) The response was very positive.
(B) Mr. Graves hasn't selected anyone yet.
(C) That seems like a reasonable deadline.

16 🔊 영국식 발음 → 호주식 발음

I have an appointment with Mr. Khan in 10 minutes.
(A) Yes, he's been expecting you.
(B) I've been appointed team leader.
(C) We were too busy at the time.

17 캐나다식 발음 → 영국식 발음

Why are there only three candidates for our job opening?
(A) Oh, Drake has the other résumés.
(B) No, I haven't found a job yet.
(C) We will open another location.

18 영국식 발음 → 호주식 발음

This evening's press conference has been rescheduled.
(A) When our collection was announced.
(B) You have to push this button.
(C) I wonder why there's a delay.

19 미국식 발음 → 캐나다식 발음

Don't we have an insufficient number of brochures?
(A) My team won't be attending the seminar.
(B) I designed some of them myself.
(C) This lighting is insufficient.

20 영국식 발음 → 미국식 발음

Why don't we ask if the flight attendant has headphones?
(A) We don't want to go to that convention.
(B) An economy class seat.
(C) I don't need any right now.

21 캐나다식 발음 → 호주식 발음

Aren't special permits required in order to park here?
(A) Yes, those changes are necessary.
(B) The outing was held at Hawthorne Park.
(C) This lot is open to the public.

22 미국식 발음 → 캐나다식 발음

What organization are we partnering with?
(A) It's been nice working with you.
(B) Actually, I organized the party.
(C) An environmental research institute.

23 호주식 발음 → 미국식 발음

When was an inspection last conducted at your establishment?
(A) Just over a month ago, I believe.
(B) The inspector left the message.
(C) I looked at it closely.

24 미국식 발음 → 호주식 발음

How does going out for dinner next week sound to you?
(A) I usually bring my lunch to work.
(B) Let me check my schedule.
(C) I had a great time.

25 영국식 발음 → 캐나다식 발음

A celebrity spokesperson has finally been selected for the company.
(A) Well, each person should get one.
(B) I was told this place is famous.
(C) Yes, Joseph mentioned that earlier.

26 영국식 발음 → 호주식 발음

Have Sam and Janie registered for the accounting workshop?
(A) These are the proper forms.
(B) One of the accounts is low on money.
(C) They'll do so after lunch.

27 캐나다식 발음 → 영국식 발음

Was Jones Industries or Peters Manufacturing contracted to produce our shoe line?
(A) Our contract expires soon.
(B) Clients waited in line for several hours.
(C) A different one was chosen.

28 호주식 발음 → 미국식 발음

Curtis is joining us for a picnic on Saturday, right?
(A) The weather was nice on Sunday.
(B) Did you bring some snacks?
(C) That's why we planned it for the morning.

29 영국식 발음 → 캐나다식 발음

Are you going to forward the memo to personnel, or should I do that?
(A) It's up to you.
(B) The entire human resources division.
(C) It discusses the new leave policy.

30 호주식 발음 → 미국식 발음

What could be the cause of our company's recent drop in sales?
(A) Because I dropped a platter.
(B) Shoppers' buying habits are changing.
(C) The sails were torn by the strong winds.

31 캐나다식 발음 → 미국식 발음

The business center is scheduled to be remodeled this fall.
(A) I heard the project could cost millions.
(B) Here's the spring catalog.
(C) We already sent her the outline.

PART 3

Questions 32-34 refer to the following conversation.

영국식 발음 → 캐나다식 발음

W: A representative of the state government just contacted me regarding our recent funding proposal. Our request was approved, so the community center is going to be the recipient of a technology grant worth $75,000.

M: Wonderful! Now we can finally afford to replace the outdated electronics in our computer lab with more modern equipment. People in the community are going to be very pleased with the news.

W: That's right. However, there are limitations on how the grant money can be spent. So, we'll have to read over the documents carefully before buying computers or other devices.

Questions 35-37 refer to the following conversation.

미국식 발음 → 캐나다식 발음

W: Good morning, Mr. Abdul. This is Alicia Ponds calling from Davenport Architecture. We received your résumé and cover letter in regard to our associate architect position. And we would like to invite you in for an interview this Thursday. Are you available in the morning?

M: Thank you for contacting me. I already have an appointment scheduled then, but I'm free that afternoon or at any time before 12 P.M. on Friday.

W: Thursday afternoon at 2 P.M. will be fine.

M: I'll mark it in my calendar. Is there anything else I should bring? Like a reference letter?

W: I'd appreciate an example of a blueprint that you created for a previous employer. Other than that, I have everything I need.

Questions 38-40 refer to the following conversation.

영국식 발음 → 호주식 발음

W: Do you know why our investor Mr. Herman hasn't gotten in touch with me yet? He was supposed to call at around 9:00 A.M. today, which is when his flight was scheduled to arrive. But it's 9:45 now, and I haven't heard from him.

M: I just received a message from his secretary indicating that his flight was delayed in Detroit. Apparently, his departure was postponed by an hour due to a severe blizzard. His flight should arrive shortly, however.

W: Oh, I see. In that case, we'll have to hold off starting the presentation on product development until this afternoon, as Mr. Herman is flying in to listen to it.

M: Yes, that looks unavoidable at this point. I'll notify the research team.

Questions 41-43 refer to the following conversation.

미국식 발음 → 캐나다식 발음

W: We're having trouble selling a lot of the sweaters, jackets, and other warm clothing in our store. Sales of these items have dropped about 20 percent in the past month.

M: Yeah, summer is approaching. Usually what we do is hold a big sale on winter and fall clothing. Jackets go for 25 percent off, sweaters for 30 percent off, and so on. I'll send you an e-mail with further information.

W: Sounds like a plan. When will the sale go into effect?

M: Usually, it starts on April 1 and goes until April 15. Over the next couple days, I'm going to start calling newspapers and inquire about advertising rates. I'm planning on placing a few full-page advertisements.

Questions 44-46 refer to the following conversation with three speakers.

호주식 발음 → 미국식 발음 → 영국식 발음

M: Good morning. I have three large parcels to bring in, and I'm wondering if someone can hold the front doors open for me.

W1: Oh, hold on a second . . . Anna, can you take care of the doors?

W2: Sure, no problem. It must be the shelves we ordered a week ago.

M: Is there a particular place where you'd like to put the boxes?

W1: Please bring them to the storage room. Oh, and be careful with our pottery displays on your way.

M: Oh, in that case, how about putting those somewhere safe first?

Questions 47-49 refer to the following conversation.

캐나다식 발음 → 영국식 발음

M: Good morning. I work at Spector Industries, and we want to convert a vacant lot on our property into a garden with a seating area. Could your landscaping company handle a job of that scale?

W: Absolutely. Although our firm mostly does residential work, we have commercial clients too. In fact, just last summer we did a large landscaping project for the Seward Grocery Store, which is located three blocks from your facility.

M: Oh, really? I pass by that building daily, and I'm always impressed with how nice its front lawn looks.

W: We certainly appreciate the compliment. Now, why don't you tell me more about the work you'd like done?

미국식 발음 → 캐나다식 발음 → 호주식 발음

W: Hello. I've come to pick up medicine prescribed to me by Dr. Vasquez. My name is Marcia Chow.

M1: Certainly. Here you are. Can I help you with anything else today?

W: Yes. Do you know if it is possible to get a free flu shot at the medical clinic next door?

M1: It costs $30, I believe.

W: I see. And where exactly should I go to get the shot? I've never been inside the clinic before.

M1: I'm not sure. Ah . . . I can ask my supervisor, though. One moment, please. Daniel, this customer is interested in getting a flu vaccination at the clinic. Where exactly should she go?

M2: Just head to the eighth floor—the area for family medicine. You can't miss it.

Questions 53-55 refer to the following conversation.

영국식 발음 → 호주식 발음

W: Mr. Dorsey, I want to get your feedback regarding next month's Oxford Commerce Convention. Should our company booth feature a poster board with images of our latest makeup products? I'm trying to figure out how to best promote our new line of products to attendees.

M: You know, we incorporated a digital slideshow last year. Many people commented on it.

W: Hmm . . . I'm not sure how to set that up, though.

M: Why don't you take a look at the one from last year? I'm sure it only needs a few minor changes. Danny Connor in marketing should have a copy.

Questions 56-58 refer to the following conversation.

미국식 발음 → 캐나다식 발음

W: As you can see, this apartment has a fully renovated kitchen. All of the counters and appliances are brand new. Take a look at that stainless steel stove.

M: That's great! I really like cooking, so having an updated kitchen is important. And this apartment is definitely better than the last one. I'd like to fill out an application today if possible.

W: Of course. I have the form right here. Oh . . . I'm not sure if you are aware, but once your application is reviewed and accepted, the deposit needs to be submitted within a week.

M: I understand. That won't be a problem.

Questions 59-61 refer to the following conversation.

호주식 발음 → 영국식 발음

M: How are negotiations going with TruCare Medical Supplies? Did the president of TruCare say whether the company agrees to our acquisition terms regarding the retention of personnel?

W: Yes. He agreed that none of our existing employees will be dismissed immediately. However, all staff will be subject to a six-month evaluation following the purchase to determine whether they will receive contract extensions.

M: Hmm . . . Well, at least everyone will have a chance to maintain their jobs. Have financial figures been discussed at all?

W: As of now, we're being offered $45 million, which our analysts tell me is a bit low. I need your approval to ask the company to pay $48 million instead.

Questions 62-64 refer to the following conversation and floor plan.

미국식 발음 → 호주식 발음

W: Roger, we have to get the auditorium lobby ready before people arrive for tonight's debut performance of the play *Going for Broke*.

M: Right, I've got the actors' photographs framed for display. What else is there to do?

W: Can you set up some tables where programs can be handed out?

M: Sure. There are a few in the basement. I'll ask Jacob to help me carry them up here. His shift starts in 15 minutes.

W: OK. And finally, we need a spot where fans can take photos with the cast after the show.

M: Let's put it where it was last year . . . in the area to the left when you enter the building, just before you reach the refreshment stand.

Questions 65-67 refer to the following conversation and form.

캐나다식 발음 → 영국식 발음

M: Hey, Pamela. There's an issue regarding the reimbursement request I filed for my recent business trip to Osaka. I was paid back for all of my costs except a meal I bought at the airport departure lounge.

W: Really? That's strange. Let me see . . . It seems you forgot the receipt for that one.

M: Oh, sorry. I'll look for it and send it to you right away. Will that resolve the matter?

W: As an accountant, I actually don't have the authority to approve specific repayments. The financial manager, Ronald Brenton, has final say over such things.

M: Oh, I see.

W: I believe he's in a meeting right now, but if you leave him a voice mail, I'm sure he'll look into it.

Questions 68-70 refer to the following conversation and flight schedule.

호주식 발음 → 미국식 발음

M: Let's hurry, Kelsey. I'm concerned we won't catch our connecting flight to our destination.

W: Wait—look here. This screen says our flight has been delayed.

M: Yeah, you're right. In that case, I'd like to find a spot in this terminal that provides Wi-Fi. I need to download the lecture notes from the sales conference we attended in Cincinnati.

W: Just so you know, there's a charge to use the airport's Internet service.

M: Really? I'd rather not pay a fee. Well, I should still have time to review the notes before our noon meeting today in Portland.

W: Yeah. Ms. Anderson probably won't ask us much about the conference anyway. She'll be more interested in whether we secured any sales contracts on our trip.

PART 4

Questions 71-73 refer to the following recorded message.

미국식 발음

Hello, Mr. Richter. This is Deloris Burke from Anytime Optical. As a friendly reminder, you have a 3:30 P.M. appointment on Saturday, January 13. Also, we moved our main office . . . It's now on Clyde Boulevard, right next door to the Devon Art Gallery. To avoid any complications during your visit, we ask that you have your current pair of glasses and a copy of your latest prescription on hand. Our optometrist will need to look at them both before conducting your eye examination. Please arrive at least 15 minutes early, as you'll need to fill out a couple of brief forms.

Questions 74-76 refer to the following talk.

호주식 발음

Good afternoon, ladies and gentlemen. I'm Erik Mackay. I'm here today to tell you the story of how I built up Starbox Incorporated . . . um, from a start-up with just three employees to a large company with a range of popular software products, not to mention offices in 25 different countries. In fact, this company now employs over 2,000 people worldwide. Yet when I was working on the prototype of our first product, Starbox Productivity, I was simply pursuing my hobby at the time. OK, now, I'd like to talk about our first product, and how it contributed to Starbox's rapid expansion.

Questions 77-79 refer to the following introduction.

영국식 발음

I'd like to begin by introducing myself. My name is Catherine Coulson, and I'm the consultant who has been hired to advise your team on marketing techniques. As far as my credentials go, I worked in the field of market research for two decades before branching out on my own to found Prime Advertising Services five years ago. Throughout my career, I've consulted for dozens of the country's largest companies with much success. Over the next two weeks, I'm going to collaborate with you all to create a series of online advertisements to ensure your firm's brand recognition among consumers. Together, I think we can greatly improve your company's standing in the market.

Questions 80-82 refer to the following advertisement.

캐나다식 발음

At Recycled Tech, we specialize in the sale of used electronics. We sell laptops, tablets, desktop computers, and much more, all of which are available at up to 60 percent off their original retail prices! Although you may be accustomed to purchasing new items, all of our products come with a one-year warranty, so you can buy with confidence! And in addition to great prices, we hold a drawing every month to give a free tablet to one lucky customer. All you need to do to enter the drawing is to make a purchase of at least $100. Both in-store and online purchases qualify for this offer, so be sure to shop at Recycled Tech today!

Questions 83-85 refer to the following talk.

미국식 발음

Western College will be holding a job fair on Saturday, September 14, for its students. The event will be an excellent way for a small investment company like ours to reach out to potential future employees. That's why I'd like to have at least two staff members operate a booth at the event. Informational pamphlets have already been made and printed. So, those who volunteer would only be responsible for attending the event, answering attendees' questions, and passing out materials. If this sounds like something you'd be willing to do, please let me know by the end of the week so that I can make the necessary arrangements.

Questions 86-88 refer to the following excerpt from a meeting.

캐나다식 발음

To begin our meeting, I have some important news to share. Our director of sales, Emily Delane, has decided to remove Visseria line of office furniture from our stores. The collection has become a bit outdated. The line will be officially removed from over 30 retail outlets next month. In the meantime, everything from the collection will be dramatically discounted. Our warehouse is currently full of stock. Um, moving on, I'd now like to share our plan for the store's new layout. We are hoping this will make it easier for customers to shop in our stores.

Questions 89-91 refer to the following telephone message.

[3]) 미국식 발음

Hello, this is Olga Nabokov. I live at 4209 Grand Avenue, and I'm calling because I'm very unhappy with the lawn care service your company recently provided. My front lawn has more weeds than usual this year, so I arranged for one of your employees to spray a chemical on it last Sunday. I was told that the substance he used would kill the weeds within a few days of its application, but now it seems like he needs to visit my home again. Please call me at 555-0583 to discuss a date and time. I would prefer next Saturday afternoon, if possible. Thank you.

Questions 92-94 refer to the following instructions.

[3]) 영국식 발음

Good morning, and thanks for attending this one-day seminar on import and export laws here in the United Kingdom. If you look at the program that was handed out earlier, you'll see that the seminar is going to be broken down into three main sections. During the first part of the meeting, I am going to give a lecture, in which I will discuss the most recent changes to the country's laws. Following that, we will focus on a handful of well-known case studies that highlight breaches of those regulations. Finally, we will conclude by holding an open forum. At that point, you all will be given an opportunity to pose questions related to your specific industries.

Questions 95-97 refer to the following talk and chart.

[3]) 호주식 발음

For those of you who don't know me, my name is Lucas Scott. I'm in charge of collecting and analyzing data about consumer trends. I've been asked to discuss the results of the survey that I e-mailed to customers on our mailing list last Wednesday. Um, we requested their opinions on our current line of products. Many were impressed with the design of our newest shoes . . . the Hornet Pumps. They said they plan to buy them even though they are more expensive than our other items. However, we got some negative feedback on our second-best-selling athletic shoes. A number of customers indicated that they felt they weren't durable enough. Now . . . please turn your attention to the screen behind me to see my slideshow.

Questions 98-100 refer to the following talk and table.

[3]) 영국식 발음

Welcome to the Sahara Wildlife Reserve. When your professor contacted us about arranging a special tour for his class members, we were happy to accommodate his request. Today, I'll be showing you around the facility and introducing you to our director and some of the other people who work here . . . like the biologists and medical staff. The reserve currently covers an area of 500 acres, but an additional 100 acres will be . . . um . . . added to it later this fall. We need all this space because we care for 200 animals from 60 different species. The first inhabitant that you're going to see arrived here 10 days ago. It is our only animal under six months old. Her enclosure is just this way.

PART 1

1 [3w] 캐나다식 발음
(A) The man is holding a power drill.
(B) The man is picking up one of the boards.
(C) The man is packing some tools.
(D) The man is cutting a piece of wood.

2 [3w] 영국식 발음
(A) They're placing their feet on a rug.
(B) They're installing an electronic device.
(C) They're watching television from a couch.
(D) They're repositioning some cushions.

3 [3w] 미국식 발음
(A) One woman is hanging up a gown.
(B) One woman is taking a measurement.
(C) A tailor is greeting some customers.
(D) A dress is being altered on a sewing machine.

4 [3w] 캐나다식 발음
(A) Some trees are being trimmed.
(B) A flag is hanging from a branch.
(C) Some people are walking on the beach.
(D) A hammock has been tied to some trees.

5 [3w] 호주식 발음
(A) Some people are entering a meeting room.
(B) A man is holding a poster.
(C) Chairs have been positioned by a window.
(D) A laptop is currently in use.

6 [3w] 영국식 발음
(A) A railroad track emerges from a tunnel.
(B) A train has arrived at a platform.
(C) A group of people has collected at a bus stop.
(D) A ticket agent is checking passes.

PART 2

7 [3w] 미국식 발음 → 호주식 발음
When are you heading to the medical convention?
(A) We've got a booth on the third floor.
(B) I'm departing on June 14.
(C) About twenty minutes from downtown.

8 [3w] 캐나다식 발음 → 미국식 발음
Who manages our corporate acquisitions?
(A) If everyone cooperates.
(B) He managed to arrive on time.
(C) That's the director's responsibility.

9 [3w] 영국식 발음 → 호주식 발음
Currently, a train ticket to Barcelona costs 40 Euros.
(A) I'll take one, please.
(B) Luggage is stored separately.
(C) The exchange rate in Europe.

10 [3w] 미국식 발음 → 캐나다식 발음
Is Klein Avenue closed down throughout the weekend?
(A) No, I don't own a truck any longer.
(B) Throughout the main hallway.
(C) Yes, a section has to be repaved.

11 [3w] 영국식 발음 → 호주식 발음
Could you ask a technician to repair our photocopier?
(A) Thank you for fixing it.
(B) I'll need 10 copies, please.
(C) One is already on the way.

12 [3w] 영국식 발음 → 캐나다식 발음
How often does the janitor mop the hallway floors?
(A) I'll grab a broom from the closet.
(B) You should ask the building manager.
(C) He is off today.

13 [3w] 호주식 발음 → 미국식 발음
Why did Ms. Collins call a meeting for this afternoon?
(A) In the main conference room at 2.
(B) There's a problem at the Dallas branch.
(C) Because she isn't available today.

14 [3w] 영국식 발음 → 캐나다식 발음
Where should we go to eat dinner following the screening?
(A) Probably around 8 P.M.
(B) I don't know where deliveries go.
(C) I was thinking of having Latin food.

15 [3w] 미국식 발음 → 캐나다식 발음
Why were you late for the consultation yesterday?
(A) There was heavy traffic on the highway.
(B) Don't worry. She'll be on time.
(C) By at least fifteen minutes or so.

16 〔3ｍ〕 호주식 발음 → 영국식 발음

Should we rent a car while we're in Morocco or rely on cabs?
(A) He's very reliable.
(B) I'd rather have a vehicle.
(C) I bought one while living in New York.

17 〔3ｍ〕 미국식 발음 → 캐나다식 발음

Which spare bookcase do you want moved into your office?
(A) Whichever binder isn't being used.
(B) A few movers just showed up.
(C) The one with lots of shelves.

18 〔3ｍ〕 호주식 발음 → 미국식 발음

Does this pair of jeans come in black as well?
(A) Every pair of sunglasses.
(B) Only blue ones are available.
(C) Come over after work.

19 〔3ｍ〕 영국식 발음 → 캐나다식 발음

Benson Lawn Care has excellent customer service.
(A) What a great company logo!
(B) I've read about it on the Internet.
(C) At the customer service desk.

20 〔3ｍ〕 호주식 발음 → 미국식 발음

How far from your house is Sharper Mall?
(A) Well, I'd like to go shopping.
(B) From noon until 1 o'clock.
(C) Let me check a map quickly.

21 〔3ｍ〕 캐나다식 발음 → 미국식 발음

When do you expect to hire a permanent assistant?
(A) It'll be permanently installed.
(B) I'm waiting for approval.
(C) The help is much appreciated.

22 〔3ｍ〕 영국식 발음 → 호주식 발음

The mayor is giving a speech today in the town square.
(A) I'm glad you decided to give a lecture.
(B) I heard it'll cover education funding.
(C) If I have enough time.

23 〔3ｍ〕 호주식 발음 → 영국식 발음

Who created the notice that's hanging in the front window?
(A) A sign was put up there?
(B) I registered to receive e-mail notifications.
(C) We can hang them next to the door.

24 〔3ｍ〕 영국식 발음 → 캐나다식 발음

Why haven't you unpacked your belongings yet?
(A) Because the price tag was removed.

(B) I was meeting with a colleague.
(C) No, we haven't done it yet.

25 〔3ｍ〕 미국식 발음 → 호주식 발음

Has the singer Jeff Bloom agreed to perform at our charity event?
(A) Cash donations are preferred.
(B) Some musicians were playing along the street.
(C) It appears that he can participate.

26 〔3ｍ〕 캐나다식 발음 → 미국식 발음

The heat in the office can be turned down, can't it?
(A) I'm not sure who can adjust it.
(B) Yes, both of these sheets.
(C) The rack is a bit too high.

27 〔3ｍ〕 호주식 발음 → 영국식 발음

We need to send out the wedding invitations for Ms. Lang and her fiancé.
(A) The ceremony is in Hall A.
(B) No, Mr. Cho is not invited.
(C) I totally forgot about that.

28 〔3ｍ〕 영국식 발음 → 캐나다식 발음

What's the problem with the flyers we printed for the seminar?
(A) There is a stack of printer paper over there.
(B) Everything seems fine.
(C) I'm flying into Madrid for the seminar.

29 〔3ｍ〕 캐나다식 발음 → 미국식 발음

Do you think we should buy a new refrigerator?
(A) Our current one still works well.
(B) Across from the break room.
(C) No, I think they're next to the stoves.

30 〔3ｍ〕 호주식 발음 → 미국식 발음

Should I order a filing cabinet with a single drawer or one with three?
(A) Extra storage is always helpful.
(B) In the top drawer.
(C) Most of the documents are in there.

31 〔3ｍ〕 영국식 발음 → 호주식 발음

While Peter is editing the slide show, we should rehearse the rest of the presentation.
(A) Why don't you go first?
(B) Everyone found it relaxing.
(C) The editor likes the manuscript.

PART 3

Questions 32-34 refer to the following conversation.
미국식 발음 → 캐나다식 발음

W: Ted, have you booked accommodations for the speakers presenting at the environmental conference on January 12 that our company is organizing?

M: I was planning to reserve rooms for all eight speakers at the Drake Inn. It's the same hotel we used when we arranged the trade show last month. But nothing is confirmed yet. Why?

W: Well, the Silkwood Hotel is offering a 15 percent discount on all deluxe suites booked next week. The details about the deal are included in the newsletter that the hotel sent out by e-mail yesterday.

M: Could you forward the message to me? I'll check it out.

Questions 35-37 refer to the following conversation with three speakers.
영국식 발음 → 호주식 발음 → 미국식 발음

W1: Our competitor is launching a free delivery service next month. To stay competitive, we should consider eliminating the fee to deliver furniture from our store to customers' homes as well. What do you think?

M: Hmm . . . I'm concerned we'd need to buy additional delivery trucks. More customers would use that service if there were no charge.

W1: Well, we could just lease them instead. That would require less initial investment.

M: I like your suggestion. Amelia, do you believe we should prepare a cost projection report before we discuss your idea with our supervisor?

W2: Yes, let's do that. Can I get my tablet back from you? I lent it to you yesterday, and it contains the report template we'll need.

Questions 38-40 refer to the following conversation.
미국식 발음 → 호주식 발음

W: Now, we can take a look at the compiled feedback from the recent diner questionnaire and see if we can find some useful information to help improve our restaurant.

M: Well, it looks like a majority of guests made positive comments about our facility's decor and layout. However, there are several complaints about the attitudes of some of our serving staff.

W: I see. I think it's best we hold a training session to remind employees about our standards of service when dealing with customers.

M: That's a thought. I can even share some great tips from the conference on the food service industry that I attended last week.

Questions 41-43 refer to the following conversation.
캐나다식 발음 → 영국식 발음

M: Hello, Ms. Carter. This is William Glover calling from Beacon Valley Health Clinic. You left a message about coming in to get a flu shot next week. How does Tuesday at 3 P.M. sound?

W: Unfortunately, I will be out of town until that evening. My bus arrives at 7 P.M. Could I visit on Wednesday?

M: Sure. Could you come to the clinic in the late afternoon?

W: I finish work at 1 P.M.

M: Great. We have an opening at 4. But please come 15 minutes early so that you can fill out some paperwork.

Questions 44-46 refer to the following conversation with three speakers.
호주식 발음 → 미국식 발음 → 영국식 발음

M: Excuse me, Ms. Hill. Do you have a few minutes to talk about the new brochure for our fitness center?

W1: We need your approval before we have it printed.

W2: I've got some time now. I was just looking through it. To be honest, it still needs some work.

M: What do you think needs to be addressed?

W2: It should include more details about the improvements we made to our facilities last month. Specifically, our weight-lifting rooms were all expanded, and skylights were installed above the indoor pool.

W1: Oh, thank you for pointing that out. We should've been more specific.

M: I agree. I can call the firm we contracted to design the brochure after lunch and request the changes.

Questions 47-49 refer to the following conversation.
미국식 발음 → 캐나다식 발음

W: Do you happen to know where Liew is? I need him to proofread the press release we're going to publish at 5 P.M., and I can't find him in his office.

M: Right now, he's in a meeting with some new employees. He is demonstrating to them how to post files and communicate using the company's systems.

W: Ah, that's annoying. I really need him to look over this press release. We always have a copy editor look over the text we're going to publish.

M: Don't worry. It should only last another 20 minutes. Just leave a copy of the press release you want him to look at on his desk.

Questions 50-52 refer to the following conversation.
영국식 발음 → 캐나다식 발음

W: Thanks for returning my call so quickly, Derrick. There's a problem with the projector in our boardroom. Someone knocked it off the table, and now it doesn't work properly.

M: Oh, no. We bought that less than a month ago. Plus, I'll need it when I give a presentation to the board of directors this afternoon.

W: That's why I'm contacting you. Fortunately, it turns on, but it's making a buzzing sound.

M: Well, at least it's operating. You know, I just heard that the IT department doesn't have many requests to deal with today. Maybe I can get someone to look at it quickly and confirm that it's fine.

Questions 53-55 refer to the following conversation.

[3》] 미국식 발음 → 호주식 발음

W: When will we be getting more units of the L7? We've been sold out of that smartphone model all week, but customers keep coming in to buy it.

M: It's hard to say. The phone is extremely popular across the country, so most stores are out of stock. Plus, the product manufacturer hasn't indicated when our next inventory order will be shipped out. However, you can offer to put shoppers who want the item on a waiting list.

W: OK. By the way, we've had high customer traffic in the store, so I think we need another staff member to work weekday evenings.

M: Good point. I'll post a notice in the break room to see if any of our employees are looking for extra hours.

Questions 56-58 refer to the following conversation.

[3》] 영국식 발음 → 캐나다식 발음

W: Excuse me. Isn't the museum featuring a special exhibit about space exploration for the next few weeks? I heard a commercial on the radio that made it sound quite interesting.

M: That's correct. The exhibit is called *Deep Universe*, and it includes several interactive displays. The most popular is a collection of instruments from an actual space shuttle. Um, these were lent to us by the National Space Agency.

W: Wow! I'd like to check that out. Is access to the exhibit included in the regular entrance fee?

M: I'm afraid not. It will be an extra $15 per person.

Questions 59-61 refer to the following conversation.

[3》] 호주식 발음 → 미국식 발음

M: I just want to see how your department is progressing with preparations for our annual clearance sale, which starts this Friday.

W: There's a slight problem. Some display racks were broken when our staff moved them from the front of the store on Tuesday. Do we have any extras in the back room?

M: Unfortunately not. We'll have to place a rush order

for more racks because we need them to arrive on Thursday.

W: But the store manager has to approve such orders, right? I'm on my way to his office now anyway, so I'll submit a formal request for him to sign off on.

M: Thanks. In the meantime, I'll double-check if we have sufficient shopping bags underneath every cash register.

Questions 62-64 refer to the following conversation and floor information.

[3》] 캐나다식 발음 → 영국식 발음

M: I'm really looking forward to going to the Brenton Sports & Leisure complex on Saturday. My friend Jessica said that she went there last year and it was a lot of fun.

W: I'm excited too. One thing, though. When we originally planned the day, we decided we would drive there together at 11 A.M. However, my mom needs a ride to the doctor that morning, so I won't be available until noon or possibly later.

M: That's OK. Why don't you just meet us there? When you enter, leave your belongings in a locker and then come upstairs. 64We'll already be in the pool by the time you arrive.

W: Where exactly?

M: Oh, the one next to the food place.

Questions 65-67 refer to the following conversation and receipt.

[3》] 호주식 발음 → 미국식 발음

M: Paula, is your dress ready for the charity fund-raiser we're attending tomorrow evening?

W: It's still at the dry cleaners, since it needed to be shortened a few inches. I'll pick it up tomorrow morning.

M: You go to Bedford Dry Cleaners, don't you? I'm thinking about switching to that one, as my current dry cleaner will shut down in June.

W: Well, Bedford's customer service is exceptional, and they even have monthly discounts. Ah . . . in May, they're providing 10 percent off work on all leather items.

M: That sounds great. Maybe I'll come with you tomorrow and drop off some of my button-down shirts.

Questions 68-70 refer to the following conversation and notice.

[3》] 캐나다식 발음 → 영국식 발음

M: Welcome to the Hartford Public Library.

W: Hi. I'd like to borrow this book. I have my library card right here.

M: OK. And just to let you know, we've increased the loan period. You can borrow books for up to three weeks now.

W: Great. Um, I also want to check out some new books that were supposed to arrive on August 13, but they aren't on the shelves.

M: I know the two you're referring to. The guidebook will be available on August 23. There's a typo on the notice. But the other one was damaged in transit, and the replacement won't arrive until September.

W: Hmm . . . Can you recommend another book on that topic?

M: Sure. I'll check our system for a similar title.

PART 4

Questions 71-73 refer to the following announcement.

[3n] 영국식 발음

Attention, all Quickstone Corporation employees. Next week, from June 9 to 13, all staff members are encouraged to make donations of clothing, books, and toys. These will be given to the Victoria Community Center to be distributed to needy families. Large plastic boxes will be placed in the lobby of our office building for workers to put items into. Four volunteers from our company are also needed to help deliver the containers to the center on Monday, June 16, at 5 P.M. Those interested should call Marcy Dwyer in the human resources department at extension 700 before the end of the day. We look forward to great participation in this charitable effort on behalf of our organization.

Questions 74-76 refer to the following telephone message.

[3n] 캐나다식 발음

This message is for Amy Yang. My name is Floyd Lamar, and I'm an employee at the Center Street DVD Shop. You rented The Brothers O'Brien five days ago, which makes it two days past due. Please return it as soon as possible. We will be closed from December 24 to 26 for the holidays, so you should use the return bin near the entrance during that period. Of course, you will have to pay a late fee. You currently owe $10, and this will increase by $5 per day until we receive the DVD. So, you should act quickly. If you have any questions, call 555-8039.

Questions 77-79 refer to the following introduction.

[3n] 호주식 발음

Could I have your attention, please? This is Sally Greenly. As I mentioned last week, I've hired Ms. Greenly to take headshots of everyone at our consultancy. These will be included with the bios of our staff members on the Web site we are currently designing. Um, it should be accessible to the public early next month and will hopefully attract more clients for our company. Anyway, Ms. Greenly needs an empty room to set up her equipment, and there are no tables in the conference room at the moment. Once she is ready, she will call you in one by one. It should only take a few minutes of your time.

Questions 80-82 refer to the following broadcast.

[3n] 미국식 발음

In tonight's Around Town segment, we're going to look at a recently completed construction project here in San Bernardino. Burke Industries opened its City Springs Mall yesterday. This 200,000 square meter facility contains more than 275 stores and restaurants. It is expected to generate annual sales of approximately $20,000 per square meter. Of course, the city government will collect more taxes as a result. The mall will also create at least 5,000 new jobs, which is important because high unemployment has been a problem in the area since Analytic Systems moved its factory abroad last year. We will now take a short commercial break. When we return, a representative from Burke Industries will join us to answer some questions.

Questions 83-85 refer to the following excerpt from a meeting.

[3n] 호주식 발음

I've called you all here to this meeting to let you know that a position will soon be vacated at our firm. Marcos Gomez will be retiring in May, leaving the role of factory supervisor open. Upon informing us of his decision, Mr. Gomez said that it would be better to promote his replacement than to fill the position with an outside candidate. We do have many competent employees at our company. Therefore, I encourage all of you to turn in an application form for this position by April 29. It's only as a last resort that I'll recruit someone from another company.

Questions 86-88 refer to the following announcement.

[3n] 영국식 발음

Welcome to the Museum of Science. We are pleased to announce that an audio tour is now available. To use this service, request a media player and headphones at the main information booth. As you move through the museum, sensors on the device will detect nearby exhibits, causing the appropriate recorded messages to be played. Please note that temporary exhibitions are not covered by the tour, including the one on the history of photography that runs until October 25. If you would like more information about this exhibition, simply pick up a brochure from the rack next to the main entrance. It includes detailed descriptions of the items on display. Thank you.

Questions 89-91 refer to the following advertisement.

[3။] 미국식 발음

Internet access should be affordable for everyone. That's why Emerson Digital is offering a special package for people living in Creston. For just $14.99 per month, you'll enjoy upload and download speeds comparable to those of more expensive packages offered by other companies. And you can try it at no risk. If you are a resident of the region, you qualify for a free, one-week evaluation period. Just visit our office at 1432 Pine Street to register today. Be advised that you will have to show an identification card that includes your current address to sign up. Don't miss out on this great offer!

Questions 92-94 refer to the following radio broadcast.

[3။] 영국식 발음

This is Brett Keller for WZEB Hampton Radio. And now for a traffic update. Unfortunately, the bridge on Jefferson Avenue is still under construction. Crews had been working overtime to finish the project before the holiday weekend, but heavy rains fell last week. Drivers who normally use this bridge should take the one on Oak Street instead. It will only change your route slightly, and you will be able to avoid delays. Up next, Jan Carlson, who runs Hampton Construction, will give us a few more details about this project.

Questions 95-97 refer to the following telephone message and sign.

[3။] 미국식 발음

Hello, Mr. Peters. It's Caley Francis from the Baldwin Performing Arts Center. I wanted to let you know that you have won two free tickets for the ballet *Bold Winter*. If you are not interested in seeing this performance, call me back immediately at 555-0939. I'll switch these tickets with those for another production. To claim your prize, you need to visit our administration office at 1201 Harbor Street . . . um, one block away from our main building on Field Street. Parking is limited, so I recommend that you take public transportation. The office is within walking distance of the Oakridge Subway Station.

Questions 98-100 refer to the following talk and table.

[3။] 호주식 발음

Just a couple of things to keep in mind this week. Our distribution center has a new floor manager, Brett Jensen. He's been hired to manage the evening shift, so his hours will be from 3 to 11 P.M. If one of you is willing to show him around the facility later this afternoon, that'd be great. Also, beginning tomorrow, we'll be receiving a number of shipments from suppliers. While the schedule posted next to the loading dock is mostly right, there's one piece of outdated information. The shipment of microwaves is going to arrive a day later—on May 15. The dishwashers and dryers scheduled to get here earlier in the week should arrive as planned, though.

PART 1

1 미국식 발음
(A) A man is adjusting his helmet.
(B) A man is staring at a coworker.
(C) They are changing some screens.
(D) They are typing on some keyboards.

2 호주식 발음
(A) She is reviewing the content of a book.
(B) She is stacking reading material on a windowsill.
(C) She is crossing her arms over her chest.
(D) She is turning the page of a publication.

3 캐나다식 발음
(A) A ball has been placed on the floor.
(B) A light fixture is hanging from the ceiling.
(C) There is a rug beneath the table.
(D) There is an air-conditioning unit behind the sofa.

4 영국식 발음
(A) A passenger boat is docked in a harbor.
(B) A handrail borders a series of steps.
(C) Some people are riding bicycles on a wharf.
(D) Water is being sprayed from a statue.

5 캐나다식 발음
(A) He is taking off an apron.
(B) He is inspecting baked goods.
(C) He is pulling a tray from an oven.
(D) He is leaning against some equipment.

6 영국식 발음
(A) Some vehicles are parked in a lot.
(B) A truck is driving along a highway.
(C) A portion of the pavement has been damaged.
(D) Some lines are being painted on a road.

PART 2

7 미국식 발음 → 호주식 발음
Who is waiting for you in your office?
(A) Mr. Sanders took the file.
(B) To wait in line.
(C) A friend from college.

8 영국식 발음 → 캐나다식 발음
Will you be able to contact me later?
(A) My assistant can go with them.
(B) Yes, I'll do so at three.
(C) No, I don't see the waiter.

9 호주식 발음 → 미국식 발음
Where would you like to sit for the concert?
(A) In the back row.
(B) A local band performed.
(C) No, I probably wouldn't.

10 영국식 발음 → 호주식 발음
You live on the east side of town, don't you?
(A) The eastern highway is blocked off.
(B) I did for a few years.
(C) I lost the key to the house.

11 캐나다식 발음 → 미국식 발음
Should we renew our lease or relocate the boutique?
(A) Not according to our rental agreement.
(B) It's a fashionable store.
(C) I want to stay in this space.

12 영국식 발음 → 캐나다식 발음
Which of those bags is yours?
(A) Use the overhead compartment.
(B) Mine is in the closet.
(C) You'll need a luggage voucher.

13 미국식 발음 → 호주식 발음
What day is your dentist appointment on?
(A) For a regular check-up.
(B) I wrote it down in my calendar.
(C) He is only available during the day.

14 캐나다식 발음 → 미국식 발음
Am I allowed to bring a beverage into the theater?
(A) It's not permitted.
(B) We are sitting close to the stage.
(C) I'll get some coffee.

15 호주식 발음 → 영국식 발음
Which employees need to attend tomorrow's training?
(A) Only people from the accounting department.
(B) At an employment agency.
(C) I'm happy to oversee it.

16 🎧 캐나다식 발음 → 영국식 발음

Could you change the bulb for this lamp?
(A) Sure, you can turn the TV on.
(B) Yes, but not immediately.
(C) All of the records we modified.

17 🎧 호주식 발음 → 미국식 발음

How do you suggest improving this manuscript?
(A) The author made a public appearance.
(B) Let's shorten it by 25 percent.
(C) Well, Novak recommends Midway Bistro.

18 🎧 캐나다식 발음 → 영국식 발음

When was the projector in the conference room fixed?
(A) I will arrange a conference call.
(B) They repaired it a week ago.
(C) Details of the project are posted on the wall.

19 🎧 미국식 발음 → 캐나다식 발음

Do you want to stop by the history museum?
(A) So long as it's free.
(B) When we stopped by the campus.
(C) The Aztec exhibit was the highlight.

20 🎧 영국식 발음 → 호주식 발음

When does the hotel restaurant normally open?
(A) Breakfast is served beginning at 6 A.M.
(B) Are you open to driving?
(C) I think the buffet is quite good.

21 🎧 캐나다식 발음 → 미국식 발음

Why haven't we received any of the new monitors?
(A) I'll check on the order's status.
(B) My manager received similar instructions.
(C) They have touchscreens as well.

22 🎧 호주식 발음 → 미국식 발음

Our firm is having a new logo designed.
(A) Yes, I often buy that brand.
(B) Hopefully, it will be appealing.
(C) Ken has resigned from his position.

23 🎧 영국식 발음 → 캐나다식 발음

Didn't Alan already proofread the newsletter that will be shared with gym members?
(A) We typically e-mail it out once per month.
(B) Read the proposal whenever you can.
(C) The draft is still being completed.

24 🎧 미국식 발음 → 호주식 발음

Payroll mistakes should be reported to Ms. Colt, right?
(A) Yes, take a souvenir.
(B) We were paid yesterday.

(C) No, Mr. Yang handles them.

25 🎧 호주식 발음 → 영국식 발음

The CEO has decided to step down in late October.
(A) An executive officer.
(B) You've made the right decision.
(C) He'll be difficult to replace.

26 🎧 캐나다식 발음 → 영국식 발음

Are you still in Atlanta, or has your train left the station?
(A) I'm heading to Denver now.
(B) I think I'll go to Atlanta for vacation.
(C) Really? My friend is from there.

27 🎧 미국식 발음 → 캐나다식 발음

Some of the shelves by the registers look low on merchandise.
(A) Yes, from our warehouse in Ohio.
(B) Shelves will be installed soon.
(C) They'll be stocked now that we have more goods.

28 🎧 호주식 발음 → 영국식 발음

Are you able to troubleshoot computer problems?
(A) That depends on the issue.
(B) You've been no trouble at all.
(C) The laptops are for business use only.

29 🎧 호주식 발음 → 미국식 발음

Why did the diners return these appetizers to the kitchen?
(A) Do you provide full refunds?
(B) My favorite dish is the mushroom pasta.
(C) Some of the chicken seems undercooked.

30 🎧 캐나다식 발음 → 영국식 발음

Where can I find a copy of the annual budget?
(A) You should talk to someone in the finance team.
(B) It was completed in April.
(C) We brought in over $20 million last year.

31 🎧 미국식 발음 → 호주식 발음

But I thought Ms. Stein had to postpone her flight to Mexico City.
(A) Airport shuttles leave every hour.
(B) That was before her plans were updated.
(C) Actually, the function went longer than expected.

PART 3

Questions 32-34 refer to the following conversation.

[음성] 캐나다식 발음 → 영국식 발음

M: I'm calling from Data-Trend Enterprises. We have a client flying in from Shanghai tomorrow morning and would like a driver from your chauffeur service to pick her up from the airport.

W: I can arrange that for you. May I have her name, flight number, and arrival time?

M: Her name is Tina Ming, and she'll be arriving on Flight DF304 at 10:20 A.M. Also, could she be taken to the Palm Hotel before being brought to our office? She'll need to drop off her luggage.

W: No problem. I'll add the pickup to our schedule, and one of our employees will be at the airport in the morning to get her.

Questions 35-37 refer to the following conversation.

[음성] 미국식 발음 → 캐나다식 발음

W: Hello. My name is Leslie Carver from Dannis Incorporated. My department will be having a luncheon on July 2 at noon. I'd like you to deliver food and drinks to the eighth-floor conference room for approximately 50 people on that day.

M: OK, Ms. Carver. Do you expect any attendees with special dietary requirements?

W: Yes, actually. I noticed on your online menu that you have vegetarian sandwiches, so could I please order 10 of those? For the remaining sandwiches, I think a combination of the chicken salad and roast beef ones would work. Also, do you offer drinks without any sugar?

Questions 38-40 refer to the following conversation.

[음성] 호주식 발음 → 미국식 발음

M: Good afternoon. My name is Frank Peters, and I have my yearly physical examination today with Dr. Murray. My appointment is at 10:45 A.M.

W: Hello, Mr. Peters. Please wait while I pull up your records. Also, did you by chance bring your health insurance card today? If so, please place it on the counter.

M: Yes, I have it right here. But may I ask what you need it for? Isn't my insurance information already on file?

W: All the state hospitals recently adopted a new record-sharing system that will keep patients like you from having to register personal information at each facility. I just want to confirm that your medical records are in order following the upgrade.

Questions 41-43 refer to the following conversation.

[음성] 캐나다식 발음 → 영국식 발음

M: Good morning, Ms. Willard. This is Hiro Kusanagi from Décor Max. I visited your booth at the Virginia Crafts Exhibition, and I was impressed with the wooden picture frames you make. Would you be willing to sell them at my store on a commission basis?

W: I'd be very interested, Mr. Kusanagi. Why don't I bring some samples to your store later this week?

M: Great. We can talk about prices and other details then as well. Um, how many frames can you produce each month?

W: About 40 . . . But I could make more if I hired a couple of assistants for my workshop.

M: That probably won't be necessary right away. But we can talk more about that when we meet.

Questions 44-46 refer to the following conversation.

[음성] 영국식 발음 → 호주식 발음

W: Alonso, are you done creating the blueprints for the Morissey Building? Our supervisor wants to review them in our meeting at 4:00 P.M.

M: Not yet. I'm still working on the presentation slideshow for the seminar I'm leading tomorrow on finding architectural inspiration. It's been taking me longer than anticipated.

W: Hmm . . . I gave a similar presentation to new hires last year. How about I finish the slideshow so that you can focus on the blueprints?

M: I'll e-mail you the presentation materials in a minute. Let me just wrap up the design for this slide and save the file to my computer. I really appreciate your assistance.

Questions 47-49 refer to the following conversation with three speakers.

[음성] 캐나다식 발음 → 미국식 발음 → 호주식 발음

M1: Yumi and Brian, will Hall A in our museum have enough room for the Egyptian art exhibition?

W: Maybe. There aren't many pieces to display, right?

M2: Just two dozen. But they're all large, so we need a big space . . . I recommend Hall C instead. Is it available?

M1: It will be. Korean tapestries are there now, but our director said to take them down on August 1.

W: Umm . . . I'm a little worried, since that only gives us three days to set up the necessary pieces.

M2: How about printing the labels for the Egyptian works beforehand? Then we could just move everything into the hall prior to the event.

W: OK. I'll grab the artwork list for us to reference now.

Questions 50-52 refer to the following conversation.

[3세] 호주식 발음 → 영국식 발음

M: Good afternoon. This is Carlos Tran, and I'm a representative from the Riverside Business Institute. I was hoping to reach Ms. Brenda Ling in regard to the advanced accounting course she completed last week.

W: This is Ms. Ling. What can I do for you?

M: I'm contacting the participants who went through the course to gather feedback. The responses we receive will help our organization to improve its services and curriculum in the future. Could you spare a moment to answer some questions? It won't take up much of your time.

W: I'm actually quite busy at the moment. I'll have some free time in the afternoon, however. Please call me back after 2 P.M.

Questions 53-55 refer to the following conversation.

[3세] 캐나다식 발음 → 미국식 발음

M: Do you know if Mr. Patel's flight has been delayed? I just heard that there was a blizzard in Edinburgh. I'm a little worried that he won't make it today.

W: Actually, he is based in Edmonton.

M: Oh, OK. It is important that he be here for the presentation this afternoon. The more investors at the meeting, the greater the chance we will get the financial support we require. Did you already set up the conference room?

W: Yes, but the projector wasn't working. I've called someone in the IT department to come take a look at it. It should be taken care of soon.

Questions 56-58 refer to the following conversation.

[3세] 캐나다식 발음 → 미국식 발음

M: I'm trying to figure out which of these colors from the catalog would look best in my office. But there are so many options. Would you be able to help me decide?

W: Of course. We have five brands in our store and hundreds of colors, so many customers find it hard to make a decision. What color is the furniture in the room?

M: The desk and chair are black, and the bookshelf is gray. I don't want the walls to be too bright or distracting.

W: There are a few products from Meyer paints that might be suitable. And we're having a sale on that particular brand. Wait here, and I'll bring back a few color samples.

Questions 59-61 refer to the following conversation with three speakers.

[3세] 캐나다식 발음 → 호주식 발음 → 영국식 발음

M1: I'd like to create a Web site for our hair salon before our grand opening. How do you two feel about that?

M2: That's a good idea. These days, it's necessary to have a well-developed site to connect with customers.

W: Right, but none of us have made a Web site before. We should pay an expert to do it.

M1: Do you know anyone who could help us?

W: Yes, actually. A former colleague . . . She's now a freelancer who designs Web sites for a living.

M2: Why don't you call her now? We should figure this out soon.

W: Sure thing. Please excuse me for just a minute or two.

Questions 62-64 refer to the following conversation and schedule.

[3세] 미국식 발음 → 호주식 발음

W: Hello. I'd like to buy a ticket to the 6:30 P.M. showing of Made in Melbourne.

M: I'm very sorry, but there aren't any seats left for that particular show time. However, you can attend the 7:45 P.M. showing.

W: No, that'll be too late for me. Hmm . . . I guess I'll see the one that starts at 6:45 P.M. instead. I heard that's very good too.

M: Certainly. That will be $9.

W: Here you go. Oh, one more thing . . . I saw on your Web site that customers can get a free movie poster today. Where can I get one?

M: Oh, there is a booth set up next to the concession stand. Just ask the employee there for one.

W: Great. I'll do that now.

Questions 65-67 refer to the following conversation and map.

[3세] 캐나다식 발음 → 영국식 발음

M: Excuse me. Where is the observation deck for the harbor located?

W: Just walk toward Starfish Beach after you exit this visitor center. The deck is on the corner. Ah . . . and it's fortunate you came today. The boardwalk will be filled with people tomorrow because of a kite-flying competition.

M: Good to know. By the way, I'll be able to see Dune Island from the deck, right?

W: Yes. New viewing machines were just installed there, and the weather is clear today.

M: Great! Also, I'm curious how much the parking fee for the nearby lot is.

W: The regular price is $20 per day. But local residents

only pay $15 because they get a 25 percent discount.

Questions 68-70 refer to the following conversation and schedule.

미국식 발음 → 호주식 발음

W: Did you see this section of the carpet? There's a rather large stain here.

M: Oh! What a mess! Maybe something was spilled during the year-end party that occurred earlier this afternoon. I'm worried because our clients from Downview Legal Associates are arriving for a meeting at 3 P.M.

W: We should use Conference Room D instead, seeing as it's unoccupied right now.

M: All right. I'll gather up our presentation handouts and bring them there. While I do that, please call the building maintenance team. They should deal with the stain in Conference Room C as soon as possible, since Janice Chung will conduct an interview there later this afternoon.

PART 4

Questions 71-73 refer to the following telephone message.

미국식 발음

Good morning, Ms. Chancy. I work at Source Incorporated, and I'm calling to inform you about a credit card that our company just released called the Gold Rewards Card. It offers a unique benefits package that caters to the spending habits of each customer. These benefits include 10 percent off at 20 major retail chains. Moreover, points accumulated through card purchases may be transferred to any of the five most popular frequent-flyer programs. If you want to take advantage of this amazing opportunity, just fill out an application form at www.sourceinc.com!

Questions 74-76 refer to the following speech.

영국식 발음

Please join me in welcoming Jason Chao to the stage, as he is being given the Employee of the Year Award. Mr. Chao was named one of our marketing firm's supervisors late last year, and he's really shown his worth to the company since then. He was responsible for all of the marketing activities we implemented for Tiger Cars, including some of our most successful magazine advertisements to date. Because of that campaign, we have attracted several new clients and have consequently seen our profits rise in recent months. So, let's give a big round of applause for Mr. Chao.

Questions 77-79 refer to the following announcement.

호주식 발음

Holmstead Bookstore is excited to announce that the final installment in author Marianne Lane's popular series of fantasy novels, *Wicked Witches*, will be released on November 10. To celebrate, our Westport branch will give away tickets to the book signing event being held there on November 30. These will be given to the first 300 customers who purchase her novel at that branch. If you are interested in this opportunity, be sure to get there early on the 10th. Ms. Lane has a lot of fans who will be thrilled about this chance to meet her. For more information regarding this and other Holmstead offers, I recommend downloading our mobile application.

Questions 80-82 refer to the following telephone message.

미국식 발음

Hello. My name is Karen Brody, and I'm calling to request your services. I will be representing the laboratory I work for at a biotech conference in Oslo. I plan to distribute a 10-page booklet to the people who attend my presentation. Therefore, I'll need 100 copies printed. How long would this take? The conference is on June 15. I'll be in a meeting for the rest of the morning, so I would appreciate it if you could get back to me after lunch today to discuss this matter. My number is 555-0292. Thank you.

Questions 83-85 refer to the following speech.

캐나다식 발음

I want to begin by saying it's been an honor to spend the final two decades of my career working in the public sector here at the State Consumer Protection Agency. As the legal department administrator, I oversaw the creation of numerous laws that helped protect the rights and safety of consumers. That's something I'm very proud of, and I'll always cherish my time here. Although I look forward to spending more time with my family, I will miss working with such a skilled group of people. Finally, let me express my gratitude to all of you for organizing this party. I had no idea that one was being planned. Thank you.

Questions 86-88 refer to the following telephone message.

영국식 발음

Mr. Hong, this is Andrea Plume calling on behalf of Hertz Construction. Thank you for replying to my initial e-mail so promptly. I reviewed your counteroffer regarding my firm's fee for the new soccer stadium project. Now it's time to discuss the project timetable. If it is convenient for you, I would like to meet later this week. Just note that I'll be out of town on Thursday. That leaves Wednesday and Friday, and I'm free throughout both afternoons. Let me know which day works best with your schedule.

Questions 89-91 refer to the following radio broadcast.

호주식 발음

Welcome to *This Week in Brooklyn* on Central Radio 96.1 FM. On Tuesday, the latest phase of a redevelopment project in the Bentham neighborhood was completed. Over the last three months, an old toy factory has been renovated to provide studios for artists. The space is going to open its doors this Friday, with painters, writers, musicians, and other artists holding a party for the grand opening event. The developer of the site—who also converted the old Wentworth Warehouse into apartments—hopes that it will serve to further improve the area. Now, we'll have a brief talk with one of the construction company's board members, Steven Godering.

Questions 92-94 refer to the following excerpt from a meeting.

미국식 발음

Could I have everyone's attention, please? I think it's a good idea to hold some kind of promotional event for the opening of our business. To that end, I'd like at least three employees to walk up and down William Street passing out coupons for discounted car washes. The coupons will be valid for one month. When you give them out to people, make sure you mention that we're open until 10 P.M. on weeknights. We'll also be running an advertisement in a local newspaper. Well, I'm not sure how many people read it. But we've got to try everything to attract customers to our new business.

Questions 95-97 refer to the following telephone message and building directory.

영국식 발음

Kenny, it's Nina Emerson. I'm calling about our conversation yesterday afternoon concerning the firm's incoming recruits. You asked if I'd be willing to take charge of their orientation session next Friday. I just remembered that I'll be out of town for a convention that day, so I can't assist you. However, Victoria Styles has directed training workshops in the past, and she's offered to help out. I suggest talking with her in person sometime today. Just note that her office is no longer on the third floor . . . She moved to the top floor when she transferred to another department. As for your comments about the Greenway Project, we'll have to discuss that when I get back.

Questions 98-100 refer to the following excerpt from a meeting and table.

캐나다식 발음

First of all, thank you for developing the new solar panel so quickly. I didn't expect the prototype to be ready for another two weeks. And it looks like this panel will be a significant improvement over our existing model. Assuming it functions as expected, we should see a 15 percent increase in power generation. Which brings me to the next stage of the project . . . The initial test of the panel will be conducted next week. The forecast calls for rain on Monday, and Tuesday is a national holiday, so we'll do it on the next clear day. My assistant—Charlotte Cruz—confirmed with the maintenance department this morning that we'll be able to gain access to the building's roof to set up our equipment. Any questions?

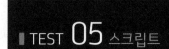

TEST 05 스크립트

* 무료 해석은 해커스토익(Hackers.co.kr)에서
  다운로드 받을 수 있습니다.

* QR 코드로
  바로가기

PART 1

1 [호주식 발음]

(A) A woman is getting out of a seat.
(B) A woman is closing a compartment.
(C) A woman is reaching for a suitcase.
(D) A woman is drawing a curtain.

2 [캐나다식 발음]

(A) A wheel is being taken off a car.
(B) A mechanic is hammering on metal.
(C) A man is pumping fuel into a vehicle.
(D) A man is wearing safety gear.

3 [영국식 발음]

(A) She is sitting on a patio.
(B) A flowerpot has fallen over.
(C) She is grasping a gardening utensil.
(D) A bouquet is being arranged.

4 [미국식 발음]

(A) A man is giving an item to a waitress.
(B) A woman is touching some jewelry on her wrist.
(C) Water is being poured in a glass.
(D) Food is being served to some diners.

5 [영국식 발음]

(A) The woman is vacuuming a floor.
(B) The woman is walking into a house.
(C) The woman is approaching an entrance.
(D) The woman is bending over a chair.

6 [미국식 발음]

(A) Words have been written on a whiteboard.
(B) A plant has been situated in a hallway.
(C) Monitors have been set up on the desks.
(D) The blinds have been shut in an office.

PART 2

7 [호주식 발음 → 영국식 발음]

How do you feel about this article?
(A) To review the editorial.
(B) I think so too.
(C) It is extremely impressive.

8 [미국식 발음 → 호주식 발음]

What movie are you going to see?
(A) At the cinema on Camus Drive.
(B) I bought the tickets already.
(C) The one starring Claire Holt.

9 [캐나다식 발음 → 영국식 발음]

Have you read through the manual yet?
(A) I found out through my secretary.
(B) Yes, you can take it.
(C) It appears to be automatic.

10 [영국식 발음 → 캐나다식 발음]

Can we have our glasses of wine refilled?
(A) No, I don't wear glasses.
(B) I didn't see who spilled it.
(C) Sure, right away.

11 [호주식 발음 → 미국식 발음]

When did you last have a chance to communicate with Mr. Lin?
(A) Friday works for me too.
(B) I ran into him today.
(C) We discussed our workflow.

12 [영국식 발음 → 캐나다식 발음]

How can we increase our sales volume this quarter?
(A) Try to lower the seat.
(B) I agree. It's very loud.
(C) By hiring more telemarketers.

13 [캐나다식 발음 → 미국식 발음]

Your café offers a vegetarian soup, doesn't it?
(A) You must be thinking of another place.
(B) Could I have a cup of coffee?
(C) All soups are made fresh daily.

14 [영국식 발음 → 캐나다식 발음]

There are several interns starting next Thursday.
(A) The Internet isn't currently working.
(B) Please make sure their work areas are ready.
(C) Why is the inspection beginning so late?

15 [호주식 발음 → 미국식 발음]

Are the safety measures clear, or should I further explain them?
(A) I understand them perfectly.
(B) Someone should clear out the lockers.
(C) I took the room's measurements.

16 [캐나다식 발음 → 호주식 발음]

How about I drive you to the amusement park?
(A) Oh, about three or four times.
(B) Aren't you riding with other friends?

(C) I thought it was a lot of fun.

17
What should I do with this box of paper?
(A) Just write it down here.
(B) Put it in the supply room.
(C) He helped me move the box.

18
Who should be put in charge of creating our spring collection?
(A) The fashion show is this coming summer.
(B) Most of the clothing is too big for me.
(C) I suggest bringing in an outside designer.

19
Won't the staff be meeting later in the week?
(A) They're slightly understaffed.
(B) Mr. Gimple didn't make it.
(C) I'll ask about that this afternoon.

20
Where will the second restroom be built?
(A) The architect has the floor plans.
(B) Some building supplies.
(C) It should be finished by tomorrow.

21
We're getting many customer complaints lately.
(A) We've gone through customs.
(B) So I've heard.
(C) There wasn't much rain today.

22
Do patients typically check in at the reception desk?
(A) We appreciate her patience.
(B) That desk is quite nice.
(C) Unless they're instructed otherwise.

23
The modified surveys were e-mailed to consumers, weren't they?
(A) That's what I was told.
(B) Questions about the company.
(C) Here is my e-mail address.

24
Who is the more qualified candidate, Jordan Fink or Erin Manifold?
(A) During the next interview.
(B) Their résumés are comparable.
(C) The quality of this item is poor.

25
I'm confused about how to prepare for the product launch.
(A) Follow these directions.
(B) It was attended by the press.
(C) I don't understand the novel either.

26
Why did you ask Kurt to organize the building tour?
(A) You can register near the entrance.
(B) Guided tours are free.
(C) He's led them in the past.

27
Where does the firm intend to open another branch?
(A) It hasn't been trimmed.
(B) A few possibilities are being considered.
(C) The president is from San Francisco.

28
One more person must be named to the executive council.
(A) I got great advice from my attorney.
(B) Can anyone be appointed?
(C) You must make the booking in advance.

29
Doesn't your photography studio specialize in portraits?
(A) All of the pictures have been framed.
(B) We perform a wide array of services.
(C) Our studio is in Las Vegas.

30
Why haven't any of these posters been placed in the storefront?
(A) Beside the information booth.
(B) OK, but contact the store first.
(C) I was wondering the same thing.

31
Are you interested in going for a short walk before our lunch break ends?
(A) As long as we have enough time.
(B) No, I've been there once.
(C) A brief meal with coworkers.

PART 3

Questions 32-34 refer to the following conversation.

호주식 발음 → 미국식 발음

M: Selina, is your phone working? I just tried to make a call, but there's a busy signal when I pick up my receiver.

W: I have the same problem. I contacted Mr. Bradford, the technical manager, and he said that the entire fourth floor has been affected. His team is fixing the phone lines now, but it looks like we'll have to rely on our mobile devices to call clients until the matter is resolved.

M: Hmm . . . That's going to be an issue because I'm supposed to participate in a conference call in 15 minutes.

W: I see. Well, maybe you should head to the third floor and use a phone in the meeting room there.

Questions 35-37 refer to the following conversation.

캐나다식 발음 → 영국식 발음

M: My family and I will be visiting the ruins of Tikal in a few hours for a guided tour. However, I forgot to arrange a ride to the site. I heard another guest talking about a shuttle service provided by the resort and would like to know more about it.

W: That's right. We have our own vehicles that take visitors to destinations in the area. Plus, there is no charge for the service for those staying at our accommodation.

M: Is it possible for us to take a shuttle at 1 P.M.? We need to be at the site around 1:30 P.M.

W: Hold on. Let me just make sure that there is a shuttle departing at that time.

Questions 38-40 refer to the following conversation with three speakers.

캐나다식 발음 → 미국식 발음 → 호주식 발음

M1: Our grocery store has been really busy this month. All of our employees have been talking about it. I wonder why we've had so many more shoppers than usual lately.

W: We were featured in a local magazine. It has a large readership among people living in the area.

M1: That's great. We should try to capitalize on that. Alex, why don't we run advertisements in the same magazine?

M2: Good idea. Maybe we could include some half-price coupons to attract new customers. Everyone likes to feel like they are getting a special deal when they go shopping.

Questions 41-43 refer to the following conversation.

영국식 발음 → 호주식 발음

W: Hi, Mr. Young. This is Fatima from *Carolina Monthly*. I've been assigned to take your picture for the article we're writing about you, and I'm wondering when you'd be free to meet with me.

M: I'll be available tomorrow at 3 P.M., Fatima. Where do you want to get together?

W: Since the article focuses on your architectural work, perhaps we could meet at the construction site of the latest building you designed, the Grand Theater. I'd like to photograph you in front of the partially finished structure.

M: That sounds good. By the way, once the building is completed next month, I'll be happy to bring you back and let you capture images of the interior as well.

Questions 44-46 refer to the following conversation.

미국식 발음 → 캐나다식 발음

W: I'm dissatisfied with Gordon Distribution Services. Our retail outlet has received incorrect shipments of goods from them on multiple occasions over the previous six months. For instance, just last Tuesday we received a dozen pairs of Eclipse basketball shoes, which is fewer than I requested. Plus, the company has yet to address my complaints.

M: Considering the ongoing troubles that we're experiencing with that company, I think it would be best for us to partner with another firm.

W: In that case, I'll reach out to other reputable distributors that provide services in the Madison area. Ah . . . but before I do that, can you help me hang up some signs about our membership program changes throughout the store?

Questions 47-49 refer to the following conversation.

호주식 발음 → 영국식 발음

M: Hi. I called in earlier regarding an event I am attending. I need a tuxedo.

W: Hmm . . . you are much taller than average. You'll need a custom-made tuxedo. The ones I have in the shop right now are all too small. Um, when do you need it by?

M: In two weeks. How much would that be?

W: It depends on the options you choose. The materials will be the greatest consideration in terms of cost. But the design will also affect the price, along with any accessories you choose . . . like bowties or vests. That being said, the total price likely won't exceed $1,000.

M: That sounds reasonable.

W: Great. I'll just need to measure you then.

Questions 50-52 refer to the following conversation with three speakers.

[3] 미국식 발음 → 호주식 발음 → 영국식 발음

W1: Tim, Laura . . . Have you had a chance to speak with Mr. Kang from Seaward Financial yet? He needs help finding employees for the new office his company is opening in San Diego.

M: Oh, yes. He stopped by this morning.

W2: Right. We explained how our firm can manage the recruiting process, and he seemed very interested.

W1: Great. So, he's decided to hire us, then?

W2: Uh, not exactly. While the meeting went smoothly, he still hasn't made up his mind. I think we need to explain more clearly how much time and money he'll save by paying us to do the work.

M: I agree. It's the only way we'll be able to convince him to become a client.

Questions 53-55 refer to the following conversation.

[3] 미국식 발음 → 호주식 발음

W: I just received a phone call from Lisa Belano's secretary. Ms. Belano is on her way to Raybury Park, so we should leave within a few minutes. We don't want to be late.

M: Great. I've already packed up our cameras and spare lenses, so we can go whenever you're ready.

W: What about our portable lighting setup? I think we should bring them for the shoot.

M: Well, it's not cloudy at all today.

W: Yeah, that's a good point. In that case, let's head to the park. My car is parked right out front.

Questions 56-58 refer to the following conversation.

[3] 영국식 발음 → 캐나다식 발음

W: I just found out about the new inventory tracking software that was installed on our computers on Tuesday. But its functions are a bit unusual, so I'm having some trouble. Have you figured out how to properly use it?

M: For the most part. Reading the user manual has been helpful. I recommend you do the same. A digital copy of it was e-mailed to everyone a few days ago.

W: Oh, really? I never received the message. Can you forward it to me so I can look it over?

M: Certainly. However, it's odd that you weren't included in the original e-mail. You should inform our manager about that to ensure you're a part of future group messages and important announcements.

Questions 59-61 refer to the following conversation.

[3] 미국식 발음 → 호주식 발음

W: Hello. My name is Padma Jodhpur. I am calling because I was charged a fee for canceling a class

even though I registered in another one right away. I'm not sure why this happened.

M: I apologize for that, but the company changed its late cancellation procedure. You can only change an existing reservation without any fee up to 12 hours before the class starts. I informed all students of this policy change through a text message a few days ago.

W: Really? I never received that.

M: Hmm . . . That's unfortunate. I can't cancel the charge, but I can give you a coupon for 10 percent off the next class you sign up for.

Questions 62-64 refer to the following conversation and table.

[3] 미국식 발음 → 호주식 발음

W: Eastside Cable. How may I help you?

M: Hi. This is Jeremy Monroe. A worker is supposed to install a new cable box at my property today, but I can't remember the appointment time.

W: Just a minute . . . Um, he'll be there at 2 P.M.

M: Thanks. I also want to change my TV package. I'm viewing your online brochure now.

W: OK . . . Well, for this month only, Package A is offered at a discount.

M: But that doesn't include the service I'm most interested in. I prefer Package B.

W: I see. Well, you're certainly free to upgrade to that one, but you'll have to pay the standard rate.

Questions 65-67 refer to the following conversation and instruction manual.

[3] 영국식 발음 → 캐나다식 발음

W: Hi, Billy. What are you doing?

M: I'm trying to assemble this table. Um, our manager told me to set up another one in this conference room.

W: Is it very complicated?

M: The instructions are pretty straightforward. I've used all the bolts to attach the legs to the tabletop. However, one of the remaining parts seems to be missing.

W: That must be frustrating. Have you contacted the company you ordered it from?

M: I called them this morning, but their customer service department was busy dealing with other issues. I'm going to try them again during my lunch hour.

Questions 68-70 refer to the following conversation and building directory.

[3] 호주식 발음 → 미국식 발음

M: Hey, sorry I'm late. The freeway was really backed up. It took twice as long as usual to get to the construction site.

W: That's fine. Were you able to stop by Timber World

and get the supplies I asked for?

M: Yeah. The lumber is in my truck now. Where do you want me to store it for the time being?

W: We're eventually going to use it in the bedrooms, but you can put everything in the living room for now . . . Oh, and another thing. This afternoon, an air purifier is going to be dropped off. If I'm not here when it comes, have the delivery people bring it into the kitchen.

PART 4

Questions 71-73 refer to the following announcement.

[3»] 캐나다식 발음

May I have your attention, please? There is a red Jupiter four-door sedan in parking lot 4D that is currently blocking the hospital's east exit. Its license plate number is DTG103. We ask the owner to please move the car immediately. Also, as a reminder, vehicles should never be left in the hospital's emergency areas. To identify these, look for red and yellow stripes on the pavement. Anyone who parks their vehicle in one of these areas will be subject to a fine of up to $500 in accordance with state laws. We appreciate your cooperation.

Questions 74-76 refer to the following telephone message.

[3»] 미국식 발음

Hello, Minho. This is Katy. I just finished meeting with our client in Philadelphia. Unfortunately, I will not be able to return this evening as scheduled, as my flight has been pushed back for several hours. Would you mind making the presentation to Techworth at 3 P.M. tomorrow? You helped create the application for them last year, so the presentation's contents should be very familiar to you. I e-mailed you the necessary files a few minutes ago. Could you confirm that you received them and can cover for me? If you need any help with this assignment, contact my assistant, Rin Richards.

Questions 77-79 refer to the following excerpt from a meeting.

[3»] 캐나다식 발음

Over the month of August, we will be painting and remodeling parts of our office. This work will take place on the third floor, and it may be a bit noisy. That's why personnel from our division are going to use temporary workstations on the fourth floor. Since the construction is scheduled to begin in a couple of weeks, preparations have already been made, with desks having been set up on the designated floor. However, staff members' work computers won't be relocated until the final week

of this month. I understand that these temporary changes will be an inconvenience, but I trust that everyone will try to make the best of the situation.

Questions 80-82 refer to the following telephone message.

[3»] 영국식 발음

Hello, Ms. Olsen. I'm calling from Vine Express to let you know that we're holding a package for you. One of our employees tried to deliver the item to your house three times, but you were not home on any of those occasions. Because the parcel needs to be signed for, you'll have to pick it up at our sorting facility at 896 West Pine Drive between 9 A.M. and 5 P.M. If you don't retrieve the package within seven days, it will be returned to the sender. For more information about the item, please feel free to call us at 555-9172. Thank you.

Questions 83-85 refer to the following broadcast.

[3»] 영국식 발음

Officials from the Dublin Electric Utility have decided to expand the city's use of renewable energy sources. The head of the company, Betty O'Rourke, shared the news at a press conference yesterday afternoon. The goal is to reduce residents' dependency on fossil fuels and move toward using solar power exclusively. The utility company has hired Renew Incorporated to install the necessary solar panels. This company has extensive experience with this type of project. Of course, some customers are concerned about higher monthly bills. But Ms. O'Rourke has stated that while this is possible, people should not worry.

Questions 86-88 refer to the following radio broadcast.

[3»] 캐나다식 발음

In business news, local firm Digital Solutions has announced plans to release the latest version of its mobile phone application, SpeakVid. The application allows users to record, edit, and share short video messages. It has become hugely popular, resulting in a sharp rise in the developer's stock prices. The upgrade is anticipated among consumers and investors alike. The general public is excited for the application's updated interface, while business analysts predict that the upgrade will expand the firm's market base. SpeakVid has attracted national media coverage already, and experts believe that interest will increase next month when the new version of the application comes out.

Questions 89-91 refer to the following announcement.

[3»] 호주식 발음

Could I have everyone's attention please? I have a quick announcement. As you all know, I texted everyone this morning to say that today's employee workshop on graphic design will be held in the main conference room. However, Mr. Bailey wants to meet with clients in there. That leaves us the break room. We will meet there at the originally scheduled time. For those of you who want to take part but have yet to sign up, there's still space. We have one more opening left. The registration form is at the reception desk.

Questions 92-94 refer to the following telephone message.

[3๗] 미국식 발음

I'm calling on behalf of Music Central in Newark, New Jersey. I apologize for this last-minute change, but I need to update the order that my store put in yesterday for a bulk shipment of electronics. As of now, the order is for 20 portable Kentmoore speakers, 25 wireless Conquest microphones, and 25 Pure Sound noise-canceling headphones. However, we need 10 more Kentmoore speakers than were originally requested. If it's not too late to add items to our order, please do so and bill us for the additional costs. Also, I'd appreciate it if you could e-mail me an updated invoice at purchasing@soundequip.com this afternoon.

Questions 95-97 refer to the following announcement and a survey.

[3๗] 호주식 발음

Thank you for participating in this focus group. The designer of the product . . . uh, Greg Henderson . . . wanted to welcome you personally, but he's dealing with a problem at our factory. Anyway, the goal today is to get your feedback on our newest product, the Flow S60. We are confident that there is a strong demand for it. In a recent survey about upcoming purchases, a large percentage of respondents indicated that they plan to buy this type of device soon. Next to air conditioners, it was the most popular choice. However, we're concerned that our model may be difficult to operate. So to start, please give your opinion about the most recent draft of the user instructions. I'll hand this document out now . . .

Questions 98-100 refer to the following advertisement and map.

[3๗] 미국식 발음

Looking for a quick and affordable way to see the sights in Boston? Then hop on the Bean Bus! Our bus stops at historical sites throughout the city. To purchase a ticket, drop by our company's information booth in the lobby of the Stanford Hotel. Tickets usually cost $20, but we will be offering a 10 percent discount during the month of May to celebrate our company's fifth anniversary. For route information, visit www.beanbus.com. Please note that the bus will not stop at the site between Boston Harbor and Bunker Hill from June 25 until July 15 due to ongoing road construction in the area. Explore Boston with the Bean Bus today!

* 무료 해석은 해커스토익(Hackers.co.kr)에서
  다운로드 받을 수 있습니다.

• QR 코드로
  바로가기

PART 1

1 ♪₩ 캐나다식 발음
   (A) The man is knocking on a door.
   (B) The man is stacking packages on a cart.
   (C) The man is carrying a box into a house.
   (D) The man is getting out of a vehicle.

2 ♪₩ 영국식 발음
   (A) A woman is typing on a keyboard.
   (B) A computer monitor is being installed.
   (C) Some men are standing near a screen.
   (D) Some books are being placed on a shelf.

3 ♪₩ 호주식 발음
   (A) He is preparing a dish.
   (B) He is holding a plate.
   (C) He is serving a customer.
   (D) He is stirring a pot.

4 ♪₩ 미국식 발음
   (A) A bag of trash has been left beside a bin.
   (B) Bushes are growing along a fence.
   (C) Some containers are being emptied.
   (D) A wall separates two buildings.

5 ♪₩ 영국식 발음
   (A) A desk is being disassembled by workers.
   (B) Safety vests are arranged on a warehouse floor.
   (C) A device has been set on a table.
   (D) Uniforms are organized on a shelf.

6 ♪₩ 캐나다식 발음
   (A) There is a painting hanging above the fireplace.
   (B) A window blind has been partially opened.
   (C) A lamp has been attached to a wall.
   (D) There is a cup on the windowsill.

PART 2

7 ♪₩ 호주식 발음 → 영국식 발음
   When does your flight arrive?
   (A) From Lisbon.
   (B) At noon.
   (C) Her flight is late.

8 ♪₩ 미국식 발음 → 캐나다식 발음
   Who is in charge of hiring interns?
   (A) Let me get back to you.
   (B) That's not one of their responsibilities.
   (C) Don't miss your turn.

9 ♪₩ 미국식 발음 → 호주식 발음
   The city's new mayor is very popular.
   (A) That's what I've heard.
   (B) The election is next week.
   (C) His office is at city hall.

10 ♪₩ 영국식 발음 → 캐나다식 발음
    When do you need me to pick you up?
    (A) I drove there earlier.
    (B) In front of Terminal A.
    (C) Friday evening around 8.

11 ♪₩ 영국식 발음 → 호주식 발음
    Where should I put the office supplies?
    (A) The storage closet over there.
    (B) We've got a few cases of paper.
    (C) No, I work in the other office.

12 ♪₩ 캐나다식 발음 → 미국식 발음
    Where was the company founded?
    (A) In San Francisco.
    (B) It is a charity foundation.
    (C) Right here on my desk.

13 ♪₩ 호주식 발음 → 영국식 발음
    What should we get Tanya for her going-away gift?
    (A) How about a bouquet?
    (B) She's a gifted person.
    (C) It's going to be very useful to her.

14 ♪₩ 미국식 발음 → 캐나다식 발음
    Isn't Angela's new apartment very beautiful?
    (A) They're just for decoration.
    (B) I was really impressed by it.
    (C) Her apartment is on the third floor.

15 ♪₩ 영국식 발음 → 호주식 발음
    Can you finish painting the room on your own, or do you need help?
    (A) Yes, I've seen that painting before.
    (B) An extra set of hands would be great.
    (C) I couldn't have it done alone.

16 ♪₩ 호주식 발음 → 미국식 발음
    Which cinema is the movie playing at?
    (A) A horror movie.
    (B) The Grand Theater.
    (C) It starts at 8 P.M.

17 ③ 캐나다식 발음 → 미국식 발음

Would you like to pay by cash or card?
(A) It's way too expensive.
(B) No, thank you.
(C) That depends on the price.

18 ③ 영국식 발음 → 호주식 발음

Why is the Mexican restaurant closed?
(A) It is being remodeled.
(B) The chef is from Mexico City.
(C) Most people order tacos.

19 ③ 캐나다식 발음 → 영국식 발음

I'm having trouble finding a venue for the banquet.
(A) It sounds like the best solution.
(B) Let me call some places.
(C) There's a bank on the corner.

20 ③ 미국식 발음 → 호주식 발음

Please be sure to submit your expense report by this afternoon.
(A) It cost more than I thought.
(B) I'll send it to you now.
(C) Sarah reported the problem.

21 ③ 영국식 발음 → 캐나다식 발음

Aren't you meeting the department manager about your promotion today?
(A) Let's meet for lunch.
(B) She is my supervisor.
(C) We already discussed it.

22 ③ 호주식 발음 → 미국식 발음

How did Louis learn about the two companies' merger talks?
(A) You'll have to ask him.
(B) He missed the meeting yesterday.
(C) Sometime last week.

23 ③ 캐나다식 발음 → 영국식 발음

Please inform all of the staff about the changes to the holiday schedule.
(A) It's full of useful information.
(B) I'll post a memo.
(C) It changes every year.

24 ③ 영국식 발음 → 캐나다식 발음

Did you visit the Louvre while you were in Paris?
(A) It's my first time in France.
(B) I might have to extend my trip.
(C) I didn't have enough time.

25 ③ 미국식 발음 → 호주식 발음

Who showed you how to use the accounting software?
(A) I attended a workshop on it.
(B) Managing accounts is time-consuming.
(C) Your experience really shows.

26 ③ 캐나다식 발음 → 영국식 발음

Mr. Colt approved the budget change, right?
(A) We need to save money.
(B) Didn't you get the e-mail?
(C) Yes, I have some right here.

27 ③ 호주식 발음 → 미국식 발음

The employee break room is the last door on the right, isn't it?
(A) I'm afraid it's broken.
(B) That's the janitor's office.
(C) Please close the door.

28 ③ 미국식 발음 → 호주식 발음

Can you make sure the package is delivered by tomorrow?
(A) By Friday.
(B) You can order it online.
(C) The overnight delivery fee is $30.

29 ③ 영국식 발음 → 캐나다식 발음

I think we'd better look for another party planner.
(A) What's wrong with the one we have?
(B) I'm looking forward to being there.
(C) The party lasted longer than expected.

30 ③ 미국식 발음 → 캐나다식 발음

What was Ms. Fulton's position at her last job?
(A) She has a master's degree.
(B) At Gable Brothers Law Firm.
(C) Marketing director.

31 ③ 호주식 발음 → 영국식 발음

Carter was named Employee of the Year.
(A) In a couple of years.
(B) He deserves it.
(C) It has 40 employees.

PART 3

Questions 32-34 refer to the following conversation.

③ 호주식 발음 → 미국식 발음

M: Good morning. Where can I take you today?

W: I'm on my way to the Spring Valley Clothing Store on 19th Street. It's right past Thompson Square.

M: OK, I know where that is. By the way, there is heavy traffic right now because part of Victoria Avenue is closed. Um, city workers are fixing a water line. I might have to take a side road. The distance will be technically longer, but we should get to your destination more quickly.

W: That's totally fine as long as I get to the store before it closes at 5 P.M. This is the last day of a sale, and I'm trying to buy a sweater.

Questions 35-37 refer to the following conversation.

🎧 캐나다식 발음 → 미국식 발음

M: Hi, Fumiko. It's Christian from HR. Could I get your self-performance review? The deadline is today.

W: Hi, Christian. Sorry, I have not had the time to do it yet. I thought I could submit it during the performance evaluation meeting.

M: That won't work. I need to review it beforehand to make sure everything is all right. You can simply go online and fill in the form. There are only multiple-choice questions.

W: I understand. I'll log in to the site now.

M: Alright. Let me know if you need any further information.

Questions 38-40 refer to the following conversation.

🎧 호주식 발음 → 영국식 발음

M: Excuse me. I'd like to sit down on this bench and read my newspaper, so can you move your bicycle?

W: Sorry about that. I wasn't sure where to leave my bike, so I just leaned it against this bench.

M: There is a bike rack near the fountain. It is the only designated area you can park your bicycle, but quite difficult to find as many people have picnics near it. By the way, do you have a bicycle lock?

W: Yes. I've got one in my backpack. Why?

M: Uh, I heard that some bikes have gone missing recently. Just make sure to use it.

W: I see. Thanks for your help.

Questions 41-43 refer to the following conversation.

🎧 영국식 발음 → 캐나다식 발음

W: Hello, I would like to order some of your lab coats . . . Uh, the model number is YE210. We have some new employees that we would like to get them for.

M: I am sorry, but we no longer sell that here at Work Solution Gear. We do have several new models available, though.

W: I would need a coat with the same material as the YE210. Do you have anything like that?

M: Yes. The YK160 is the one I would recommend. It has the same material and design. However, extra pockets were added for convenience.

W: OK. I'll order 15 of them.

Questions 44-46 refer to the following conversation with three speakers.

🎧 캐나다식 발음 → 호주식 발음 → 미국식 발음

M1: Kyle, have you noticed that shoppers haven't shown much interest in the new line of salad dressings we've got in stock?

M2: Yes, I'm a bit worried that the ones on our shelves are nearing their expiration date. And there's a full box in our storeroom. What should we do?

M1: How about marking down the price and setting up a special display near the cashier counters? Could you handle that, Beth?

W: Sure. I'll also make some eye-catching signs. How much of a discount are you thinking of?

M2: How about 30 percent? Would it be too much?

Questions 47-49 refer to the following conversation.

🎧 미국식 발음 → 캐나다식 발음

W: Hi, Robert. This is Dominica Jones from Fresh Advertising Solutions. I am happy to offer you the TV commercial copywriter position you interviewed for. We would like for you to start next Monday.

M: Oh, thank you. I'm happy to hear that. I have another couple of weeks left at my current job, but then I will be ready to start.

W: That is later than we had anticipated, but still works. In the meantime, I will send you a copy of our employee manual. Please go through the company policies carefully and feel free to contact me if any of them are unclear.

M: I'll be sure to do that.

Questions 50-52 refer to the following conversation.

🎧 영국식 발음 → 호주식 발음

W: I just finished setting up the Coleman X20 Standing Desk that I purchased online. I thought the height would be adjustable, but it isn't. It's too short for me. I would like to send this one back and get the taller model from the same company.

M: Unfortunately, X20 is the only Coleman model we have. We could have a technician put in an extra part in order to make the model you purchased work for you.

W: Hmm . . . I would rather just get one that is the right size for me. So please take this one back.

M: Absolutely. I'll just need your name and order number so that I can refund your payment.

Questions 53-55 refer to the following conversation.

🎧 미국식 발음 → 캐나다식 발음

W: Hi, this is Cathy Conde from Wave Credit Card. I am responding to an inquiry you made on our Web site. What exactly is the nature of your problem?

M: There is an unexpected charge of $14 labeled as a

fee on my card. Could you explain to me what that is?

W: That fee is for making your monthly minimum payment a day late.

M: Oh, I see. I got kind of busy last month, and it just slipped my mind.

W: To avoid this problem in the future, why don't you sign up for our auto-payment program? Your credit card will be linked to a bank account of your choice.

M: That sounds great. I'll do that right now.

Questions 56-58 refer to the following conversation.

[3•] 미국식 발음 → 호주식 발음

W: Have you finished writing our company's annual report, Marvin? We'll need to send out copies to shareholders before December 20.

M: The summary of our profits and losses is done, but I'm still struggling with the section on what we've achieved this year. We failed to achieve one of our main goals, and I'm quite sure that our shareholders won't be happy about that.

W: Focus on the aspects of our business that have the most potential. The Edgar Telecom project, and, um. . . I'm sure you can think of other opportunities that will interest our investors.

M: Good idea. Thanks for your advice.

Questions 59-61 refer to the following conversation with three speakers.

[3•] 영국식 발음 → 호주식 발음 → 캐나다식 발음

W: OK, let's talk about Vickie's retirement. Do you have any ideas?

M1: We should really get something nice for her because she has been an integral part of this team for so many years.

W: Maybe we should throw her a party.

M1: Good idea. I could reserve a private room at a restaurant.

M2: Also, it would be nice if we got her a gift card. We could ask everyone on the team to pitch in a few dollars. Would you mind doing that, Greg?

M1: All right. I will send everyone an e-mail about it. Let's try to keep it a secret from Vickie, though.

Questions 62-64 refer to the following conversation and tag.

[3•] 캐나다식 발음 → 영국식 발음

M: Welcome. Do you have a room reservation?

W: Yeah. Here's my confirmation form.

M: Thank you, Ms. Graham. We have you booked for two nights, and you'll be staying in one of our executive suites. Um. . . I'm afraid the room won't be ready until 3 P.M. You can wait in the hotel lounge if you like.

W: That's OK. I can do some window shopping while I

wait. Could I leave my suitcase here?

M: Not a problem. Please keep this baggage claim check. You'll need to present it here when you return.

W: Oh, on second thought, I'd like to leave my backpack as well.

M: That's fine.

Questions 65-67 refer to the following conversation and list.

[3•] 미국식 발음 → 호주식 발음

W: Lewis, since you weren't in the meeting yesterday, I want to let you know that we've decided to stop handing out loyalty cards to customers.

M: Really? How are we going to encourage customers to keep coming back to our restaurant then?

W: Well, we're going to introduce a membership app for smartphones, just like one of our competitors has done.

M: That'll be a lot of work. Are there any advantages to launching an application?

W: Well, having an app will appeal to more customers and be very convenient for them.

M: Hmm . . . And I suppose the app will also help our company gather customer data.

W: That's right.

Questions 68-70 refer to the following conversation and map.

[3•] 영국식 발음 → 캐나다식 발음

W: You've reached the tourist information hotline. How may I help you?

M: Hi. Someone suggested that I visit the Sugary Dessert Bar while I'm here in Melbourne. However, that restaurant doesn't have a Web site. Could you let me know where it is?

W: Just a moment . . . Um, the business you are looking for is on the corner of Brunswick Street and Warren Avenue.

M: Oh, that's actually very convenient for me. I have to participate in a workshop at the Westwood Conference Center on Nolan Avenue until 2 P.M. today. That's just a block away. Thank you so much for your help.

W: It was my pleasure. Enjoy your time in Melbourne.

PART 4

Questions 71-73 refer to the following advertisement.

[3•] 캐나다식 발음

Do you frequently handle documents in a foreign language or speak with clients overseas? In important situations like these, you don't want to deal with unreliable translations. Here at Commslink, we provide the expert services you need to ensure good communication. We can translate documents in over 20 languages at reasonable prices. We can also supply interpreters to attend lectures and conferences. Visit our Web site at commslink.com to read reviews from our customers and to see a list of companies that have worked with us in the past.

Questions 74-76 refer to the following announcement.
[3»] 미국식 발음

Every year, we hold a baseball game against our store's competitor, Fredericksburg Mattresses. This year, it will happen at Marshall Field, just three blocks from here, on Saturday, April 7. I encourage all of you to join our team. I believe Cindy is ordering us some T-shirts we can wear. We're also going to need someone to keep track of the game's score, so if you're not interested in playing, I suggest volunteering for that job. I'm also pleased to announce that Redwood Department Store is willing to provide a $25 gift certificate to each member of the winning team.

Questions 77-79 refer to the following introduction.
[3»] 호주식 발음

While I have your attention, I'd like to introduce our newest team member, Lynn Falken. She'll be in charge of setting up and maintaining our databases. And she'll have a lot of other roles as well. Um . . . We recently had an incident that led to a lot of important data being lost—I'm sure you all remember. Well, Lynn will work to prevent that sort of thing from happening again. You'll be relying on her quite frequently, so I recommend writing down her office extension—it's 7784.

Questions 80-82 refer to the following telephone message.
[3»] 미국식 발음

Hi, Mr. Evans, this is Linda Blake. I'm calling regarding an issue with your art exhibit at our establishment. One of the paintings you asked us to display, *Wisconsin Summer*, is actually too big to fit on any of our walls. What would you like us to do with this painting? We can send it back to you, or we can have it shipped to one of our partner galleries in the area. We still have plenty of great paintings to display, and we think the exhibit is going to draw the largest crowd in our gallery's history. We hope this issue won't dampen your enthusiasm for working with us.

Questions 83-85 refer to the following announcement.
[3»] 호주식 발음

Attention, customers. I regret to inform you that we have opted to suspend cable car operations for the rest of the day. The wind is too strong, and we have your

safety in mind. To return to the base of Quail Mountain, you may either take the trail or the road down from this café. But whichever way you choose, the walk will take about 40 minutes. It should not be attempted after dark. If you bought a return ticket for the cable car, you can get a partial refund at the ticket window. If you need assistance walking down the mountain, please visit the information desk. Thank you.

Questions 86-88 refer to the following broadcast.
[3»] 영국식 발음

Welcome to the Tech Stuff podcast. Today, I want to talk a bit about Scion Incorporated. This firm expanded to become the largest in the digital communications field after purchasing its main rival last year. At a recent press conference, a spokesperson said that the company's current CEO will be replaced by the noted software developer Mitchell Horner. He plans to begin working at Scion next week. It was also announced that Scion's popular social media application has been updated. I will now take a few minutes to explain to you how some of the new features work.

Questions 89-91 refer to the following telephone message.
[3»] 캐나다식 발음

Hi, Jasmine. This is Richard Hill following up on your interview for our childhood education specialist position. We've decided that you're a great fit for our institution. In terms of credentials, no one else comes close. You're matchless when it comes to using the tools and platforms that are a big part of the job. What we'd like to know at this stage is when you'd be able to start. Our school year begins in June. Please call me back at this number, or send an e-mail if you prefer.

Questions 92-94 refer to the following telephone message.
[3»] 영국식 발음

Hi, Mr. Ahmad. This is Cynthia from *Car Digest Monthly*. We received your change of address form, and we will begin shipping our magazines to your new apartment starting January 1. I would also like to remind you that you have free access to all of our online content, including back issues of our magazine. We encourage you to check out our previous stories about famous car manufacturers, championship races throughout history, competitive drivers, and more. If you would like to access this online content, just go to our Web site, click "Set Up an Online Account," and you will be guided from there.

Questions 95-97 refer to the following talk and screenshot.

호주식 발음

I would like to thank everyone for participating in Vistant Securities' online workshop on personal investment strategies. My name is Kevin Coleman, and I have been assigned to fill in for your regular instructor, uh, Laura Welch. She can't take part in today's session because there is a problem with the Internet connection at her home office. There is one more thing I have to mention before we get started. The video conferencing software we use for this class will be updated later this week. Once this happens, you will no longer find the option to save the video. This is being done to address concerns about privacy.

Questions 98-100 refer to the following talk and map.

영국식 발음

OK, listen up everyone. I hope you enjoyed today's tour of Chinatown. We really lucked out with the weather . . . So, um, if you look at our schedule, you'll see that tomorrow is a free day. That means that you get to explore the city on your own. If you'd like to do some shopping for souvenirs, I suggest visiting Kingsway Mall. It includes a number of stores that sell local products. You will find it on Davis Avenue between the Hillside Library and Elmwood Park. Oh, and before I forget . . . If you are planning on having lunch in the hotel restaurant, you should book a table in advance. It gets really busy on Saturdays and Sundays.

PART 1

1 〔3ᵚ〕 캐나다식 발음
(A) The man is wiping a fan.
(B) The man is twisting a metal knob.
(C) The man is washing a cup.
(D) The man is drinking water.

2 〔3ᵚ〕 영국식 발음
(A) The woman is dressing a mannequin.
(B) The woman is looking at her reflection.
(C) The woman is collecting some hangers.
(D) The woman is putting away some merchandise.

3 〔3ᵚ〕 호주식 발음
(A) One of the women is wearing a headset.
(B) One of the women is shaking hands with the man.
(C) They are posting a document on a notice board.
(D) They are working at different stations.

4 〔3ᵚ〕 미국식 발음
(A) Textbooks are being distributed in a lecture hall.
(B) Some people are giving a presentation.
(C) Some people are leaving an auditorium.
(D) A pen is being pointed at a page.

5 〔3ᵚ〕 호주식 발음
(A) One of the men is pulling up a chair.
(B) A beverage is being poured from a pitcher.
(C) One of the men is serving some food.
(D) A plate is being passed around a table.

6 〔3ᵚ〕 미국식 발음
(A) A window frame of a house is being painted.
(B) A mailbox has fallen on the ground.
(C) A residential garage door has been raised.
(D) A railing has been erected near an entrance.

PART 2

7 〔3ᵚ〕 캐나다식 발음 → 미국식 발음
When would it be convenient for you to have dinner?
(A) I can meet at 7 o'clock.

(B) Yes, we definitely have.
(C) At the new sushi restaurant.

8 〔3ᵚ〕 영국식 발음 → 호주식 발음
Hasn't Ms. Kramer's plane already landed?
(A) Her passport hasn't expired.
(B) It gets in soon.
(C) She has plain black luggage.

9 〔3ᵚ〕 캐나다식 발음 → 영국식 발음
Why am I getting so many advertisements in my e-mail?
(A) We get a lot of packages too.
(B) I prefer the other commercial.
(C) Have you tried unsubscribing from mailing lists?

10 〔3ᵚ〕 호주식 발음 → 영국식 발음
What's the price of bananas at the grocery store?
(A) A worker will restock the store shelves.
(B) According to this flyer, 50¢ each.
(C) Most of this fruit is still not ripe.

11 〔3ᵚ〕 미국식 발음 → 호주식 발음
Mr. Draper will be taking over the Seattle branch next week, won't he?
(A) His promotion hasn't been finalized yet.
(B) We have an office in Oakland as well.
(C) Yes, he has been in that position for two years.

12 〔3ᵚ〕 캐나다식 발음 → 미국식 발음
Where did you work during the first half of your career?
(A) Primarily at Champlain Law Office.
(B) Throughout most of the last decade.
(C) My superior makes the hiring decisions.

13 〔3ᵚ〕 미국식 발음 → 캐나다식 발음
How do you plan to get to the airport on Saturday?
(A) Flight 208 will depart at 8 A.M.
(B) My trip was canceled, actually.
(C) We should get a taxi to the hotel.

14 〔3ᵚ〕 영국식 발음 → 호주식 발음
Should we try to renegotiate the price or switch suppliers?
(A) Give him the lease agreement.
(B) Our supply is low.
(C) I'm fine with either strategy.

15 〔3ᵚ〕 캐나다식 발음 → 미국식 발음
Has a band been booked for the event?
(A) Concert tickets are $20 each.
(B) At a nearby venue.
(C) A jazz group is going to perform.

16 [3회] 영국식 발음 → 호주식 발음

Which products have been discounted?
(A) Everything in Aisle 4.
(B) A special promotion.
(C) Yes, I have an account.

17 [3회] 캐나다식 발음 → 미국식 발음

When should we inform the audience about upcoming shows?
(A) There's an intermission in 30 minutes.
(B) In the main auditorium.
(C) Over 30 of the people here.

18 [3회] 호주식 발음 → 미국식 발음

Why haven't you ever owned a vehicle?
(A) Bring it to the automotive shop.
(B) My city has a great public transit system.
(C) I guess we can drive.

19 [3회] 영국식 발음 → 호주식 발음

Please don't forget to give me the files I requested.
(A) Don't worry about the ticket.
(B) You should pile the supplies in the corner.
(C) I wrote myself a reminder.

20 [3회] 캐나다식 발음 → 영국식 발음

How did the conference attendees like your lecture about social media?
(A) Their Web site is due for upgrades.
(B) By heading to Conference Room 1.
(C) Overall, it was a success.

21 [3회] 미국식 발음 → 캐나다식 발음

Are all the servers required to wear a uniform?
(A) They served snacks this afternoon.
(B) It is standard procedure.
(C) I think your outfit looks very nice.

22 [3회] 미국식 발음 → 호주식 발음

Should we order one or two desks for the office?
(A) I'm undecided.
(B) I will wait in the office.
(C) There are three lamps.

23 [3회] 영국식 발음 → 캐나다식 발음

Wouldn't you rather share a taxi to save money?
(A) We only accept cash.
(B) I'm riding with some friends.
(C) Taxes are going to increase.

24 [3회] 호주식 발음 → 영국식 발음

We're not sure how to make copies on this odd paper size.
(A) The tray has to be adjusted.
(B) You have a good idea.

(C) Our hats come in one size.

25 [3회] 캐나다식 발음 → 미국식 발음

A representative must inspect our factory in China, right?
(A) Some of the labor regulations.
(B) That won't be necessary.
(C) Yes, across from the plant.

26 [3회] 호주식 발음 → 영국식 발음

Do you know what the fastest route downtown is?
(A) Take Sonny Street.
(B) Oh, just set them down.
(C) I know how they feel.

27 [3회] 미국식 발음 → 캐나다식 발음

Will the architect be able to stop by for a consultation today?
(A) Well, the building has modern furnishings.
(B) A tour of the architecture in Delaware.
(C) Her assistant made an appointment for 3 P.M.

28 [3회] 영국식 발음 → 호주식 발음

How can I access my online bank account while I'm overseas?
(A) Our financial institution has expanded.
(B) Just log in using your normal information.
(C) You'll thoroughly enjoy traveling abroad.

29 [3회] 미국식 발음 → 캐나다식 발음

What is the plan for replacing Ms. Jenkins after her retirement?
(A) We're hoping to hire internally.
(B) Formal attire is required at the party.
(C) She's been with us for 30 years.

30 [3회] 호주식 발음 → 미국식 발음

This rental space is very conveniently located.
(A) It's on top of the microwave.
(B) I have a feeling it's overpriced.
(C) No, another parking space.

31 [3회] 영국식 발음 → 캐나다식 발음

Are you willing to write a reference letter on my behalf?
(A) All the résumés were left in that folder.
(B) If you don't need one until next week.
(C) Yes, both reference manuals.

PART 3

Questions 32-34 refer to the following conversation.

3₄) 영국식 발음 → 호주식 발음

W: Now that we've finished weeding the existing flowerbed, the new rose bushes must be planted along the front of the customer's house. This task will take us a couple of hours at most to complete, so we'll be done with it by lunchtime.

M: OK, but before we unload the plants, holes need to be dug for the bushes. I'll pull our shovels and work gloves out of the truck.

W: Could you also bring over the small cart? We'll use it to carry away the excess dirt.

M: Oh! I didn't remember to pack that this morning. I'd better go get it from our company's shed. Sorry about that.

Questions 35-37 refer to the following conversation.

3₄) 캐나다식 발음 → 미국식 발음

M: Welcome to Harvey Home Goods. How can I help you?

W: Yes. I need hooks that adhere to the wall—not ones that are drilled in—to hang paintings in my apartment.

M: Those are in Aisle 13, which is where we keep hardware and fixtures. Is there anything else I can give you a hand locating?

W: Thanks, but I'm pretty sure I remember where the other products I need are located.

M: All right. Just in case you have trouble finding other products, there's a . . . um . . . computer that you can use to search for store merchandise. The machine indicates where specific goods are shelved as well as whether they're in stock. It's situated near the front doors.

Questions 38-40 refer to the following conversation with three speakers.

3₄) 영국식 발음 → 호주식 발음 → 캐나다식 발음

W: I'm supposed to work at this cash register today, but the scanner isn't working. Do you think it might be broken?

M1: That's odd. Bill, could you help us out?

M2: Oh, I switched off the scanner this morning while cleaning the checkout area. You just need to switch it back on before your shift starts to reset it.

W: I see. How do I turn it back on?

M2: The switch is located on the left side of the scanner. Um, this is all in the manual under the register.

W: Thanks. I should probably review that again.

M1: That's a good idea. There's some other information in there that you need to know.

Questions 41-43 refer to the following conversation.

3₄) 캐나다식 발음 → 영국식 발음

M: I want to talk about the banquet Crest Financial hired us to organize. I'm worried that Goldfish, the band we hired, won't be able to perform. Have you heard from them?

W: I got an e-mail this morning. But that reminds me . . . Do we need to buy extra decorations for them?

M: I think the flowers and banners are enough.

W: Great. In that case, we don't have any more expenses to factor in, as our client has hired a catering company to provide the food.

M: Right. Our client will be pleased to know the budget is larger than necessary.

Questions 44-46 refer to the following conversation.

3₄) 미국식 발음 → 호주식 발음

W: Thank you for setting aside some time to talk with me, Mr. Gabo. Now, I'll explain why your retail outlet should stock the DirtDuster vacuum cleaner. First, the DirtDuster has a motor attached to the wheels, making it self-propelled. Plus, it can be used on hard surfaces as well as carpets.

M: I don't know. We already have the SwiftClean, which works well on wood floors.

W: But unlike the SwiftClean, the DirtDuster is guaranteed not to leave scratches on any surfaces. Consumer polls indicate that people really appreciate this aspect of the vacuum.

M: Well, I'd like you to demonstrate how the machine operates before I decide. You can use it on the floor in our staff kitchen, just down the hall.

Questions 47-49 refer to the following conversation with three speakers.

3₄) 캐나다식 발음 → 호주식 발음 → 미국식 발음

M1: Look at this. Someone must have accidentally poured a beverage on the lobby sofa.

M2: Yeah, I see what you mean. It still looks pretty wet, so it probably happened recently.

W: We should let the hotel receptionist know, so it can be dealt with.

M2: OK. I'll tell them about it now while we wait for our rooms to be prepared for us.

W: And could you ask them when the pool closes? I'd like to swim this evening before I head out for the music festival.

M1: Unfortunately, the singer we want to see starts performing at 8:30 P.M.—just an hour from now. So, I don't think we'll have time.

Questions 50-52 refer to the following conversation.

[3)] 캐나다식 발음 → 영국식 발음

M: Good morning, Michaela. Do you have all the information you'll need to make a notice for passengers about the subway system's new transit cards?

W: I think so. But just to confirm, the cards will be able to hold up to $500 worth of credit, right?

M: Correct. And funds can be added to them at the automated machines in each station. Riders can also put money on their cards by making an account on the transportation authority's Web site.

W: Great. Is there anything else that we need to tell people about?

M: The upcoming closure of Line 5 tomorrow, from 10 A.M. until noon.

W: Oh, yeah. I forgot all about that. I'll be sure to note it too.

Questions 53-55 refer to the following conversation.

[3)] 영국식 발음 → 호주식 발음

W: Good afternoon, Vincent. I want to let you know that Martin Marquez, the recently appointed manager of the Northeast district, is expected to come to our headquarters. The visit will give him an opportunity to acquaint himself with our CEO. He'll arrive on November 3—one month from now.

M: Hasn't a consultant been hired to give a talk about productivity to some of our staff on that date? If so, it might be hard to fit everything into the schedule, as there will be many activities going on.

W: I've actually requested that Mr. Marquez stop by on the same day so he can attend the lecture. I think he'd benefit from it because it will be targeted at middle management.

Questions 56-58 refer to the following conversation.

[3)] 미국식 발음 → 호주식 발음

W: Jake and I have been asked to take five workers who are visiting from our partner corporation in Japan out next week. And we're struggling to think of something fun to do with them rather than simply dining at a fancy restaurant.

M: How about renting a boat and taking them sailing for an evening? If you go around sunset, you can enjoy views of the Miami cityscape.

W: That's a wonderful suggestion, but would our boss approve something so costly?

M: It's more affordable than you'd expect. Boats can be rented from local businesses for as little as $1,200 a day. Our company has spent more than that on expensive meals for similarly sized groups.

Questions 59-61 refer to the following conversation.

[3)] 미국식 발음 → 캐나다식 발음

W: Preston, did you hear that I moved to a new office? I'm now in Room 206 . . . right opposite to the lift at the end of this hallway.

M: Mr. Collins mentioned that to me. Have you set everything up yet?

W: Actually, I still need to move a cabinet. Could you give me a hand?

M: Um, I'm experiencing some pain in my wrist. I'm not sure what happened, though.

W: I'm sorry to hear that. Have you seen a doctor?

M: Not yet. I'm hoping the pain will go away on its own.

W: Maybe you should give it some rest. I'm sure our manager could find someone to cover for you over the next few days if you ask.

Questions 62-64 refer to the following conversation and floor plan.

[3)] 캐나다식 발음 → 영국식 발음

M: Thanks again for letting me into the building on such short notice, Ms. Molden. I thought I was done working on the blueprints for your renovation project, but then I discovered that I was missing some information.

W: Oh, no problem. I'm just sorry I didn't answer your phone call right away. I was in a meeting all morning.

M: Don't worry about it. . . Now, as I mentioned in my message, I need to measure a wall to make sure the window you requested will fit properly. Once I do that, I'll be on my way.

W: Certainly. Which room do you need access to?

M: The one right across the lobby. It should only take a few minutes.

Questions 65-67 refer to the following conversation and map.

[3)] 호주식 발음 → 미국식 발음

M: During Wednesday's hiking trip, let's rest and have a picnic lunch before reaching the observation point on Mt. Evans.

W: Great suggestion. I can swing by a convenience store and buy some snacks and soft drinks for us. I'll just do that on my way to meet you at Grove Station on Wednesday morning.

M: Sounds good. I'll pack sandwiches too. How about having our picnic at a waterfall alongside Ridge Road?

W: I recently heard that path is blocked off. Apparently, last week's storm knocked down some large trees on it that have yet to be cleared away. But there's another spot at the intersection of Breeze Road and Peak Road. I think it'll be comfortable there.

3 캐나다식 발음 → 영국식 발음

M: Hannah, did you end up ordering new jackets to be used in the photo shoot for our magazine's October issue?

W: Yes, Raymond. They'll be delivered on August 16. I also submitted a complaint about the shirts that arrived on August 9. I mentioned that they had tears in them in an e-mail to Nextwear's manager, Ken Powers. He responded a few days later and attached a discount coupon.

M: Nicely done. Oh, by the way, have you received an e-mail from the photographer, Linda Wright? She had a question about whether she can be compensated for the cost of her taxi ride to the shoot location.

W: I replied to that right after this morning's press conference regarding our October edition.

PART 4

3 영국식 발음

Hello, Ms. Han. This is Sunmi Park calling from Edge Designs. I want to inform you about an issue regarding the project you commissioned us to do. Although the T-shirts that my firm is designing for your organization are supposed to be ready by this Thursday, they will not be done by then. One of our staff members was sick the last two days, so the work is taking longer than expected to finish. As a result, we won't be able to send the completed products to you until Friday. I'm very sorry, and we intend to take 10 percent off your final bill to make up for the delay. If you have any inquiries, please reach out to me. I'd be happy to answer them.

3 캐나다식 발음

I have an important announcement for all administrative staff. Over the weekend, a technician installed a new operating system on all of the computers in our clinic. Unfortunately, some data was lost in the process. Patient medical records were not affected, but the schedule for the upcoming week was accidentally deleted. So, we have to contact our patients immediately to find out the dates and times of their appointments. This is currently our top priority, as we don't know who has an appointment tomorrow. Our lead receptionist—Janet Lee—will now hand out a list of patients and their contact information. You each will be assigned 70 of them to call.

3 미국식 발음

Hello, Mr. Campbell. It's Denise Reynolds. I may have found a suitable tenant for the apartment you are trying to lease out through my firm. A visiting researcher at Forest University named Brad Patterson contacted me about it. He wants to rent your home until September 1. Um, you asked me to find someone to take the apartment until the end of September, but . . . most people don't want to stay long. Mr. Patterson would like to visit your place this week. I know you work on Thursday and Friday, so how about on the weekend? He mentioned that he was free on Saturday afternoon. Call me at 555-0394 to let me know what time would be best.

3 호주식 발음

Our CEO organized this four-day retreat for managers in order to express gratitude for the hard work you have done. She recognizes that you all strive to perform at a high level and wants you to know that you are essential to the firm's success. Now, in addition to relaxing and enjoying this beautiful resort, we're going to carry out a few team-building exercises together over the next few days. While the exercises are designed to be lighthearted and fun, they will also give you a chance to enhance your communication abilities. One more thing . . . The CEO would like a picture of everyone together. So, please meet in the resort's main event room at 4 P.M.

3 미국식 발음

In local news, the Meyerville city council voted to tear down the historic city hall building on July 12. The decision comes after an inspection last year uncovered cracks in the foundation. For months, the government debated whether to undertake costly renovations or simply demolish the facility. Mayor John Hamilton held a press conference this morning, during which he announced plans to build a public park in the building's lot. The city council will hold a special session to discuss the design of the new park this Friday at 7 P.M. at Fairview High School. Residents are encouraged to attend and share their ideas.

3 호주식 발음

Thank you all for coming this evening. During the next hour, we're going to be discussing some of the exciting new projects Burlington Associates is involved with, including a shopping center near the waterfront and an office tower on the north side. We hope that these investment opportunities will interest you. Right now, I'm passing out copies of a pamphlet that goes into further detail about these projects. Please take the time to go through it carefully. Overall, this has been our most productive year yet, with over eight developments in progress. We've really come a long way since our founding five years ago.

Questions 89–91 refer to the following speech.

영국식 발음

The Snow and Ice Festival has grown considerably in recent years, and it now attracts many visitors from overseas. This increase in the number of international travelers has a very positive impact on Brenton City's economy. Your goal for today is to figure out how to promote the festival to foreign tourists and continue this trend. Just keep in mind that most guests find the snow sculptures and ice palace to be the two most impressive features of the festival. So, those attractions should be emphasized in our campaign. All right, I'd now like everyone to split up into small groups and brainstorm ideas. Then, in about half an hour, break for lunch.

Questions 92–94 refer to the following excerpt from a workshop.

캐나다식 발음

I'm Milo Forsythe, and I was hired to provide training on how to manage complaints. As new employees of the customer service department, it's important that you know how to effectively respond when someone is unhappy with one of the company's products. This is because handling a complaint well can actually lead to increased customer satisfaction and loyalty. To better demonstrate this point, I'd like to do a simple role-play exercise. One of you will be an upset customer, and I'll be the company representative. Pay close attention to how I deal with the situation by validating the other person's experience. You may be surprised by the results. Hopefully, you will use this technique when interacting with customers.

Questions 95–97 refer to the following advertisement and schedule.

호주식 발음

Are you looking for ways to save money on airfare and accommodations? Then be sure to tune in to 108.6 FM's newest program, *The Frugal Traveler*. Hosted by Jeff Wallace, who ran his own travel agency for 25 years before retiring, the program will provide tips on how to stretch your budget while on vacation. Jeff will set aside time each day to respond to questions from listeners, and callers will have their names entered into a monthly draw to win a flight to any major city in Europe with Omega Air. *The Frugal Traveler* will air Wednesday afternoons, starting May 2. It will fill the time slot immediately after our local traffic update. Make sure to check it out!

Questions 98–100 refer to the following telephone message and receipt.

영국식 발음

My name is Janis Lyle, and I rented a car from your company when I visited a client in Manchester last week. While filling out an application for reimbursement from my company, I noticed an error on my receipt. I was told that if I upgraded to a larger vehicle, I would receive the navigation system for free, but I realize now that I was charged for it. I'd like to have that amount refunded to my credit card. In addition, I . . . ah . . . I've got one more request. Your Web site mentions that your company has a rewards program. Could you send me a brochure that describes the benefits of membership? I'm going to be taking a lot of business trips this year, so I might sign up. Thanks.

* 무료 해석은 해커스토익(Hackers.co.kr)에서 다운로드 받을 수 있습니다.

* QR 코드로 바로가기

PART 1

1 호주식 발음

(A) People are pouring some beverages.
(B) People are spreading out platters.
(C) People are holding wine glasses.
(D) People are sitting across from each other.

2 영국식 발음

(A) A glass door is being cleaned.
(B) Some stools are unoccupied.
(C) Tables are arranged in a row.
(D) Some menus are open on the counter.

3 캐나다식 발음

(A) A woman is waving at a group.
(B) A woman is photographing a tree.
(C) The men are setting up a camera.
(D) The men are posing for a picture.

4 미국식 발음

(A) A power tool has been left in a case.
(B) An electrical cord is being coiled.
(C) A worker is cutting the base of a pole.
(D) A ladder has been propped against a wall.

5 영국식 발음

(A) She's removing fabric from a machine.
(B) She's connecting a pipe to a device.
(C) She's pulling a laundry cart.
(D) She's laying a sheet on the floor.

6 캐나다식 발음

(A) Some equipment is being carried indoors.
(B) A monitor is mounted on the wall.
(C) A room has been decorated with patterned paper.
(D) Some weights have been stored in a box.

PART 2

7 미국식 발음 → 호주식 발음

When can I buy tickets for a semi-final game?
(A) No, I'm fine.
(B) Right now, the score is tied.
(C) The first week of June.

8 캐나다식 발음 → 영국식 발음

What's included in the gift bag for visitors?
(A) Thank you for the present.
(B) Items displaying our company's name.
(C) Give Kevin a few more plates.

9 미국식 발음 → 캐나다식 발음

Have you finished the report on our competitor's new product yet?
(A) There was a lot of competition.
(B) Mr. Madden is looking it over.
(C) I want to buy a newer model.

10 호주식 발음 → 미국식 발음

Who is going to talk first at the economics forum?
(A) It begins at 9:30 tomorrow morning.
(B) The president of the research firm.
(C) Yes, I've got the transcript here.

11 영국식 발음 → 호주식 발음

Can't we go to the theater later in the week?
(A) It's not my second visit.
(B) A new play by a local writer.
(C) No, we reserved seats for this evening.

12 미국식 발음 → 캐나다식 발음

Has the package been delivered yet?
(A) There is no charge for delivery.
(B) Check with the other receptionist.
(C) I ordered it online.

13 영국식 발음 → 캐나다식 발음

What's the matter with your briefcase?
(A) That's very interesting.
(B) Juice was spilled on it.
(C) My car is fine.

14 영국식 발음 → 호주식 발음

How would you like to spend the afternoon?
(A) If you'd like to.
(B) Because I spent too much money.
(C) I haven't given it much thought.

15 영국식 발음 → 미국식 발음

Should we distribute awards to staff now or after dinner?
(A) Not everyone has arrived yet.
(B) I'll have the tomato soup.
(C) Our main distribution center.

16 미국식 발음 → 캐나다식 발음

Mr. Willis from the payroll department called for me, right?
(A) All the supplies have been paid for.
(B) Here's my extension number.
(C) No, he was looking for Andrea.

17 캐나다식 발음 → 영국식 발음

Are employees cataloging complaints that we receive from customers?
(A) It's the product catalog.
(B) That's what I've been told.
(C) Only a few workers were disappointed.

18 미국식 발음 → 호주식 발음

Don't purchases over €75 qualify for free shipping?
(A) Payments can be made over the phone.
(B) Take these parcels as well.
(C) We no longer offer that service.

19 호주식 발음 → 영국식 발음

When can you update the bulletin board?
(A) Generally, Steven takes care of it.
(B) The most up-to-date medications.
(C) We upgraded the network last month.

20 영국식 발음 → 캐나다식 발음

Mr. Adams, where should we discuss the Ford Project?
(A) As soon as I return from my meeting.
(B) The second-floor conference room isn't being used.
(C) Everyone is pleased with the project.

21 미국식 발음 → 캐나다식 발음

Supervisors must strictly adhere to established regulations.
(A) The store was established a decade ago.
(B) What about in special circumstances?
(C) Management provided lunch.

22 영국식 발음 → 호주식 발음

Did Ms. LaPlante request extra towels and pillows, or just pillows?
(A) Because I'm going to the pool.
(B) Additional interns.
(C) She'd like both.

23 캐나다식 발음 → 미국식 발음

Have you had a chance to train the new waitress?
(A) Not as of yet.
(B) No, we'd better head to Platform 2.
(C) There's a chance it might snow.

24 영국식 발음 → 캐나다식 발음

Are you aware that we can't use our normal route to work?
(A) There's a way to fix the device.
(B) You'll find them quite useful.
(C) Yes, a lane is being added to Highway 43.

25 미국식 발음 → 호주식 발음

Which of these printers has wireless capabilities?
(A) As far as I know, that's right.
(B) A small section of wire.
(C) They all do.

26 호주식 발음 → 영국식 발음

None of our guests have dietary restrictions, do they?
(A) We've been granted restricted access.
(B) Those details are written on this sheet.
(C) None of the vehicles.

27 캐나다식 발음 → 미국식 발음

Some of this produce is beginning to spoil.
(A) I just started this week.
(B) Factory production levels.
(C) Please replace it with fresh vegetables.

28 캐나다식 발음 → 영국식 발음

Why didn't you ask me for a ride from the airport?
(A) I made other arrangements.
(B) I asked for a window seat.
(C) At the international airport.

29 호주식 발음 → 미국식 발음

This wristwatch has to be engraved with a client's name.
(A) My wrist still hurts.
(B) OK, but it can't be done until tomorrow.
(C) Yes, watch out for the beam.

30 캐나다식 발음 → 영국식 발음

Why don't I ask the engineers to improve this prototype?
(A) No, we don't own any.
(B) Tell them to apply our feedback.
(C) Research and development costs.

31 미국식 발음 → 호주식 발음

These machines ought to be unloaded immediately.
(A) We should order them soon.
(B) Do you mean the dishwashers?
(C) All downloads are free of charge.

PART 3

Questions 32-34 refer to the following conversation.

[3(1)] 영국식 발음 → 캐나다식 발음

W: Hi, Mark. Our department head wants me to arrange the corporation's year-end party. However, I'm not sure when it should be hosted. How about December 21?

M: Could you think about choosing another day? The 21st is when the Tampa Bay Hurricanes plays in the championship ice hockey game, and I know a lot of staff plan to watch that.

W: Thanks for reminding me. Would December 22 be better, then?

M: Definitely. Also, I can help out by sending a notice to fellow employees. So, let me know once you settle on a specific time and the other details.

Questions 35-37 refer to the following conversation.

[3(1)] 영국식 발음 → 호주식 발음

W: Excuse me, I'd like to see the 8:00 P.M. screening of *Voyage Across Australia*.

M: I'm sorry. But tickets for that and all other show times tonight have been sold out. You may book a seat for tomorrow night, however.

W: I didn't realize the movie was that popular. I have to be at the office tomorrow night. Will the film still be playing at the theater next week?

M: Yes. In fact, Andy Baker, the director, will be present for a question and answer session following the screening next Wednesday at 3:30 P.M. You can find out more information about that by reading the flyer posted behind you.

Questions 38-40 refer to the following conversation.

[3(1)] 미국식 발음 → 캐나다식 발음

W: Hello. I need a car for next week. I know it's a holiday weekend, but will your company have any available?

M: Well, no. But, we will have a van. Do you mind driving a larger vehicle?

W: I've driven a van before. But we only have a $400 budget for this.

M: I've got a 10-seat van available for $360 a week. Would you like to get started on the paperwork? There are a couple of forms you need to complete.

W: Sure. Here's my driver's license.

Questions 41-43 refer to the following conversation.

[3(1)] 호주식 발음 → 영국식 발음

M: Did you hear about the policy change for business travel expenses? Employees will have to submit relevant receipts within at least three days following the end date of a trip.

W: But that means I'll need to get the paperwork from my recent visit to our warehouse in Dubai in order by today. I won't have time for that.

M: Don't worry. The rule doesn't take effect until the end of next month.

W: That's a relief. Why is the policy being modified?

M: The goal is to improve efficiency within the financial department.

W: Makes sense. Last week, the head of the division was actually telling me how hard it is to track costs when people aren't timely about turning in their receipts.

Questions 44-46 refer to the following conversation.

[3(1)] 미국식 발음 → 호주식 발음

W: Excuse me. I checked out some novels here earlier today, and I may have left my wallet somewhere near this circulation desk. Has one been found recently?

M: Not to my knowledge. However, I think you'd better visit our lost-and-found center just one floor up. Someone could have possibly picked it up and brought it there.

W: I see. Also, I'm wondering if it's possible to borrow these DVDs without my library card. Unfortunately, my card was also in my wallet.

M: Certainly. We have your account in our system, so I can go ahead and do that for you. May I ask for your account number?

Questions 47-49 refer to the following conversation.

[3(1)] 영국식 발음 → 캐나다식 발음

W: The Sporting Supplier. This is Wanda. What can I help you with?

M: I'd like to ask about a tennis racquet I found on your homepage—the Kendell Swift XE. I'm wondering if these racquets come with spare grips for the handle or if those would need to be purchased separately.

W: All tennis racquets come with just one standard grip. But we offer a variety of other grips that absorb shock and reduce hand strain. Those can be added on for an extra charge.

M: OK. I'm interested in the shock-absorbing types, so I'll take another look online this afternoon and see what specific options are available. Thanks.

Questions 50-52 refer to the following conversation.

[3(1)] 미국식 발음 → 호주식 발음

W: Hi, Charlie. I'm having dinner with our investment consultant in Brownville in 30 minutes, but I forgot my day planner at the office. It contains the name and address of the restaurant we agreed to meet at, which I need.

M: Yes, it's right here on your desk. Is it OK if I open it and find those details?

W: Please do. Is there a sticky note attached to the page with the information for the meeting with Charles Grand?

M: Indeed. It says that you have a table booked at El Toro Bistro on 45 Weston Avenue.

Questions 53-55 refer to the following conversation.

영국식 발음 → 캐나다식 발음

W: Hi, Michael. Mr. Hoffman, the marketing director, asked me to book the flights for the conference in San Francisco. Do you think a 6 A.M. departure on May 23 would be too early?

M: The first day of the conference will likely be really busy. I'd rather get there the night before so we are well rested. Would that be possible?

W: Mr. Hoffman mentioned a team meeting scheduled for May 22.

M: Hmm . . . I wasn't aware of that. Actually, May 23 doesn't sound that bad. I'll pack a smaller bag for the trip.

Questions 56-58 refer to the following conversation with three speakers.

호주식 발음 → 캐나다식 발음 → 미국식 발음

M1: Alright, I think I'm ready to head over to Manfred Park for lunch with our cycling group.

M2: I'm ready as well. In fact, I've already put the drinks in my car.

W: Wait. There's one problem. I left the cheese on the counter all night by mistake, and now it's no good.

M2: Oh, that's a shame. Why don't Mitch and I get more on the way to the park?

M1: Hmm . . . I don't think we will pass by a place to buy cheese.

W: That's OK. I'll grab some when I pick up Mr. Pearson. His apartment is next door to a supermarket.

Questions 59-61 refer to the following conversation with three speakers.

호주식 발음 → 미국식 발음 → 영국식 발음

M: I just got back from the banquet hall where our CEO will give his address tomorrow. Um . . . I'm worried that the hall we rented will be uncomfortably warm for the participants.

W1: I noticed that too. I tried to lower the temperature on the air-conditioning, but it seems to be locked on one setting.

M: Who do we contact about this?

W2: I was told to call Mr. Bentley, the head of the facility's maintenance department, if we need help setting things up.

M: Alright, then. Jordy, could you dial him up for me? I don't have his number.

W1: Sure. Just one second.

Questions 62-64 refer to the following conversation and schedule.

캐나다식 발음 → 영국식 발음

M: Sarah, I saw that the Langley Community Center has started holding lectures this month. Some of the topics seem really interesting. Do you want to check one out this week?

W: Unfortunately, I'm flying to Dallas tomorrow for a class reunion. It's been years since I've seen most of my old friends from school. I probably won't return until the end of the week.

M: Too bad. Do you need a ride to the airport?

W: That would be great. Thanks! And why don't we attend a lecture next week?

M: OK. I should have some time on Monday or Tuesday.

W: Hmm . . . I think I'm more interested in learning how to take care of my plants than decorating my home.

Questions 65-67 refer to the following conversation and floor directory.

미국식 발음 → 캐나다식 발음

W: Welcome to Desmond Electronics. How can I help you today?

M: I have a parcel for Donald Grayson. I went to the third floor as the address indicates, but I couldn't find him.

W: Just let me check. . . OK, Mr. Grayson's department recently moved one floor up. One of the staff members will direct you to his office.

M: Thanks so much for you help.

W: No problem. One question, though . . . Is your truck out front? If it is, you'll need to park it behind the building.

M: Really? Why's that?

W: You will have to pay a fine if you leave it on the street for more than 15 minutes.

Questions 68-70 refer to the following conversation and graph.

호주식 발음 → 미국식 발음

M: Gina, has the environmental assessment that Skylark Incorporated commissioned our research firm to conduct been completed?

W: It has. I was in charge of carrying it out, and everything went smoothly.

M: Good. If I remember correctly, the company is concerned with rainfall levels.

W: That's right—in four counties that it's considering constructing an amusement park.

M: So, I assume you recommend that the firm build at the driest location of the ones analyzed.

W: No, actually. That one isn't suitable, since land costs there exceed Skylark's budget. As a result, we recommended the next best option.

#### PART 4

Questions 71-73 refer to the following telephone message.

[3w] 미국식 발음

Cynthia, it's Haley Vincent. I know you're busy preparing for the convention in Orlando you'll be attending on behalf of our investment company, but I could really use your help. I'm presenting some information about a couple of stocks to a client on Monday. I'm a little nervous because I've never done that before. It'd be great if you could go over my notes and visual materials with me beforehand. I want to make sure everything is in order. Oh, also, do you happen to know of any good vegetarian places in town? I might go for lunch with the client after the meeting, and he doesn't eat meat. Thanks in advance, and I'll talk to you soon.

Questions 74-76 refer to the following speech.

[3w] 호주식 발음

Thank you all very much for being here to celebrate the release of our company's latest device, the Access Portable Charger. I would like to give Patricia Sanderson from the design team special praise today. She came up with the idea to include a flashlight function in the charger. This feature has proven popular with online reviewers who were given the device in advance. They say it makes this the perfect charger for a camping trip, which should result in more sales. Now, please turn your attention to the screen at the front of the room . . . A commercial for the Access Portable Charger will air on several major TV networks starting tomorrow, and I'd like to give you a sneak preview.

Questions 77-79 refer to the following excerpt from a meeting.

[3w] 영국식 발음

Let me address the following before we finish the meeting. Thanks to the laptop promotion that we recently introduced, our quarterly sales have increased by 10 percent. There are many students studying at universities in this state. I know we originally planned to offer discounted rates for only three months, but I think we should keep them for at least another year . . . and maybe even consider making them permanent. If students become accustomed to using our products, they are likely to remain our customers once they graduate. Please brainstorm some new ideas on how to attract even more students. Let's meet again tomorrow to discuss those.

Questions 80-82 refer to the following talk.

[3w] 미국식 발음

OK . . . My name is Sarah Edwards, and I'll be showing you around our tire manufacturing facility today. As new employees, it's important that you be familiar with the various sections. Now, we usually visit the tire testing laboratory first during these orientation tours. But, since researchers are currently wrapping up an urgent study, I've been asked to do the tour in reverse order today. So, we'll start by heading to the viewing deck of our assembly line room. Throughout the tour, please refrain from placing your hands or fingers on any of the machines. Are there any questions before we begin?

Questions 83-85 refer to the following instructions.

[3w] 호주식 발음

In the last part of our training for new employees today, I'll talk about taking a cash deposit. To do this, you should first give customers a deposit slip to fill out. While they write on the form, you can pull up their bank account information. If the information cannot be found by looking at the customer's bank card, you should just call a supervisor. Um, we have been having some issues with our computer system. Next, count the money carefully and put it in the drawer by your desk. Remember, after every shift, all of the cash in this container should be moved to the secured area in the back of the bank. Any questions?

Questions 86-88 refer to the following advertisement.

[3w] 캐나다식 발음

Are you a singer or musician looking for your first big break? Then Star Broadcast Network's newest program is for you! *Music Icon* is a talent competition that will end with one participant receiving a contract with a major entertainment company. On the show, a panel of celebrity judges—which varies every week—will eliminate one contestant. And once there are only three participants left, the viewers alone will get to select the winner. We'll be holding auditions across the country from May 11 until June 15 to select our competitors. So sign up for the one in the city closest to you today! Visit our Web site for a list of audition sites.

Questions 89-91 refer to the following talk.

[3w] 호주식 발음

I'd like to start by saying that it's a great honor to be able to participate in this lecture series at James College. Several speakers have already given excellent talks, and I hope that you'll find mine as engaging as theirs. Now . . . the focus of my lecture is the impact that fiction has on society. Specifically, I'm going to look at how one popular novel . . . um, *The Looking Glass* by Jack Coyle . . . led to several reforms to the legal system. If you haven't read Coyle's book, don't panic. I'll hand out the relevant excerpts from it now, so you can refer to them during my lecture.

Questions 92–94 refer to the following telephone message.

미국식 발음

Hi, Mr. Davidson. My name is Theresa Short, and I teach marketing at Chicago Business College. I was wondering if you'd be interested in speaking to my class of marketing graduate students. I recently stumbled across a video of one of your advertising lectures, and I found it very instructive. And, according to your Web site, you're currently available to give guest talks. I'm sure my students would greatly benefit from your knowledge and experience. Let me know if and when you're available and what your speaking fee would be. My class ends at the beginning of December.

Questions 95–97 refer to the following announcement and floor plan.

영국식 발음

Attention, everyone. Before we open today, I just want to remind you that our clothing store is having a sale this week in honor of the holidays. Make sure to tell customers that over 20 of our best-selling sportswear items are marked down. The display has been set up in the aisle closest to the main entrance, so it will be the first thing people see when they enter the store. Oh . . . one more thing. We're going to close down for two days toward the end of the month so that our checkout area can be expanded. I'll announce the dates tomorrow after I have met with a representative of the interior design firm doing the work.

Questions 98–100 refer to the following announcement and chart.

캐나다식 발음

Ever since we started working on the Raymon Arena Project last month, things have been very busy. The tight deadlines have created problems for some of you architects, which we need to address. If you look at this flow chart, you'll see that our normal work process for drafting blueprints includes five steps. However, for the rest of this project, I want you to draft blueprints right after meeting with clients. I think eliminating one step will expedite the work process. Now, I want to say a few things about a new city regulation that we need to take into account when designing the stadium. It'll only take a few minutes.

* 무료 해석은 해커스토익(Hackers.co.kr)에서
다운로드 받을 수 있습니다.

* QR 코드로
바로가기

PART 1

1 호주식 발음
(A) He's carrying some jackets.
(B) He's riding an escalator.
(C) He's weighing a suitcase.
(D) He's waiting for an elevator.

2 영국식 발음
(A) Some men are operating devices.
(B) Some men are moving a couch.
(C) Some men are clearing a table.
(D) Some men are setting up a computer.

3 캐나다식 발음
(A) She is plugging a cable into a printer.
(B) She is copying some pages.
(C) She is placing a book on a shelf.
(D) She is sliding paper into a tray.

4 미국식 발음
(A) Some outfits are on display.
(B) A shelf has been disassembled.
(C) A mannequin is being set up.
(D) Some clothing is being folded.

5 영국식 발음
(A) They are stepping down from a curb.
(B) They are tying their shoelaces.
(C) They are lifting bags with their hands.
(D) They are walking next to each other.

6 미국식 발음
(A) Containers are being piled up on a deck.
(B) Passengers are disembarking from a ship.
(C) A vessel is sailing through the water.
(D) Storage crates are being unloaded from
   a boat.

PART 2

7 호주식 발음 → 미국식 발음
When did you start seeking another job?
(A) A few days ago.
(B) It's a good start.

(C) At the employment agency.

8 영국식 발음 → 캐나다식 발음
How long did medical school take for you to
complete?
(A) I'm glad they're finally done.
(B) Dr. Robinson is my physician.
(C) Almost six years.

9 캐나다식 발음 → 미국식 발음
What date should we get together?
(A) Let me get a table.
(B) We left on July 21.
(C) I'm not really sure.

10 영국식 발음 → 호주식 발음
Who left these tools out all night?
(A) Yes, put them in here.
(B) The entire evening.
(C) I did.

11 미국식 발음 → 영국식 발음
Was the moving company willing to reschedule on
short notice?
(A) I appreciate your being so flexible.
(B) It fortunately was.
(C) By moving the furniture.

12 호주식 발음 → 미국식 발음
Don't you want to apply to become the department
head?
(A) Toward the head of the line.
(B) A late departure time.
(C) I don't feel ready for it.

13 캐나다식 발음 → 영국식 발음
How did tennis with Mitch go on Monday?
(A) Youth tennis courses are popular.
(B) We both enjoyed it.
(C) Can he drive on Tuesday instead?

14 호주식 발음 → 영국식 발음
Why is the CEO leaving early?
(A) He has to take part in a workshop.
(B) Probably around 8:30.
(C) His name is Steve Erickson.

15 미국식 발음 → 캐나다식 발음
I plan to purchase a house later this fall.
(A) I want to see your place once you move.
(B) In the bedroom.
(C) The blueprints have gone missing.

16. 캐나다식 발음 → 미국식 발음

What event did you and Jonas go to last weekend?
(A) There's a fashion show tomorrow.
(B) We saw a concert in New Jersey.
(C) He decided to.

17. 호주식 발음 → 영국식 발음

Aren't we operating a booth at the agricultural convention?
(A) Our overseas operations.
(B) There weren't any spaces available.
(C) Driving would be more convenient.

18. 캐나다식 발음 → 미국식 발음

Have you enrolled in a photography class yet?
(A) Glass items should be recycled.
(B) He takes nice pictures.
(C) Yes, it begins tomorrow.

19. 호주식 발음 → 영국식 발음

I'm supposed to film a video of the guest speaker, right?
(A) You can use this equipment.
(B) The video was very well produced.
(C) I suppose we'll require a vehicle.

20. 영국식 발음 → 캐나다식 발음

The gym on Halifax Road is now open.
(A) Just close the door.
(B) I'll stop by later today.
(C) No, I canceled my membership.

21. 미국식 발음 → 호주식 발음

Why don't we update the information on our Web site?
(A) You can order it online.
(B) The site on Oak Street.
(C) Yes, that's long overdue.

22. 캐나다식 발음 → 영국식 발음

The fabric for the new curtain will arrive very soon.
(A) That's good to know.
(B) The window in the kitchen.
(C) The shuttle bus hasn't arrived.

23. 호주식 발음 → 미국식 발음

When must my existing credit card balance be paid?
(A) I believe I've been overcharged.
(B) You gave me those cards.
(C) By the end of the month.

24. 영국식 발음 → 캐나다식 발음

Is Brandon still taking his break, or did he return to work?
(A) We took Flight 362.
(B) I still need supplies.
(C) He's at his desk right now.

25. 호주식 발음 → 영국식 발음

We should hold a training session for new employees.
(A) All former personnel.
(B) I've already organized one.
(C) Basic software skills.

26. 영국식 발음 → 호주식 발음

Is the marketing presentation going to be completed by Friday?
(A) We're actually ahead of schedule.
(B) I didn't attend the seminar.
(C) Wilbur's Supermarket has specials every day.

27. 캐나다식 발음 → 미국식 발음

Will you take care of the office plants or should I ask Karen to do it?
(A) A pot of flowers.
(B) I'd be happy to help.
(C) I'll be more careful next time.

28. 호주식 발음 → 미국식 발음

Where can I set up a workstation?
(A) The statue has been erected.
(B) I thought you were assigned to another division.
(C) Anytime after lunch.

29. 영국식 발음 → 캐나다식 발음

The sales forecast has changed due to the shortage of raw materials.
(A) It's a pretty short documentary.
(B) I just heard the weather forecast.
(C) By how much?

30. 캐나다식 발음 → 영국식 발음

Are your current sneakers as comfortable as your previous pair?
(A) I'd say they're fairly similar.
(B) This color suits you better.
(C) She bought them yesterday.

31. 호주식 발음 → 미국식 발음

Which type of cake should we bring to Louis's birthday party?
(A) He was very pleased with the gift.
(B) Yes, try the ice cream too.
(C) I had to choose last time.

PART 3

Questions 32-34 refer to the following conversation.

미국식 발음 → 캐나다식 발음

W: I just heard that Malinda can't stay until 5 P.M. Her son isn't feeling well, so she has to leave work early in order to get him from school. Would you be able to cover her duties?

M: Sure. But can you be more specific about what I'll need to do?

W: She's currently checking in gym members and answering phone calls at the main desk, so I'd like you to do that. Seeing as you used to be a receptionist at an advertising company, you should be able to handle everything.

M: Well, I'm not very familiar with our registration system, but I'm sure I'll manage.

Questions 35-37 refer to the following conversation.

영국식 발음 → 호주식 발음

W: It seems as if more people have been stopping by our store in recent weeks. That's probably because we've started selling albums that are hard to find on the Internet.

M: Yes, I think you're right. But we're still losing a lot of customers to online music retailers. To ensure that people keep coming, we should ask some regional bands and singers to appear here at our business.

W: Funny you should suggest that. I've already reached out to several jazz and blues musicians in the area to see if they could come and sign autographs here. That's what many customers indicated they want in our satisfaction survey.

Questions 38-40 refer to the following conversation.

영국식 발음 → 캐나다식 발음

W: Excuse me. I'd like to leave my car in this indoor parking lot for a couple of hours while I run some errands. My husband works at a dental clinic down the street, and he gave me his parking pass. Can I use it here?

M: Unfortunately, it looks like your husband's pass expired two days ago. You'll have to pay to use our space.

W: Oh, OK. How does the payment process work?

M: The fee for parking is $3.50 an hour. Here . . . I'll print a new ticket for you. When you leave, you can insert it into the machine located near the exit and pay using cash or credit card.

Questions 41-43 refer to the following conversation.

미국식 발음 → 호주식 발음

W: Tyler, have you read the quarterly budget report yet?

M: No. I'm planning to look through it on Thursday. I have to fly to Birmingham this afternoon for a trade show, and I won't be back until Wednesday evening. Why? Is there a problem?

W: Actually, there is. The company's operating expenses have skyrocketed over the past few months. The CEO wants our team to develop some cost-cutting measures and introduce them in a staff meeting tomorrow morning. We don't have much time to prepare, so I could really use a hand.

M: I'll take a later flight, then.

Questions 44-46 refer to the following conversation.

영국식 발음 → 캐나다식 발음

W: I'm thinking of getting lunch at the cafeteria in our office building today. Do you want to join me?

M: No, thanks. I ate there when I started working here, and the food wasn't very good. I would prefer to dine at a restaurant.

W: Did you know that the food service company at our facility was changed last month in response to feedback from staff? Beatrice Dining now provides meals. I find their dishes to be delicious.

M: I probably missed that piece of news while I was on vacation three weeks ago. In that case, I'd be happy to come along. Just let me finish writing this e-mail message first.

Questions 47-49 refer to the following conversation.

호주식 발음 → 미국식 발음

M: Hi. Are you here to pick up a repaired item?

W: No, I'm not. I'd like to have my phone looked at. It's a Gentro M4. Um, the battery doesn't last very long anymore. I'm trying to decide whether to just replace the battery or to buy a new phone.

M: It'll only cost you $35 for a replacement battery, and that should last at least half a year. The new Gentro model will be released next quarter.

W: Oh, OK. Thanks for letting me know.

M: Also, there are steps you can take to manage your phone's power consumption. Here, I'll show you how to change some settings. We just need to open the Options menu.

Questions 50-52 refer to the following conversation.

캐나다식 발음 → 영국식 발음

M: My name is Stanley Coburn. When I logged in to my library account today, I saw that I have an overdue book. But I never received a voice mail reminder about this. I'm a little upset about the situation.

W: We switched to sending notices by e-mail last month, Mr. Coburn. You should've received a message about the development.

M: Really? I check my e-mails regularly, and I never

received one. Maybe the library hasn't been using my correct e-mail address.

W: I apologize for the inconvenience. Umm . . . here's what I can do . . . If you return the book today, you won't have to pay a late fee.

Questions 53-55 refer to the following conversation with three speakers.

美 미국식 발음 → 캐나다식 발음 → 호주식 발음

W: Before we wrap up this meeting, let's talk about the position we need to fill in the bookkeeping department. After going through the applications, I think Sheryl Johnson looks promising.

M1: I agree. I was really impressed by her responses during the interview on Monday. What do you think, Dave?

M2: I don't know. She doesn't have much experience working in the financial field.

W: It shouldn't be an issue, though. It's an entry-level position.

M1: Right. She'll receive on-the-job training.

M2: That's a good point. I don't have any objections to hiring her, then.

W: OK. But I should talk to the department head before making a final decision. I'll do that now.

Questions 56-58 refer to the following conversation with three speakers.

美 캐나다식 발음 → 영국식 발음 → 미국식 발음

M: Do you know why we're shutting down rides in the park an hour early tonight?

W1: There will be fireworks in the main plaza this evening.

M: I didn't know about that. Did you, Amy?

W2: Sure did. This month, we're celebrating the first anniversary of our opening. As a result, there's a special event each week. The schedule is posted in the staff break room.

M: Oh, odd. I never saw that throughout the week.

W1: I see. Well, it's in there. OK, we'd better get back to work. Don't forget to place closing signs near the ride entrances in 20 minutes.

Questions 59-61 refer to the following conversation.

美 미국식 발음 → 캐나다식 발음

W: Hi. I'd like to buy a watch as a gift for my assistant, since he was really helpful while I was creating my latest clothing line.

M: Certainly. Our store has a number of great choices. For instance, this piece has a leather band and costs $145.

W: I really like that. But . . . It looks like the face on it is cracked. See here? Do you have any others in stock? If so, I'll take it.

M: My apologies. Yes, let me grab another from our back room.

W: By the way, I'd appreciate it if you could gift-wrap it too. That'll save me the hassle of doing it myself.

Questions 62-64 refer to the following conversation and graph.

美 영국식 발음 → 호주식 발음

W: I was wondering, Adam . . . Have our subscriber numbers risen since we expanded our streaming service's selection of sports in May?

M: Not as much as we'd hoped. At our strategy meeting, we set the goal of reaching 100,000 subscribers in each country that our service is available in. We've hit this target in the country we first launched in. But we're not there yet in the other ones.

W: We could try advertising more in those three countries. Would that be effective?

M: Only in the country where we have the fewest subscribers. For other countries, we'd better look into some numbers first, such as our ratio of sales to advertising costs.

Questions 65-67 refer to the following conversation and employee directory.

美 미국식 발음 → 호주식 발음

W: Josh, I heard you're staying late tonight to help with the marketing department's relocation to the fifth floor.

M: Yeah. I'm setting up the computers. I was given this list detailing which desks I'm supposed to set up. However, it includes only 25 staff members despite there being 30 in the department. I need the rest of the information to finish the job.

W: Why don't you call the five employees who aren't included in the list and ask which workstations they're moving to?

M: I don't know their names, and our online directory doesn't include employees' departments.

W: Well, everyone in marketing has an extension starting with nine. Just sort by extension number, and you'll be able to see everyone in that department.

Questions 68-70 refer to the following conversation and receipt.

美 영국식 발음 → 호주식 발음

W: I'm wondering if you might be able to help me. I stopped by this shop yesterday to buy some clothing. After I left, though, I realized I was overcharged for one of the garments.

M: Really? I'm very sorry. If you show me your receipt, I'm sure I can assist you.

W: Here it is. The issue is with the footwear. I've got it here, in fact. The price tag shows half the amount that I was charged.

M: Let me check . . . Oh, I see what you mean. I'll refund you the proper amount right away. I'll also give you a free pair of our sports socks.

PART 4

Questions 71-73 refer to the following announcement.

[3ᵉ] 미국식 발음

Attention, Flight 876 passengers. This is your captain speaking. Thanks to some favorable air currents, we will reach Los Angeles approximately 20 minutes ahead of schedule. So we will arrive at 5:20 P.M. local time instead of 5:40 P.M. The weather at our destination is partly cloudy and is expected to stay that way for the rest of the day. Since this is an international flight, many of you will need to submit an immigration form upon arrival, so I suggest filling it out now. The seatbelt sign will be turned on in 10 minutes, at which time you will need to return to your seats and remain there until we land.

Questions 74-76 refer to the following advertisement.

[3ᵉ] 미국식 발음

At Durand Incorporated, we believe that cleaning supplies should not include harmful chemicals. That's why we created the LeMon line of environmentally friendly household cleaners. Made from all-natural ingredients, these products will never damage countertops, stoves, or any other surfaces. Starting this March, LeMon brand items will be even easier to find, as they will be available in all Davis Market stores across the United States. In the meantime, you can order any of our products at www.durandincorp.com, where all of our goods are currently 5 percent off.

Questions 77-79 refer to the following telephone message.

[3ᵉ] 호주식 발음

This is Michael Danton calling from Harford Legal Services. It's regarding the retirement party for another attorney at my firm that your company is catering tonight. I just spoke to one of your employees who is setting up at the banquet hall we rented, and she mentioned that there will be sufficient food for 50 people. But over 75 guests will be attending this event. I'm not sure how this mistake happened . . . I was very clear when I met with you to organize the party, and the contract I signed states the number of attendees. I expect to see you here at the hall within the hour with a plan to deal with this situation.

Questions 80-82 refer to the following announcement.

[3ᵉ] 캐나다식 발음

This is an urgent announcement from the National Weather Bureau. Be advised the city of Toronto will experience a severe heat wave on August 6 and 7. Daytime temperatures during this period are expected to exceed 36 degrees Celsius. Residents should avoid physically demanding activities, such as jogging or playing sports. In addition, pets and young children should not be left unattended in parked vehicles. Information about the symptoms of heatstroke and methods of treatment is available on our Web site, along with tips for coping with the heat. Rain is forecasted for the area on August 8, which will lead to a significant drop in temperature.

Questions 83-85 refer to the following advertisement.

[3ᵉ] 호주식 발음

Are you confused by all the different types of investments? Worried about making the wrong choices? Then contact Fieldstone Services, the largest wealth management firm in the country. Established in 1945, our company is the nation's most popular source of investment advice, as demonstrated by our number one ranking in the National Brand Survey for seven consecutive years. This is because clients know that our employees can be trusted. They do not receive commissions, so they never try to sell unnecessary products or services. If you would like to make an appointment with one of our trained professionals, call our 24-hour hotline.

Questions 86-88 refer to the following telephone message.

[3ᵉ] 미국식 발음

Hello, Gary. I have some good news. I entered my name in a contest last week, and I won two tickets to see Danielle Powers in concert on Wednesday night. I remember you told me once that you were a big fan of hers. Let me know by tomorrow if you want to use the other ticket. Uh, this is supposedly her final tour. If you decide you want to go, I would appreciate your giving me a ride to the venue. You could pick me up at my apartment building at 7:30. The concert starts at 8 P.M.

Questions 89-91 refer to the following instructions.

[3ᵉ] 영국식 발음

Thank you for this opportunity to give a sales presentation on my company's newest application. I think it'll be perfect for your insurance firm. Um, Scheduler 2.0 is an integrated online platform that makes it easy to manage client appointments. A customer who visits your Web site will be prompted to select an appointment time, and the program will then automatically assign an agent.

Uh, the employee will be able to access the client's information to prepare for the meeting. For managers, this system can be used to see how many clients each team member is meeting and what products they have sold. OK . . . let me show you how it works. Then, I'll answer any questions you might have.

Questions 92-94 refer to the following excerpt from a meeting.

캐나다식 발음

My next update is on the new shampoo our company is developing. We were getting close to finalizing the formula, but then we discovered an issue with the jasmine scent. It turned out that this synthetic fragrance can cause allergies in some people. We looked into replacing it with natural oil, but that would have raised the cost. So, I realize this may come as a surprise to many of you, but, well . . . fragrance-free products are popular these days. We can take advantage of this trend.

Questions 95-97 refer to the following broadcast and map.

호주식 발음

This is Colin Edwards reporting live from the 20th Annual Pottery Expo, which is being held in Canberra this year. Hundreds of people have gathered here at Melville Hall to see the work of artists from 12 different countries. Today, I'll be interviewing Matthew Walsh, the owner of the popular local studio Rustic Ceramics. Be sure to check out his booth next to the stairway on the ground floor to view some of his creations. Before I introduce him, though, I want to let you know that free pottery lessons are being offered to all attendees. If this interests you, just stop by the information desk to sign up for a session. Now, let's meet Mr. Walsh . . .

Questions 98-100 refer to the following telephone message and table.

영국식 발음

Good morning, Mr. Davis. This is Marsha Foster. I'm calling about my interview on Tuesday. Unfortunately, I have a family emergency to deal with, and I won't be available until the following week. Would it be possible to reschedule the interview? Also, I received an e-mail from Aiden Parker asking me for another example of my work. Um, I dropped it off at the reception desk on Wednesday. If he hasn't received the sample yet, it should be waiting for him there. Of course, should my application be missing anything else, I'll be happy to send it.

* 무료 해석은 해커스토익(Hackers.co.kr)에서
다운로드 받을 수 있습니다.

* QR 코드로
바로가기

PART 1

1 미국식 발음
(A) The man's gripping a railing.
(B) The man's digging dirt out of a vase.
(C) The man's kneeling down.
(D) The man's watering some plants.

2 캐나다식 발음
(A) The grass is being watered.
(B) Lines have been painted on a road.
(C) Pedestrians are walking alongside of a path.
(D) Bicycles are being ridden toward an
intersection.

3 호주식 발음
(A) He is loading a trunk with baggage.
(B) He is replacing a tire.
(C) He is opening a car door.
(D) He is unzipping a backpack.

4 영국식 발음
(A) The man is removing some tires.
(B) Safety gear is being cleaned.
(C) The man has a mask on his face.
(D) A vehicle is being disassembled.

5 호주식 발음
(A) Some seats are occupied in a courtyard.
(B) Chairs are positioned under umbrellas.
(C) Some leaves have fallen onto a patio.
(D) Steps lead into a swimming pool.

6 미국식 발음
(A) Carts are being pushed down a path.
(B) Cyclists are biking on a racetrack.
(C) Buildings border a street.
(D) A signboard has been attached to a gate.

PART 2

7 영국식 발음 → 호주식 발음
Whose eyeglasses are these?
(A) A new prescription.
(B) Classes are held weekly.
(C) They look like Mira's.

8 미국식 발음 → 캐나다식 발음
When will Unit 23 be vacated?
(A) A lease for a rental space.
(B) The tenant moved out yesterday.
(C) In that apartment complex.

9 캐나다식 발음 → 미국식 발음
Where can I find a restaurant nearby?
(A) Washburn Café is at the end of the block.
(B) Just for a quick bite to eat.
(C) I was able to find my license.

10 호주식 발음 → 영국식 발음
You work at Riley Industries, don't you?
(A) That's correct.
(B) Her shift will be starting soon.
(C) No, I don't have those tools.

11 호주식 발음 → 미국식 발음
Who told you about this art festival?
(A) One of my coworkers.
(B) It runs pretty late.
(C) My art teacher is from Spain.

12 미국식 발음 → 캐나다식 발음
Where will actress Marie Lawson be signing
autographs?
(A) She appeared in a television drama.
(B) You can write your name here.
(C) At the Guthrie Theater.

13 캐나다식 발음 → 영국식 발음
Will you place an event program on each chair?
(A) Dr. Delahanty's sitting in this row.
(B) The event was in Rome.
(C) I can do it in a minute.

14 미국식 발음 → 호주식 발음
Has Mr. Harrison forwarded you the memo about
holiday bonuses?
(A) No, he never asked about the costumes.
(B) I just received it.
(C) It'll be shut down over the holidays.

15 캐나다식 발음 → 영국식 발음
The speech was very informative, don't you think
so?
(A) I'm giving one at 5 P.M.
(B) When will it most likely start?
(C) The lecturer was quite knowledgeable.

16 미국식 발음 → 캐나다식 발음
Is Crystal Spa still in business?
(A) Some of these business cards.
(B) We're here until June 24.

(C) You'll have to check its Web site.

17 [3d] 호주식 발음 → 영국식 발음

This budget report seems to have some numerical errors.
(A) He works at a pharmaceutical company.
(B) Can you point them out to me?
(C) I'm having a problem with my phone.

18 [3d] 캐나다식 발음 → 미국식 발음

Haven't you already thrown out the garbage?
(A) An updated recycling policy.
(B) Park it in the garage.
(C) Only half of it.

19 [3d] 호주식 발음 → 영국식 발음

The path to Mount Cape is this way.
(A) He's heading our way.
(B) With my hiking gear.
(C) Are you positive about that?

20 [3d] 영국식 발음 → 호주식 발음

What materials have been prepared for the trade fair?
(A) Someone else is handling that.
(B) The fares are reasonable.
(C) Yes, a booth has been reserved.

21 [3d] 미국식 발음 → 캐나다식 발음

How often are performance reviews held?
(A) Hold on. I'll give you a tour.
(B) The counters are washed every day.
(C) Usually once per year.

22 [3d] 영국식 발음 → 미국식 발음

Which assignment should I prioritize next?
(A) Before I get home.
(B) I agree. You should.
(C) Please edit this press release.

23 [3d] 캐나다식 발음 → 호주식 발음

The lounge area is located on the ground floor, isn't it?
(A) Yes, down the hall from the elevator.
(B) No, the floors have been mopped.
(C) The lounge is spacious.

24 [3d] 캐나다식 발음 → 영국식 발음

Why are you returning this monitor?
(A) Keep monitoring the situation.
(B) I'm interested in something larger.
(C) Whenever you get back.

25 [3d] 호주식 발음 → 미국식 발음

When will the company merger be officially announced?
(A) I have a question about the new regulation.
(B) With another manufacturing firm.
(C) At the shareholder meeting.

26 [3d] 영국식 발음 → 호주식 발음

Does this cruise ship feature live entertainment?
(A) It's an entertaining radio program.
(B) This pamphlet should say.
(C) Passengers require boarding passes.

27 [3d] 캐나다식 발음 → 영국식 발음

The spare bedroom needs to be cleaned out.
(A) Have James give you a hand.
(B) A double mattress.
(C) The kitchen looks clean to me.

28 [3d] 호주식 발음 → 미국식 발음

Would you rather keep your reward points, or use them for a room upgrade?
(A) Well, the banquet was rather long.
(B) Both resorts have views of the mountains.
(C) I'll save them for my next visit.

29 [3d] 캐나다식 발음 → 영국식 발음

I can put in some overtime this evening.
(A) Go ahead and set them here.
(B) Patrick offered to make some desserts.
(C) Let's discuss the matter later this afternoon.

30 [3d] 영국식 발음 → 캐나다식 발음

Would you like some milk in your tea as well?
(A) I ordered coffee.
(B) We provide tea and snacks to clients.
(C) I don't like the new menus.

31 [3d] 미국식 발음 → 호주식 발음

How will we transport the furniture to the new office?
(A) Let's meet near the exit.
(B) They tested out the same chairs.
(C) It comes fully furnished.

PART 3

Questions 32-34 refer to the following conversation.

[3d] 미국식 발음 → 호주식 발음

W: By the way, an employee from the state sanitation department will be coming here to our electronics production facility tomorrow. He will inspect the waste management equipment. It'd be nice if you could give me a hand making sure there aren't any known issues with the machinery.

M: Yeah, but I'm busy at the moment with repairing our conveyor belt, as you told me to do this morning.

W: Just let me know as soon as you're free. I want to take care of everything today since we won't have much time to get ready tomorrow morning.

Questions 35-37 refer to the following conversation.

[3ᵃ] 영국식 발음 → 캐나다식 발음

W: Good afternoon. I'm interested in buying a new TV. A friend of mine recently told me about his Intrepid LS, which seems like a nice product.

M: Well, we have the Intrepid LD. The LS Model is almost four years old at this point. The LD model is a significant upgrade, so I'm sure you'll like it. The screen of it is extremely nice.

W: I see. Is it possible for me to test one out before making up my mind?

M: Certainly. Just follow me over to the display area and I'll show you how it works.

Questions 38-40 refer to the following conversation.

[3ᵃ] 호주식 발음 → 미국식 발음

M: Our department is struggling to finalize the necessary financial reports for the upcoming shareholders' meeting. I'm sorry to ask on short notice, but can you work on them over the weekend?

W: I'll be out of town from Saturday through next Tuesday. I'm visiting Charleston for my sister's birthday party. You approved my leave last month.

M: Oh, that's right. We've been so busy lately that I completely forgot. In that case, I'll have to ask someone else from your team to do it.

W: Try checking with Catherine Dawkins. Just last week, she said that she'd be open to working more overtime, as she's saving money to go to Europe.

Questions 41-43 refer to the following conversation.

[3ᵃ] 캐나다식 발음 → 영국식 발음

M: Hi. This is Larry Bates. I ordered a textbook from your store two weeks ago, but it still hasn't arrived at my apartment. My order confirmation number is 42345.

W: According to the tracking information, your book was delivered almost three days ago. However, the courier must not have brought it directly to your door, since you didn't include a specific apartment number with the shipping information.

M: Hmm . . . But I never saw the item by my complex's main door either.

W: Why don't you talk to your building manager to find out whether the package is being held for you? Otherwise, you can get in touch with the courier service, Package Express. They may be able to

help you.

Questions 44-46 refer to the following conversation.

[3ᵃ] 미국식 발음 → 호주식 발음

W: Did you hear the managers decided to change our uniforms? Ms. Campos just showed me the designs.

M: Oh, that's good. The ones we wear now look a little outdated.

W: Yeah, we will be wearing black pants and black button-up shirts. They look very professional and modern.

M: I agree. Plus, black will hide stains better. I somehow got some pen marks on my white shirt while working last week. Luckily, there was an extra in the storage closet. Which day will we make the switch?

W: I'm actually not sure about that. I'm just excited to not wear the old uniforms anymore.

Questions 47-49 refer to the following conversation.

[3ᵃ] 캐나다식 발음 → 영국식 발음

M: You're in charge of organizing tomorrow's architecture team gathering, correct?

W: Yeah. I've finalized all the activities that are gonna take place. Those details will be included in the reminder e-mail that I'll be sending to attendees before lunch. But why do you ask? Does anything need to be changed?

M: Yes, actually. Helen's presentation on modern design is going to be longer than originally expected, so please allow her an extra 15 minutes. Also, Oliver will be unable to attend. He must give a consultation to an important client instead. So, we should remove him from the agenda entirely.

W: No problem. I'll take care of those updates right now.

Questions 50-52 refer to the following conversation with three speakers.

[3ᵃ] 캐나다식 발음 → 미국식 발음 → 호주식 발음

M1: Good afternoon. Can I help you with something?

W: Yes. I'm looking for a product to relieve my back pain. Do you sell some sort of cream or gel that can do that?

M1: What's our best seller in that category, Alex?

M2: That would be FiberSoothe. But how much discomfort are you experiencing?

W: Hmm . . . It hurts when I bend over and also when I walk.

M2: Well, FiberSoothe might help a little, but you should really see a specialist and get a proper prescription.

W: OK. I'll do that this afternoon. Thanks for your advice.

Questions 53-55 refer to the following conversation with three speakers.

[3번] 호주식 발음 → 미국식 발음 → 영국식 발음

M: Excuse me. I'm hoping to learn more about your Chinese language classes, since many of my clients are based in China.

W1: Our course of business Chinese should be perfect for you. Oh, the instructor is coming down the hallway now. Jenny, can you provide some details about your class?

W2: Sure. We focus on expressions used in corporate settings. We meet twice weekly for two months. And the next course starts on June 2—this Friday.

M: Hmm . . . Two months? That'll be difficult for me, as I'm traveling to Hong Kong in July.

W2: In that case, there's another one starting in August.

W1: Yes, and you'll also be eligible for an advance registration discount if you enroll at our institute before July 10.

M: Great. I'll sign up for it now.

Questions 56-58 refer to the following conversation.

[3번] 영국식 발음 → 캐나다식 발음

W: Hi Garrett. I'm meeting with the CEO of Quebec Industrial at their offices in 20 minutes, but I don't have last year's sales report with me. I printed out a copy, but I must have left it on my desk.

M: Oh, I have it here. Would you like me to scan and e-mail it to you?

W: That would be great. I was hoping to have a paper copy, but that will do.

M: Alright. But, uh, do you need it right this minute? Brad is using the scanner.

W: Don't worry. As long as I get it before the meeting . . . Thanks!

Questions 59-61 refer to the following conversation.

[3번] 캐나다식 발음 → 영국식 발음

M: Ms. Martinez, it's Phillip Gray calling from Kerman and Associates. Have you had a chance to review the revised contract we sent you last week?

W: Our legal team is taking a look at it now, Mr. Gray. They've told me most of the contract looks satisfactory, but some small changes will need to be made to the section on licensing fees.

M: That sounds great. By the way, I heard that your corporation's soft drink Orange Lite has become quite popular in Mexico ever since it was introduced this spring. Congratulations on the success thus far.

W: Thank you. Yes, sales have definitely outperformed our expectations. We hope to make the most of the drink's popularity by continuing to expand distribution in the coming quarters.

Questions 62-64 refer to the following conversation and table.

[3번] 호주식 발음 → 미국식 발음

M: Ms. Lynch, I just checked the pharmacy's inventory, and we're running low on cough medicine.

W: I'm not surprised. We're entering the flu season, and we've already had many people coming in to buy that.

M: Should I contact the pharmaceutical manufacturers and place additional orders?

W: Please do. Also, let's get extra pain relief drugs, since our supply of that needs to be replenished, too. I meant to order more last week but forgot to.

M: I'll do that. And as for the pain relief medicine, I'll get the one with the lowest per-pill cost, as customers seem to prefer that brand.

Questions 65-67 refer to the following conversation and map.

[3번] 캐나다식 발음 → 영국식 발음

M: Thanks for calling Tuscan Sun Excursions. What can I help you with today?

W: Do you offer guided tours of art galleries around the area? I'm hoping to view some during my four-day trip here.

M: Absolutely. Our art tour stops by the city's three major museums. It takes place twice daily and begins right outside our office on Truro Avenue.

W: Oh, I'm actually hoping to browse smaller galleries. There's one at the intersection of Riviera Street and Fresco Road . . . umm . . . just opposite the theater downtown.

M: Hmm . . . Our company doesn't provide tours there, unfortunately. But I can give you the phone number of Complete Activities—another tourism firm in the area. They offer tours of those locations.

Questions 68-70 refer to the following conversation and label.

[3번] 미국식 발음 → 호주식 발음

W: This vending machine sells Dalton Pretzels. They contain very little sugar and a lot of carbohydrates, so they're a great way to get a boost of energy. I'm gonna buy some here in the terminal before we board our plane. Do you want a bag of them too?

M: Although I'm getting a bit hungry, I'll pass. I've had those pretzels before. They're really tasty, but they include too much fat. I'm trying to be careful about what I eat at the moment.

W: Oh, no worries. There're other options if you're interested—nuts and dried fruit snacks.

M: That's OK. We'll be receiving lunch once we take off, so I should be fine until then.

PART 4

Questions 71-73 refer to the following talk.

호주식 발음

We've now reached what's probably the most famous painting in this museum's collection, *The Flames of Clouds*. It was created by Guido Mariano and is believed to date back to 1821. As you can see, the picture uses a combination of bright orange and yellow paint, which was quite uncommon at the time it was made. This innovative technique gained Mariano a lot of praise from fellow painters and art critics of his era. OK, let's move on and view some of our 20th century artworks. They're located in the next gallery at the end of the hallway. Please follow me.

Questions 74-76 refer to the following advertisement.

캐나다식 발음

Want to beat the hot weather? Stop by Stevie's Frozen Yogurt for a cold, refreshing treat! We offer 22 flavors, such as vanilla, chocolate, peanut butter, and coffee. Moreover, we're the only frozen yogurt shop in town that allows customers to add as many toppings as they'd like for no additional charge. Be sure to check out our social media page, where we'll be holding promotions throughout July. There, you'll find a new deal featured daily, including amazing discounts and free items. You won't want to miss out on our incredible offers!

Questions 77-79 refer to the following talk.

호주식 발음

I'd like to welcome everyone to the Cairo Business Center's weekly seminar for entrepreneurs. Today's guest speaker is Mark Larson, whose company designs clothes for several department stores. Before we get started, though, I have a quick announcement to make. If you are planning to attend next week's session, make sure to go to Room 120 in the center's annex. Uh, the main building is scheduled to be painted. Anyway, I'll now turn the microphone to Mr. Larson. He intends to focus on effective methods to find and hire talented workers for your growing business. He'll answer any questions you might have at the end of his presentation.

Questions 80-82 refer to the following radio broadcast.

영국식 발음

Welcome to *Top Science* on WRP 101.5. I'm your host, Nina Esteban. As part of our ongoing podcast series on the impact of climate change, I've invited Dr. Luis Mattson from Fillmore College to the show. Dr. Mattson teaches in the school's ecology department and, just this Monday, published a paper in a respected journal. The paper examines the rise of sea levels along the

United States coastline as a result of melting glaciers. Throughout today's program, our guest is going to discuss his findings and respond to a few critiques that his research has received. Dr. Mattson, do you mind starting by outlining the results of your research?

Questions 83-85 refer to the following excerpt from a meeting.

미국식 발음

One last thing . . . I want to discuss the product testing for our upcoming lipstick line. We posted an advertisement seeking paid test subjects to participate in the research, and . . . well, now we've got a problem. A lot more people than we need signed up. I don't want to turn anyone away, though. Instead, let's see if they'd be willing to take part in other studies. I just spoke to our research manager Beth Meyers, and she told me that more people are needed to test some eye makeup that we're developing. She's going to reach out to those who applied to see whether they'd be open to trying those products instead.

Questions 86-88 refer to the following introduction.

영국식 발음

I'd like you all to meet Ivan Schwartz. Mr. Schwartz is the head application developer at our company's Vienna branch, and he has traveled to Liverpool to undergo training with our IT department. While here, he will be shown how to operate the data collection program that we will be rolling out across all of our branches in March. As you all know, the program is quite complicated, which is why we've asked Mr. Schwartz to travel here and work with our staff in person rather than virtually. Please be sure to make him feel welcome over the next five days and answer any questions that he may have. OK, that's all for now.

Questions 89-91 refer to the following broadcast.

미국식 발음

It's time for your Radio 98 traffic report. Following the completion of the new pedestrian overpass, Gilbert Avenue is now open to vehicles. As a result, 90traffic is moving smoothly throughout downtown at the moment. However, the championship football game will begin at noon . . . Make sure to take this into consideration if you plan to visit the area this afternoon. Now, it's time for a short commercial break. When we return, you'll hear an interesting report by journalist Tory Knight on this afternoon's event. She was able to interview several of the home team's star players. Stay tuned!

Questions 92-94 refer to the following radio broadcast.

캐나다식 발음

According to a recent press conference held by the city's mayor, Shenzhen will be launching a major campaign to attract foreign businesses. A local publicity firm has created the campaign, which focuses on the city's low corporate tax rates and large labor market. Moreover, it draws attention to how Shenzhen's growing population offers an excellent consumer base for multiple enterprises. Although Shenzhen is already well known among Chinese entrepreneurs, officials feel the city has yet to reach its full business potential. They are optimistic that the campaign will generate more attention from international companies, as well as increase tourism in the region. For further information about the campaign or to view any of its promotional materials, you can visit www.shenzhenbusiness.gov.cn.

Questions 95-97 refer to the following telephone message and form.

3에 미국식 발음

My name is Miranda Cruz, and I'm calling regarding *Elegant Fashion Magazine*. About a week ago, I was e-mailed a subscription renewal form for the publication. At the time, I signed up for a year-and-a-half subscription. However, I learned yesterday that I'll be traveling to France in December for a work project. Since the length of my stay in the country is open-ended, I . . . uh . . . I can only commit to a one-year subscription to the magazine. Of course, I would like the amount I overpaid to be returned to me. If you have any questions, you can reach me at 555-2197.

Questions 98-100 refer to the following excerpt from a meeting and table.

3에 호주식 발음

I called this meeting to discuss some changes that are going to be made to our company's speaker models. After talking to our firm's president this morning, it's clear that we need to improve profitability. The newly released HK21 is in great demand, but our second-most expensive product has been a poor seller in our target market. Young consumers find its price too high. So, we've decided to change strategies and market the product to older consumers. Of course, this is going to have a significant impact on our marketing costs. I'd like to take a few minutes now to talk about that.

Answer Sheet

TEST 02

LISTENING (Part I~IV)

#					#					#					#					#				
1	Ⓐ	Ⓑ	Ⓒ	Ⓓ	21	Ⓐ	Ⓑ	Ⓒ	Ⓓ	41	Ⓐ	Ⓑ	Ⓒ		61	Ⓐ	Ⓑ	Ⓒ	Ⓓ	81	Ⓐ	Ⓑ	Ⓒ	Ⓓ
2	Ⓐ	Ⓑ	Ⓒ	Ⓓ	22	Ⓐ	Ⓑ	Ⓒ	Ⓓ	42	Ⓐ	Ⓑ	Ⓒ		62	Ⓐ	Ⓑ	Ⓒ	Ⓓ	82	Ⓐ	Ⓑ	Ⓒ	Ⓓ
3	Ⓐ	Ⓑ	Ⓒ	Ⓓ	23	Ⓐ	Ⓑ	Ⓒ	Ⓓ	43	Ⓐ	Ⓑ	Ⓒ		63	Ⓐ	Ⓑ	Ⓒ	Ⓓ	83	Ⓐ	Ⓑ	Ⓒ	Ⓓ
4	Ⓐ	Ⓑ	Ⓒ	Ⓓ	24	Ⓐ	Ⓑ	Ⓒ	Ⓓ	44	Ⓐ	Ⓑ	Ⓒ		64	Ⓐ	Ⓑ	Ⓒ	Ⓓ	84	Ⓐ	Ⓑ	Ⓒ	Ⓓ
5	Ⓐ	Ⓑ	Ⓒ	Ⓓ	25	Ⓐ	Ⓑ	Ⓒ	Ⓓ	45	Ⓐ	Ⓑ	Ⓒ		65	Ⓐ	Ⓑ	Ⓒ	Ⓓ	85	Ⓐ	Ⓑ	Ⓒ	Ⓓ
6	Ⓐ	Ⓑ	Ⓒ	Ⓓ	26	Ⓐ	Ⓑ	Ⓒ	Ⓓ	46	Ⓐ	Ⓑ	Ⓒ		66	Ⓐ	Ⓑ	Ⓒ	Ⓓ	86	Ⓐ	Ⓑ	Ⓒ	Ⓓ
7	Ⓐ	Ⓑ	Ⓒ		27	Ⓐ	Ⓑ	Ⓒ	Ⓓ	47	Ⓐ	Ⓑ	Ⓒ		67	Ⓐ	Ⓑ	Ⓒ	Ⓓ	87	Ⓐ	Ⓑ	Ⓒ	Ⓓ
8	Ⓐ	Ⓑ	Ⓒ		28	Ⓐ	Ⓑ	Ⓒ	Ⓓ	48	Ⓐ	Ⓑ	Ⓒ		68	Ⓐ	Ⓑ	Ⓒ	Ⓓ	88	Ⓐ	Ⓑ	Ⓒ	Ⓓ
9	Ⓐ	Ⓑ	Ⓒ		29	Ⓐ	Ⓑ	Ⓒ	Ⓓ	49	Ⓐ	Ⓑ	Ⓒ		69	Ⓐ	Ⓑ	Ⓒ	Ⓓ	89	Ⓐ	Ⓑ	Ⓒ	Ⓓ
10	Ⓐ	Ⓑ	Ⓒ		30	Ⓐ	Ⓑ	Ⓒ	Ⓓ	50	Ⓐ	Ⓑ	Ⓒ	Ⓓ	70	Ⓐ	Ⓑ	Ⓒ	Ⓓ	90	Ⓐ	Ⓑ	Ⓒ	Ⓓ
11	Ⓐ	Ⓑ	Ⓒ		31	Ⓐ	Ⓑ	Ⓒ	Ⓓ	51	Ⓐ	Ⓑ	Ⓒ	Ⓓ	71	Ⓐ	Ⓑ	Ⓒ	Ⓓ	91	Ⓐ	Ⓑ	Ⓒ	Ⓓ
12	Ⓐ	Ⓑ	Ⓒ		32	Ⓐ	Ⓑ	Ⓒ	Ⓓ	52	Ⓐ	Ⓑ	Ⓒ	Ⓓ	72	Ⓐ	Ⓑ	Ⓒ	Ⓓ	92	Ⓐ	Ⓑ	Ⓒ	Ⓓ
13	Ⓐ	Ⓑ	Ⓒ		33	Ⓐ	Ⓑ	Ⓒ	Ⓓ	53	Ⓐ	Ⓑ	Ⓒ	Ⓓ	73	Ⓐ	Ⓑ	Ⓒ	Ⓓ	93	Ⓐ	Ⓑ	Ⓒ	Ⓓ
14	Ⓐ	Ⓑ	Ⓒ		34	Ⓐ	Ⓑ	Ⓒ	Ⓓ	54	Ⓐ	Ⓑ	Ⓒ	Ⓓ	74	Ⓐ	Ⓑ	Ⓒ	Ⓓ	94	Ⓐ	Ⓑ	Ⓒ	Ⓓ
15	Ⓐ	Ⓑ	Ⓒ		35	Ⓐ	Ⓑ	Ⓒ	Ⓓ	55	Ⓐ	Ⓑ	Ⓒ	Ⓓ	75	Ⓐ	Ⓑ	Ⓒ	Ⓓ	95	Ⓐ	Ⓑ	Ⓒ	Ⓓ
16	Ⓐ	Ⓑ	Ⓒ		36	Ⓐ	Ⓑ	Ⓒ	Ⓓ	56	Ⓐ	Ⓑ	Ⓒ	Ⓓ	76	Ⓐ	Ⓑ	Ⓒ	Ⓓ	96	Ⓐ	Ⓑ	Ⓒ	Ⓓ
17	Ⓐ	Ⓑ	Ⓒ		37	Ⓐ	Ⓑ	Ⓒ	Ⓓ	57	Ⓐ	Ⓑ	Ⓒ	Ⓓ	77	Ⓐ	Ⓑ	Ⓒ	Ⓓ	97	Ⓐ	Ⓑ	Ⓒ	Ⓓ
18	Ⓐ	Ⓑ	Ⓒ		38	Ⓐ	Ⓑ	Ⓒ	Ⓓ	58	Ⓐ	Ⓑ	Ⓒ	Ⓓ	78	Ⓐ	Ⓑ	Ⓒ	Ⓓ	98	Ⓐ	Ⓑ	Ⓒ	Ⓓ
19	Ⓐ	Ⓑ	Ⓒ		39	Ⓐ	Ⓑ	Ⓒ	Ⓓ	59	Ⓐ	Ⓑ	Ⓒ	Ⓓ	79	Ⓐ	Ⓑ	Ⓒ	Ⓓ	99	Ⓐ	Ⓑ	Ⓒ	Ⓓ
20	Ⓐ	Ⓑ	Ⓒ	Ⓓ	40	Ⓐ	Ⓑ	Ⓒ	Ⓓ	60	Ⓐ	Ⓑ	Ⓒ	Ⓓ	80	Ⓐ	Ⓑ	Ⓒ	Ⓓ	100	Ⓐ	Ⓑ	Ⓒ	Ⓓ

맞은 문제 개수: ＿＿ / 100

TEST 02의 점수를 환산한 후 목표 달성기에 TEST 02의 점수를 표시합니다.
점수 환산표는 문제집 167페이지, 목표 달성기는 교재의 첫 장에 있습니다.

✂ ····· 자르는 선

Answer Sheet

TEST 01

LISTENING (Part I~IV)

#					#					#					#					#				
1	Ⓐ	Ⓑ	Ⓒ		21	Ⓐ	Ⓑ	Ⓒ	Ⓓ	41	Ⓐ	Ⓑ	Ⓒ		61	Ⓐ	Ⓑ	Ⓒ	Ⓓ	81	Ⓐ	Ⓑ	Ⓒ	Ⓓ
2	Ⓐ	Ⓑ	Ⓒ		22	Ⓐ	Ⓑ	Ⓒ	Ⓓ	42	Ⓐ	Ⓑ	Ⓒ		62	Ⓐ	Ⓑ	Ⓒ	Ⓓ	82	Ⓐ	Ⓑ	Ⓒ	Ⓓ
3	Ⓐ	Ⓑ	Ⓒ		23	Ⓐ	Ⓑ	Ⓒ	Ⓓ	43	Ⓐ	Ⓑ	Ⓒ		63	Ⓐ	Ⓑ	Ⓒ	Ⓓ	83	Ⓐ	Ⓑ	Ⓒ	Ⓓ
4	Ⓐ	Ⓑ	Ⓒ		24	Ⓐ	Ⓑ	Ⓒ	Ⓓ	44	Ⓐ	Ⓑ	Ⓒ		64	Ⓐ	Ⓑ	Ⓒ	Ⓓ	84	Ⓐ	Ⓑ	Ⓒ	Ⓓ
5	Ⓐ	Ⓑ	Ⓒ		25	Ⓐ	Ⓑ	Ⓒ	Ⓓ	45	Ⓐ	Ⓑ	Ⓒ		65	Ⓐ	Ⓑ	Ⓒ	Ⓓ	85	Ⓐ	Ⓑ	Ⓒ	Ⓓ
6	Ⓐ	Ⓑ	Ⓒ		26	Ⓐ	Ⓑ	Ⓒ	Ⓓ	46	Ⓐ	Ⓑ	Ⓒ		66	Ⓐ	Ⓑ	Ⓒ	Ⓓ	86	Ⓐ	Ⓑ	Ⓒ	Ⓓ
7	Ⓐ	Ⓑ	Ⓒ	Ⓓ	27	Ⓐ	Ⓑ	Ⓒ	Ⓓ	47	Ⓐ	Ⓑ	Ⓒ		67	Ⓐ	Ⓑ	Ⓒ	Ⓓ	87	Ⓐ	Ⓑ	Ⓒ	Ⓓ
8	Ⓐ	Ⓑ	Ⓒ	Ⓓ	28	Ⓐ	Ⓑ	Ⓒ	Ⓓ	48	Ⓐ	Ⓑ	Ⓒ		68	Ⓐ	Ⓑ	Ⓒ	Ⓓ	88	Ⓐ	Ⓑ	Ⓒ	Ⓓ
9	Ⓐ	Ⓑ	Ⓒ		29	Ⓐ	Ⓑ	Ⓒ	Ⓓ	49	Ⓐ	Ⓑ	Ⓒ		69	Ⓐ	Ⓑ	Ⓒ	Ⓓ	89	Ⓐ	Ⓑ	Ⓒ	Ⓓ
10	Ⓐ	Ⓑ	Ⓒ		30	Ⓐ	Ⓑ	Ⓒ	Ⓓ	50	Ⓐ	Ⓑ	Ⓒ	Ⓓ	70	Ⓐ	Ⓑ	Ⓒ	Ⓓ	90	Ⓐ	Ⓑ	Ⓒ	Ⓓ
11	Ⓐ	Ⓑ	Ⓒ		31	Ⓐ	Ⓑ	Ⓒ	Ⓓ	51	Ⓐ	Ⓑ	Ⓒ	Ⓓ	71	Ⓐ	Ⓑ	Ⓒ	Ⓓ	91	Ⓐ	Ⓑ	Ⓒ	Ⓓ
12	Ⓐ	Ⓑ	Ⓒ		32	Ⓐ	Ⓑ	Ⓒ	Ⓓ	52	Ⓐ	Ⓑ	Ⓒ	Ⓓ	72	Ⓐ	Ⓑ	Ⓒ	Ⓓ	92	Ⓐ	Ⓑ	Ⓒ	Ⓓ
13	Ⓐ	Ⓑ	Ⓒ		33	Ⓐ	Ⓑ	Ⓒ	Ⓓ	53	Ⓐ	Ⓑ	Ⓒ	Ⓓ	73	Ⓐ	Ⓑ	Ⓒ	Ⓓ	93	Ⓐ	Ⓑ	Ⓒ	Ⓓ
14	Ⓐ	Ⓑ	Ⓒ		34	Ⓐ	Ⓑ	Ⓒ	Ⓓ	54	Ⓐ	Ⓑ	Ⓒ	Ⓓ	74	Ⓐ	Ⓑ	Ⓒ	Ⓓ	94	Ⓐ	Ⓑ	Ⓒ	Ⓓ
15	Ⓐ	Ⓑ	Ⓒ		35	Ⓐ	Ⓑ	Ⓒ	Ⓓ	55	Ⓐ	Ⓑ	Ⓒ	Ⓓ	75	Ⓐ	Ⓑ	Ⓒ	Ⓓ	95	Ⓐ	Ⓑ	Ⓒ	Ⓓ
16	Ⓐ	Ⓑ	Ⓒ		36	Ⓐ	Ⓑ	Ⓒ	Ⓓ	56	Ⓐ	Ⓑ	Ⓒ	Ⓓ	76	Ⓐ	Ⓑ	Ⓒ	Ⓓ	96	Ⓐ	Ⓑ	Ⓒ	Ⓓ
17	Ⓐ	Ⓑ	Ⓒ		37	Ⓐ	Ⓑ	Ⓒ	Ⓓ	57	Ⓐ	Ⓑ	Ⓒ	Ⓓ	77	Ⓐ	Ⓑ	Ⓒ	Ⓓ	97	Ⓐ	Ⓑ	Ⓒ	Ⓓ
18	Ⓐ	Ⓑ	Ⓒ		38	Ⓐ	Ⓑ	Ⓒ	Ⓓ	58	Ⓐ	Ⓑ	Ⓒ	Ⓓ	78	Ⓐ	Ⓑ	Ⓒ	Ⓓ	98	Ⓐ	Ⓑ	Ⓒ	Ⓓ
19	Ⓐ	Ⓑ	Ⓒ		39	Ⓐ	Ⓑ	Ⓒ	Ⓓ	59	Ⓐ	Ⓑ	Ⓒ	Ⓓ	79	Ⓐ	Ⓑ	Ⓒ	Ⓓ	99	Ⓐ	Ⓑ	Ⓒ	Ⓓ
20	Ⓐ	Ⓑ	Ⓒ		40	Ⓐ	Ⓑ	Ⓒ	Ⓓ	60	Ⓐ	Ⓑ	Ⓒ	Ⓓ	80	Ⓐ	Ⓑ	Ⓒ	Ⓓ	100	Ⓐ	Ⓑ	Ⓒ	Ⓓ

맞은 문제 개수: ＿＿ / 100

TEST 01의 점수를 환산한 후 목표 달성기에 TEST 01의 점수를 표시합니다.
점수 환산표는 문제집 167페이지, 목표 달성기는 교재의 첫 장에 있습니다.

무료 토익·토스·오픽·지텔프 자료 제공
Hackers.co.kr

Answer Sheet

TEST 04

LISTENING (Part I~IV)

1	Ⓐ Ⓑ Ⓒ Ⓓ	21	Ⓐ Ⓑ Ⓒ	41	Ⓐ Ⓑ Ⓒ	61	Ⓐ Ⓑ Ⓒ Ⓓ	81	Ⓐ Ⓑ Ⓒ Ⓓ
2	Ⓐ Ⓑ Ⓒ Ⓓ	22	Ⓐ Ⓑ Ⓒ	42	Ⓐ Ⓑ Ⓒ	62	Ⓐ Ⓑ Ⓒ Ⓓ	82	Ⓐ Ⓑ Ⓒ Ⓓ
3	Ⓐ Ⓑ Ⓒ Ⓓ	23	Ⓐ Ⓑ Ⓒ	43	Ⓐ Ⓑ Ⓒ	63	Ⓐ Ⓑ Ⓒ Ⓓ	83	Ⓐ Ⓑ Ⓒ Ⓓ
4	Ⓐ Ⓑ Ⓒ Ⓓ	24	Ⓐ Ⓑ Ⓒ	44	Ⓐ Ⓑ Ⓒ	64	Ⓐ Ⓑ Ⓒ Ⓓ	84	Ⓐ Ⓑ Ⓒ Ⓓ
5	Ⓐ Ⓑ Ⓒ Ⓓ	25	Ⓐ Ⓑ Ⓒ	45	Ⓐ Ⓑ Ⓒ	65	Ⓐ Ⓑ Ⓒ Ⓓ	85	Ⓐ Ⓑ Ⓒ Ⓓ
6	Ⓐ Ⓑ Ⓒ Ⓓ	26	Ⓐ Ⓑ Ⓒ	46	Ⓐ Ⓑ Ⓒ	66	Ⓐ Ⓑ Ⓒ Ⓓ	86	Ⓐ Ⓑ Ⓒ Ⓓ
7	Ⓐ Ⓑ Ⓒ	27	Ⓐ Ⓑ Ⓒ	47	Ⓐ Ⓑ Ⓒ	67	Ⓐ Ⓑ Ⓒ Ⓓ	87	Ⓐ Ⓑ Ⓒ Ⓓ
8	Ⓐ Ⓑ Ⓒ	28	Ⓐ Ⓑ Ⓒ	48	Ⓐ Ⓑ Ⓒ	68	Ⓐ Ⓑ Ⓒ Ⓓ	88	Ⓐ Ⓑ Ⓒ Ⓓ
9	Ⓐ Ⓑ Ⓒ	29	Ⓐ Ⓑ Ⓒ	49	Ⓐ Ⓑ Ⓒ	69	Ⓐ Ⓑ Ⓒ Ⓓ	89	Ⓐ Ⓑ Ⓒ Ⓓ
10	Ⓐ Ⓑ Ⓒ	30	Ⓐ Ⓑ Ⓒ	50	Ⓐ Ⓑ Ⓒ Ⓓ	70	Ⓐ Ⓑ Ⓒ Ⓓ	90	Ⓐ Ⓑ Ⓒ Ⓓ
11	Ⓐ Ⓑ Ⓒ	31	Ⓐ Ⓑ Ⓒ	51	Ⓐ Ⓑ Ⓒ Ⓓ	71	Ⓐ Ⓑ Ⓒ Ⓓ	91	Ⓐ Ⓑ Ⓒ Ⓓ
12	Ⓐ Ⓑ Ⓒ	32	Ⓐ Ⓑ Ⓒ	52	Ⓐ Ⓑ Ⓒ Ⓓ	72	Ⓐ Ⓑ Ⓒ Ⓓ	92	Ⓐ Ⓑ Ⓒ Ⓓ
13	Ⓐ Ⓑ Ⓒ	33	Ⓐ Ⓑ Ⓒ	53	Ⓐ Ⓑ Ⓒ Ⓓ	73	Ⓐ Ⓑ Ⓒ Ⓓ	93	Ⓐ Ⓑ Ⓒ Ⓓ
14	Ⓐ Ⓑ Ⓒ	34	Ⓐ Ⓑ Ⓒ	54	Ⓐ Ⓑ Ⓒ Ⓓ	74	Ⓐ Ⓑ Ⓒ Ⓓ	94	Ⓐ Ⓑ Ⓒ Ⓓ
15	Ⓐ Ⓑ Ⓒ	35	Ⓐ Ⓑ Ⓒ	55	Ⓐ Ⓑ Ⓒ Ⓓ	75	Ⓐ Ⓑ Ⓒ Ⓓ	95	Ⓐ Ⓑ Ⓒ Ⓓ
16	Ⓐ Ⓑ Ⓒ	36	Ⓐ Ⓑ Ⓒ	56	Ⓐ Ⓑ Ⓒ Ⓓ	76	Ⓐ Ⓑ Ⓒ Ⓓ	96	Ⓐ Ⓑ Ⓒ Ⓓ
17	Ⓐ Ⓑ Ⓒ	37	Ⓐ Ⓑ Ⓒ	57	Ⓐ Ⓑ Ⓒ Ⓓ	77	Ⓐ Ⓑ Ⓒ Ⓓ	97	Ⓐ Ⓑ Ⓒ Ⓓ
18	Ⓐ Ⓑ Ⓒ	38	Ⓐ Ⓑ Ⓒ	58	Ⓐ Ⓑ Ⓒ Ⓓ	78	Ⓐ Ⓑ Ⓒ Ⓓ	98	Ⓐ Ⓑ Ⓒ Ⓓ
19	Ⓐ Ⓑ Ⓒ	39	Ⓐ Ⓑ Ⓒ	59	Ⓐ Ⓑ Ⓒ Ⓓ	79	Ⓐ Ⓑ Ⓒ Ⓓ	99	Ⓐ Ⓑ Ⓒ Ⓓ
20	Ⓐ Ⓑ Ⓒ	40	Ⓐ Ⓑ Ⓒ	60	Ⓐ Ⓑ Ⓒ Ⓓ	80	Ⓐ Ⓑ Ⓒ Ⓓ	100	Ⓐ Ⓑ Ⓒ Ⓓ

맞은 문제수: ____/100

TEST 04의 점수를 환산한 후 목표 달성기에 TEST 04의 점수를 표시합니다.
점수 환산표와 문제집 167페이지, 목표 달성기는 교재의 첫 장에 있습니다.

✂ ----- 자르는 선

Answer Sheet

TEST 03

LISTENING (Part I~IV)

1	Ⓐ Ⓑ Ⓒ Ⓓ	21	Ⓐ Ⓑ Ⓒ	41	Ⓐ Ⓑ Ⓒ	61	Ⓐ Ⓑ Ⓒ Ⓓ	81	Ⓐ Ⓑ Ⓒ Ⓓ
2	Ⓐ Ⓑ Ⓒ Ⓓ	22	Ⓐ Ⓑ Ⓒ	42	Ⓐ Ⓑ Ⓒ	62	Ⓐ Ⓑ Ⓒ Ⓓ	82	Ⓐ Ⓑ Ⓒ Ⓓ
3	Ⓐ Ⓑ Ⓒ Ⓓ	23	Ⓐ Ⓑ Ⓒ	43	Ⓐ Ⓑ Ⓒ	63	Ⓐ Ⓑ Ⓒ Ⓓ	83	Ⓐ Ⓑ Ⓒ Ⓓ
4	Ⓐ Ⓑ Ⓒ Ⓓ	24	Ⓐ Ⓑ Ⓒ	44	Ⓐ Ⓑ Ⓒ	64	Ⓐ Ⓑ Ⓒ Ⓓ	84	Ⓐ Ⓑ Ⓒ Ⓓ
5	Ⓐ Ⓑ Ⓒ Ⓓ	25	Ⓐ Ⓑ Ⓒ	45	Ⓐ Ⓑ Ⓒ	65	Ⓐ Ⓑ Ⓒ Ⓓ	85	Ⓐ Ⓑ Ⓒ Ⓓ
6	Ⓐ Ⓑ Ⓒ Ⓓ	26	Ⓐ Ⓑ Ⓒ	46	Ⓐ Ⓑ Ⓒ	66	Ⓐ Ⓑ Ⓒ Ⓓ	86	Ⓐ Ⓑ Ⓒ Ⓓ
7	Ⓐ Ⓑ Ⓒ	27	Ⓐ Ⓑ Ⓒ	47	Ⓐ Ⓑ Ⓒ	67	Ⓐ Ⓑ Ⓒ Ⓓ	87	Ⓐ Ⓑ Ⓒ Ⓓ
8	Ⓐ Ⓑ Ⓒ	28	Ⓐ Ⓑ Ⓒ	48	Ⓐ Ⓑ Ⓒ	68	Ⓐ Ⓑ Ⓒ Ⓓ	88	Ⓐ Ⓑ Ⓒ Ⓓ
9	Ⓐ Ⓑ Ⓒ	29	Ⓐ Ⓑ Ⓒ	49	Ⓐ Ⓑ Ⓒ	69	Ⓐ Ⓑ Ⓒ Ⓓ	89	Ⓐ Ⓑ Ⓒ Ⓓ
10	Ⓐ Ⓑ Ⓒ	30	Ⓐ Ⓑ Ⓒ	50	Ⓐ Ⓑ Ⓒ Ⓓ	70	Ⓐ Ⓑ Ⓒ Ⓓ	90	Ⓐ Ⓑ Ⓒ Ⓓ
11	Ⓐ Ⓑ Ⓒ	31	Ⓐ Ⓑ Ⓒ	51	Ⓐ Ⓑ Ⓒ Ⓓ	71	Ⓐ Ⓑ Ⓒ Ⓓ	91	Ⓐ Ⓑ Ⓒ Ⓓ
12	Ⓐ Ⓑ Ⓒ	32	Ⓐ Ⓑ Ⓒ	52	Ⓐ Ⓑ Ⓒ Ⓓ	72	Ⓐ Ⓑ Ⓒ Ⓓ	92	Ⓐ Ⓑ Ⓒ Ⓓ
13	Ⓐ Ⓑ Ⓒ	33	Ⓐ Ⓑ Ⓒ	53	Ⓐ Ⓑ Ⓒ Ⓓ	73	Ⓐ Ⓑ Ⓒ Ⓓ	93	Ⓐ Ⓑ Ⓒ Ⓓ
14	Ⓐ Ⓑ Ⓒ	34	Ⓐ Ⓑ Ⓒ	54	Ⓐ Ⓑ Ⓒ Ⓓ	74	Ⓐ Ⓑ Ⓒ Ⓓ	94	Ⓐ Ⓑ Ⓒ Ⓓ
15	Ⓐ Ⓑ Ⓒ	35	Ⓐ Ⓑ Ⓒ	55	Ⓐ Ⓑ Ⓒ Ⓓ	75	Ⓐ Ⓑ Ⓒ Ⓓ	95	Ⓐ Ⓑ Ⓒ Ⓓ
16	Ⓐ Ⓑ Ⓒ	36	Ⓐ Ⓑ Ⓒ	56	Ⓐ Ⓑ Ⓒ Ⓓ	76	Ⓐ Ⓑ Ⓒ Ⓓ	96	Ⓐ Ⓑ Ⓒ Ⓓ
17	Ⓐ Ⓑ Ⓒ	37	Ⓐ Ⓑ Ⓒ	57	Ⓐ Ⓑ Ⓒ Ⓓ	77	Ⓐ Ⓑ Ⓒ Ⓓ	97	Ⓐ Ⓑ Ⓒ Ⓓ
18	Ⓐ Ⓑ Ⓒ	38	Ⓐ Ⓑ Ⓒ	58	Ⓐ Ⓑ Ⓒ Ⓓ	78	Ⓐ Ⓑ Ⓒ Ⓓ	98	Ⓐ Ⓑ Ⓒ Ⓓ
19	Ⓐ Ⓑ Ⓒ	39	Ⓐ Ⓑ Ⓒ	59	Ⓐ Ⓑ Ⓒ Ⓓ	79	Ⓐ Ⓑ Ⓒ Ⓓ	99	Ⓐ Ⓑ Ⓒ Ⓓ
20	Ⓐ Ⓑ Ⓒ	40	Ⓐ Ⓑ Ⓒ	60	Ⓐ Ⓑ Ⓒ Ⓓ	80	Ⓐ Ⓑ Ⓒ Ⓓ	100	Ⓐ Ⓑ Ⓒ Ⓓ

맞은 문제수: ____/100

TEST 03의 점수를 환산한 후 목표 달성기에 TEST 03의 점수를 표시합니다.
점수 환산표와 문제집 167페이지, 목표 달성기는 교재의 첫 장에 있습니다.

무료 토익·토스·오픽·지텔프 자료 제공
Hackers.co.kr

Answer Sheet

TEST 06

LISTENING (Part I~IV)

맞은 문제 개수: ____ /100

TEST 06의 점수를 환산한 후 목표 달성기에 TEST 06의 점수를 표시합니다.
점수 환산표는 문제집 16페이지, 목표 달성기는 교재의 첫 장에 있습니다.

✂ 자르는 선

Answer Sheet

TEST 05

LISTENING (Part I~IV)

맞은 문제 개수: ____ /100

TEST 05의 점수를 환산한 후 목표 달성기에 TEST 05의 점수를 표시합니다.
점수 환산표는 문제집 16페이지, 목표 달성기는 교재의 첫 장에 있습니다.

무료 토익·토스·오픽·지텔프 자료 제공
Hackers.co.kr

Answer Sheet
TEST 08

LISTENING (Part I~IV)

#		#		#		#	
1	Ⓐ Ⓑ Ⓒ Ⓓ	21	Ⓐ Ⓑ Ⓒ Ⓓ	41	Ⓐ Ⓑ Ⓒ Ⓓ	81	Ⓐ Ⓑ Ⓒ Ⓓ
2	Ⓐ Ⓑ Ⓒ Ⓓ	22	Ⓐ Ⓑ Ⓒ Ⓓ	42	Ⓐ Ⓑ Ⓒ Ⓓ	82	Ⓐ Ⓑ Ⓒ Ⓓ
3	Ⓐ Ⓑ Ⓒ Ⓓ	23	Ⓐ Ⓑ Ⓒ Ⓓ	43	Ⓐ Ⓑ Ⓒ Ⓓ	83	Ⓐ Ⓑ Ⓒ Ⓓ
4	Ⓐ Ⓑ Ⓒ Ⓓ	24	Ⓐ Ⓑ Ⓒ Ⓓ	44	Ⓐ Ⓑ Ⓒ Ⓓ	84	Ⓐ Ⓑ Ⓒ Ⓓ
5	Ⓐ Ⓑ Ⓒ Ⓓ	25	Ⓐ Ⓑ Ⓒ Ⓓ	45	Ⓐ Ⓑ Ⓒ Ⓓ	85	Ⓐ Ⓑ Ⓒ Ⓓ
6	Ⓐ Ⓑ Ⓒ Ⓓ	26	Ⓐ Ⓑ Ⓒ Ⓓ	46	Ⓐ Ⓑ Ⓒ Ⓓ	86	Ⓐ Ⓑ Ⓒ Ⓓ
7	Ⓐ Ⓑ Ⓒ	27	Ⓐ Ⓑ Ⓒ	47	Ⓐ Ⓑ Ⓒ Ⓓ	87	Ⓐ Ⓑ Ⓒ Ⓓ
8	Ⓐ Ⓑ Ⓒ	28	Ⓐ Ⓑ Ⓒ	48	Ⓐ Ⓑ Ⓒ Ⓓ	88	Ⓐ Ⓑ Ⓒ Ⓓ
9	Ⓐ Ⓑ Ⓒ	29	Ⓐ Ⓑ Ⓒ	49	Ⓐ Ⓑ Ⓒ Ⓓ	89	Ⓐ Ⓑ Ⓒ Ⓓ
10	Ⓐ Ⓑ Ⓒ	30	Ⓐ Ⓑ Ⓒ Ⓓ	50	Ⓐ Ⓑ Ⓒ Ⓓ	90	Ⓐ Ⓑ Ⓒ Ⓓ
11	Ⓐ Ⓑ Ⓒ	31	Ⓐ Ⓑ Ⓒ Ⓓ	51	Ⓐ Ⓑ Ⓒ Ⓓ	91	Ⓐ Ⓑ Ⓒ Ⓓ
12	Ⓐ Ⓑ Ⓒ	32	Ⓐ Ⓑ Ⓒ Ⓓ	52	Ⓐ Ⓑ Ⓒ Ⓓ	92	Ⓐ Ⓑ Ⓒ Ⓓ
13	Ⓐ Ⓑ Ⓒ	33	Ⓐ Ⓑ Ⓒ Ⓓ	53	Ⓐ Ⓑ Ⓒ Ⓓ	93	Ⓐ Ⓑ Ⓒ Ⓓ
14	Ⓐ Ⓑ Ⓒ	34	Ⓐ Ⓑ Ⓒ Ⓓ	54	Ⓐ Ⓑ Ⓒ Ⓓ	94	Ⓐ Ⓑ Ⓒ Ⓓ
15	Ⓐ Ⓑ Ⓒ	35	Ⓐ Ⓑ Ⓒ Ⓓ	55	Ⓐ Ⓑ Ⓒ Ⓓ	95	Ⓐ Ⓑ Ⓒ Ⓓ
16	Ⓐ Ⓑ Ⓒ	36	Ⓐ Ⓑ Ⓒ Ⓓ	56	Ⓐ Ⓑ Ⓒ Ⓓ	96	Ⓐ Ⓑ Ⓒ Ⓓ
17	Ⓐ Ⓑ Ⓒ	37	Ⓐ Ⓑ Ⓒ Ⓓ	57	Ⓐ Ⓑ Ⓒ Ⓓ	97	Ⓐ Ⓑ Ⓒ Ⓓ
18	Ⓐ Ⓑ Ⓒ	38	Ⓐ Ⓑ Ⓒ Ⓓ	58	Ⓐ Ⓑ Ⓒ Ⓓ	98	Ⓐ Ⓑ Ⓒ Ⓓ
19	Ⓐ Ⓑ Ⓒ	39	Ⓐ Ⓑ Ⓒ Ⓓ	59	Ⓐ Ⓑ Ⓒ Ⓓ	99	Ⓐ Ⓑ Ⓒ Ⓓ
20	Ⓐ Ⓑ Ⓒ	40	Ⓐ Ⓑ Ⓒ Ⓓ	60	Ⓐ Ⓑ Ⓒ Ⓓ	100	Ⓐ Ⓑ Ⓒ Ⓓ

맞은 문제 개수: ___ /100

TEST 08의 점수를 환산한 후 목표 달성기에 TEST 08의 점수를 표시합니다.
점수 환산표는 문제집 167페이지, 목표 달성기는 교재의 첫 장에 있습니다.

✂ 자르는 선

Answer Sheet
TEST 07

LISTENING (Part I~IV)

#		#		#		#	
1	Ⓐ Ⓑ Ⓒ Ⓓ	21	Ⓐ Ⓑ Ⓒ Ⓓ	41	Ⓐ Ⓑ Ⓒ Ⓓ	81	Ⓐ Ⓑ Ⓒ Ⓓ
2	Ⓐ Ⓑ Ⓒ Ⓓ	22	Ⓐ Ⓑ Ⓒ Ⓓ	42	Ⓐ Ⓑ Ⓒ Ⓓ	82	Ⓐ Ⓑ Ⓒ Ⓓ
3	Ⓐ Ⓑ Ⓒ Ⓓ	23	Ⓐ Ⓑ Ⓒ Ⓓ	43	Ⓐ Ⓑ Ⓒ Ⓓ	83	Ⓐ Ⓑ Ⓒ Ⓓ
4	Ⓐ Ⓑ Ⓒ Ⓓ	24	Ⓐ Ⓑ Ⓒ Ⓓ	44	Ⓐ Ⓑ Ⓒ Ⓓ	84	Ⓐ Ⓑ Ⓒ Ⓓ
5	Ⓐ Ⓑ Ⓒ Ⓓ	25	Ⓐ Ⓑ Ⓒ Ⓓ	45	Ⓐ Ⓑ Ⓒ Ⓓ	85	Ⓐ Ⓑ Ⓒ Ⓓ
6	Ⓐ Ⓑ Ⓒ Ⓓ	26	Ⓐ Ⓑ Ⓒ Ⓓ	46	Ⓐ Ⓑ Ⓒ Ⓓ	86	Ⓐ Ⓑ Ⓒ Ⓓ
7	Ⓐ Ⓑ Ⓒ	27	Ⓐ Ⓑ Ⓒ	47	Ⓐ Ⓑ Ⓒ Ⓓ	87	Ⓐ Ⓑ Ⓒ Ⓓ
8	Ⓐ Ⓑ Ⓒ	28	Ⓐ Ⓑ Ⓒ	48	Ⓐ Ⓑ Ⓒ Ⓓ	88	Ⓐ Ⓑ Ⓒ Ⓓ
9	Ⓐ Ⓑ Ⓒ	29	Ⓐ Ⓑ Ⓒ	49	Ⓐ Ⓑ Ⓒ Ⓓ	89	Ⓐ Ⓑ Ⓒ Ⓓ
10	Ⓐ Ⓑ Ⓒ	30	Ⓐ Ⓑ Ⓒ Ⓓ	50	Ⓐ Ⓑ Ⓒ Ⓓ	90	Ⓐ Ⓑ Ⓒ Ⓓ
11	Ⓐ Ⓑ Ⓒ	31	Ⓐ Ⓑ Ⓒ Ⓓ	51	Ⓐ Ⓑ Ⓒ Ⓓ	91	Ⓐ Ⓑ Ⓒ Ⓓ
12	Ⓐ Ⓑ Ⓒ	32	Ⓐ Ⓑ Ⓒ Ⓓ	52	Ⓐ Ⓑ Ⓒ Ⓓ	92	Ⓐ Ⓑ Ⓒ Ⓓ
13	Ⓐ Ⓑ Ⓒ	33	Ⓐ Ⓑ Ⓒ Ⓓ	53	Ⓐ Ⓑ Ⓒ Ⓓ	93	Ⓐ Ⓑ Ⓒ Ⓓ
14	Ⓐ Ⓑ Ⓒ	34	Ⓐ Ⓑ Ⓒ Ⓓ	54	Ⓐ Ⓑ Ⓒ Ⓓ	94	Ⓐ Ⓑ Ⓒ Ⓓ
15	Ⓐ Ⓑ Ⓒ	35	Ⓐ Ⓑ Ⓒ Ⓓ	55	Ⓐ Ⓑ Ⓒ Ⓓ	95	Ⓐ Ⓑ Ⓒ Ⓓ
16	Ⓐ Ⓑ Ⓒ	36	Ⓐ Ⓑ Ⓒ Ⓓ	56	Ⓐ Ⓑ Ⓒ Ⓓ	96	Ⓐ Ⓑ Ⓒ Ⓓ
17	Ⓐ Ⓑ Ⓒ	37	Ⓐ Ⓑ Ⓒ Ⓓ	57	Ⓐ Ⓑ Ⓒ Ⓓ	97	Ⓐ Ⓑ Ⓒ Ⓓ
18	Ⓐ Ⓑ Ⓒ	38	Ⓐ Ⓑ Ⓒ Ⓓ	58	Ⓐ Ⓑ Ⓒ Ⓓ	98	Ⓐ Ⓑ Ⓒ Ⓓ
19	Ⓐ Ⓑ Ⓒ	39	Ⓐ Ⓑ Ⓒ Ⓓ	59	Ⓐ Ⓑ Ⓒ Ⓓ	99	Ⓐ Ⓑ Ⓒ Ⓓ
20	Ⓐ Ⓑ Ⓒ	40	Ⓐ Ⓑ Ⓒ Ⓓ	60	Ⓐ Ⓑ Ⓒ Ⓓ	100	Ⓐ Ⓑ Ⓒ Ⓓ

맞은 문제 개수: ___ /100

TEST 07의 점수를 환산한 후 목표 달성기에 TEST 07의 점수를 표시합니다.
점수 환산표는 문제집 167페이지, 목표 달성기는 교재의 첫 장에 있습니다.

무료 토익·토스·오픽·지텔프 자료 제공
Hackers.co.kr

Answer Sheet

TEST 10

LISTENING (Part I~IV)

#					#					#					#				
1	A B C D				21	A B C				41	A B C D				61	A B C D			
2	A B C D				22	A B C				42	A B C D				62	A B C D			
3	A B C D				23	A B C				43	A B C D				63	A B C D			
4	A B C D				24	A B C				44	A B C D				64	A B C D			
5	A B C D				25	A B C				45	A B C D				65	A B C D			
6	A B C D				26	A B C				46	A B C D				66	A B C D			
7	A B C				27	A B C				47	A B C D				67	A B C D			
8	A B C				28	A B C				48	A B C D				68	A B C D			
9	A B C				29	A B C				49	A B C D				69	A B C D			
10	A B C				30	A B C D				50	A B C D				70	A B C D			
11	A B C				31	A B C D				51	A B C D				71	A B C D			
12	A B C				32	A B C D				52	A B C D				72	A B C D			
13	A B C				33	A B C D				53	A B C D				73	A B C D			
14	A B C				34	A B C D				54	A B C D				74	A B C D			
15	A B C				35	A B C D				55	A B C D				75	A B C D			
16	A B C				36	A B C D				56	A B C D				76	A B C D			
17	A B C				37	A B C D				57	A B C D				77	A B C D			
18	A B C				38	A B C D				58	A B C D				78	A B C D			
19	A B C				39	A B C D				59	A B C D				79	A B C D			
20	A B C				40	A B C D				60	A B C D				80	A B C D			
81	A B C D																		
82	A B C D																		
83	A B C D																		
84	A B C D																		
85	A B C D																		
86	A B C D																		
87	A B C D																		
88	A B C D																		
89	A B C D																		
90	A B C D																		
91	A B C D																		
92	A B C D																		
93	A B C D																		
94	A B C D																		
95	A B C D																		
96	A B C D																		
97	A B C D																		
98	A B C D																		
99	A B C D																		
100	A B C D																		

맞은 문제 개수: ___/100

TEST 10의 점수를 환산한 후 목표 달성기에 TEST 10의 점수를 표시합니다.
점수 환산표는 문제집 16페이지, 목표 달성기는 교재의 첫 장에 있습니다.

✂ 자르는 선

Answer Sheet

TEST 09

LISTENING (Part I~IV)

#					#					#					#				
1	A B C D				21	A B C				41	A B C				61	A B C D			
2	A B C D				22	A B C				42	A B C				62	A B C D			
3	A B C D				23	A B C				43	A B C				63	A B C D			
4	A B C D				24	A B C				44	A B C				64	A B C D			
5	A B C D				25	A B C				45	A B C				65	A B C D			
6	A B C D				26	A B C				46	A B C				66	A B C D			
7	A B C				27	A B C				47	A B C				67	A B C D			
8	A B C				28	A B C				48	A B C				68	A B C D			
9	A B C				29	A B C				49	A B C				69	A B C D			
10	A B C				30	A B C				50	A B C D				70	A B C D			
11	A B C				31	A B C				51	A B C D				71	A B C D			
12	A B C				32	A B C				52	A B C D				72	A B C D			
13	A B C				33	A B C				53	A B C D				73	A B C D			
14	A B C				34	A B C				54	A B C D				74	A B C D			
15	A B C				35	A B C				55	A B C D				75	A B C D			
16	A B C				36	A B C				56	A B C D				76	A B C D			
17	A B C				37	A B C				57	A B C D				77	A B C D			
18	A B C				38	A B C				58	A B C D				78	A B C D			
19	A B C				39	A B C				59	A B C D				79	A B C D			
20	A B C				40	A B C				60	A B C D				80	A B C D			
81	A B C D																		
82	A B C D																		
83	A B C D																		
84	A B C D																		
85	A B C D																		
86	A B C D																		
87	A B C D																		
88	A B C D																		
89	A B C D																		
90	A B C D																		
91	A B C D																		
92	A B C D																		
93	A B C D																		
94	A B C D																		
95	A B C D																		
96	A B C D																		
97	A B C D																		
98	A B C D																		
99	A B C D																		
100	A B C D																		

맞은 문제 개수: ___/100

TEST 09의 점수를 환산한 후 목표 달성기에 TEST 09의 점수를 표시합니다.
점수 환산표는 문제집 16페이지, 목표 달성기는 교재의 첫 장에 있습니다.

무료 토익·토스·오픽·지텔프 자료 제공
Hackers.co.kr

MEMO

최신 기출유형으로 실전 완벽 마무리

해커스 토익 LC

실전 1000제 3

LISTENING

문제집

개정 2판 7쇄 발행 2024년 9월 2일
개정 2판 1쇄 발행 2022년 6월 28일

지은이	해커스 어학연구소
펴낸곳	㈜해커스 어학연구소
펴낸이	해커스 어학연구소 출판팀

주소	서울특별시 서초구 강남대로61길 23 ㈜해커스 어학연구소
고객센터	02-537-5000
교재 관련 문의	publishing@hackers.com
동영상강의	HackersIngang.com

ISBN	978-89-6542-484-0 (13740)
Serial Number	02-07-01

외국어인강 1위, 해커스인강
HackersIngang.com

🔼 해커스인강

· 해커스 토익 스타강사의 **본 교재 인강**
· 단기 리스닝 점수 향상을 위한 **무료 받아쓰기&쉐도잉 프로그램**
· 최신 출제경향이 반영된 **무료 온라인 실전모의고사**
· 들으면서 외우는 **무료 단어암기장 및 단어암기 MP3**
· 빠르고 편리하게 채점하는 **무료 정답녹음 MP3**

영어 전문 포털, 해커스토익
Hackers.co.kr

🔼 해커스토익

· 본 교재 **무료 지문 및 문제 해석**
· **무료 매월 적중예상특강 및 실시간 토익시험 정답확인/해설강의**
· **매일 실전 RC/LC 문제 및 토익 기출보카 TEST, 토익기출 100단어** 등 다양한 무료 학습 콘텐츠

헤럴드 선정 2018 대학생 선호브랜드 대상 '대학생이 선정한 외국어인강' 부문 1위